Flowers

for

Brother Mudd

Flowers

for

Brother Mudd

One Woman's Path from
Jim Crow to Career Diplomat

Judith Mudd-Krijgelmans

Rev. date: 04/30/2018

To order additional copies of this book, contact:
Xlibris
1-888-795-4274
www.Xlibris.com
Orders@Xlibris.com
539593

CONTENTS

Part III: Belonging

Dedication

To Rekha Kaula, my daughter, and Jon-Mingus Horton, my grandson;
For the descendants and relatives of
William and Julia Harris Mudd

ACKNOWLEDGMENTS

Memoir is messy. Describing the big picture while recreating cameos that made my early life unique was tricky. Although I have changed some names and expressions for privacy, to avoid hate speech, or because of the inability to recall, this book is a true story. I've done my best to recount the way things were, but for the inevitable inconsistencies, I ask the reader's understanding.

Family and friends were essential: Cousin Alphonso Mudd generously shared his genealogy research, as did new found cousin Adrian Wells. My sister Helene Mudd Rowan provided essential photographs; nephew Brandon Allen gave freely of his time sending a key narrative. My daughter Rekha Kaula's time and care in designing the book jacket and preparing the graphics was crucial. My husband Claude Krijgelmans' example of how a writer protects his artistic vision was invaluable. Family friend Ronald Burchi's interest and generosity were priceless. Memoir students, especially published writers Hon Lee, Patricia Lenz, Frederick Bley, and Eleanor Akahloun greatly inspired me. They all, with the spirit of my ancestors, beckoned me to tell my story.

Believing

"*Behold,*
the only thing greater than yourself."
from *Roots* by ALEX HALEY

1

Far from My Sweet Kentucky Home

"Is this Baltimore?" After twenty-two hours of sitting on the train, I had summoned the courage to speak to another person. "Straight ahead," said the porter walking beside me in his shiny buttoned, black uniform and matching cap. He looked like someone my parents could have known. Motioning straight ahead, he stopped to collect my four-foot-wide steamer trunk from the luggage hold beneath: "You claim it inside."

The words coming from this brown-skinned gentleman were like those of an uncle welcoming me into his home. The silvery padlock dangled from the trunk as we approached the inside of the station. I had to go to the bathroom; I hadn't in a day. But I took one more breath to "hold it in" a little longer, and soon I was in a taxi on the way to Morgan State College.

Since leaving Louisville, I had not risen from my seat, afraid of walking in the moving train. I had seen many trains pass by on the tracks, but this was the first time in my eighteen-year-old life that I had ridden one. Before I boarded, Daddy had run into a man—he seemed to know everyone in Louisville's "Negro community"—who introduced me to his daughter who was going on the same train. The two dads agreed that the man's daughter could look after me. In her muted colors and pressed hair styled neatly against her head, she seemed to know everything, certainly more than me in my straight rust brown skirt (paid for on layaway) and plain gray-green blouse. It was the last week of August 1964, and my soft, curly hair, which I had taken pains to arrange and lacquer in place, was changing shape like a ball of cotton as I stood in the heat and humidity. I was trying not to have second thoughts about the whole prospect of leaving home and was on the verge of tears. The man's daughter said, "Sure," she'd look after me on the journey. Then, fixing her eyes on me, she said, "They have good breakfasts. You'll love the pancakes." But after we got on the train, I never saw her again.

After being glued to my seat for almost a day, getting up and off the train was a monumental gathering of my will. I don't know how I came to my senses, but when I heard, "Next stop Baltimore," I stood up. Freeze frozen in my brain was the parting pose of my family as they had said goodbye: Daddy, looking so unlike his usual more formally dressed self, wore a straw hat tilted back on his head and curled up at the side, his face red and sad. Mother, in a cotton checked printed blouse and navy blue skirt, looked more confident. She did not cry. My six brothers and sisters—Billy, 20; Andrea, 15; Anita, 13; Helene, 6; and Rodney, 4—had hugged and kissed me, packing me off in a deep cushion of caring. Baby Evelyn, we called her Poochie, was only ten months old. As I rubbed her bare back, she rested her head against Daddy's broad right shoulder. Her sunlit diapered bottom in the shade of Daddy's embrace was the last thing I saw as the locomotive pulled away. Going so far from the firm embrace of my sweet Kentucky home was hard, but I had to do it to be free.

Me at age three with Billy, Preston Street

2

Little Mudd

When World War II ended, my parents got together to celebrate the victory, and nine months later I rolled into the world—or so I like to imagine. Marked with a dark brown spot at the top of my behind and the stub of a sixth finger growing from my right hand, I was not going to be confused for another baby. This despite being one of thousands of newborns crowding hospitals all over the United States on June 5, 1946, in that generation that would revolutionize the world: the Baby Boomers. Born as I was a month and a day before the Fourth of July was near enough to that star-spangled date to make me feel close to Uncle Sam. Like Judy Garland, who inspired my name, in the film *Strike up the Band,* as far back as I can recall, I had a burning fervor for the "red, white, and blue." D-day, when the allied troops landed in Normandy on June 6, 1944, to begin ending the war, was just short of two years before I came into the world. The flag was like a comforting blanket. Never mind that I was black. That great things were going to happen was whispered in my ear. While I doubt that becoming a United States career diplomat traveling and living in faraway places was one of them, I knew I had to be ready.

The Korean War was going on when I was four. When it stopped in July 1953, my brother, sister, and I danced around in a circle singing, "The war is over! The war is over!" By then there was so much chatter swirling around my perked-up ears about the Iron Curtain and the Atom Bomb that I thought the Korean War and the Second World War were one and the same. The whole world was painting its backdrop on my life's diorama.

Coming into the world when I did in the USA was good timing. As an American of African descent whose ancestors were enslaved, the past, no matter how romantic, was not as good as the future could be. Even in the heyday of jazz, one of the United States' most outstanding contributions to American and world culture, black Americans couldn't go to the clubs that made money from the music they created. Had I been born earlier, I would have looked forward to a much dimmer future. In 1946, masses of coffee- and tawny-skinned people throughout the world were sloughing off years of colonial domination. I was among them.

In America, women went back to the kitchen, but their time on the assembly lines during the war made it impossible for them just to do dishes again. Black Americans, in large part, influenced by the protests of black men who had fought in the war, were finally seeing a brighter horizon after a harsh half century that made a mockery of the emancipation granted eighty years before. Now they might find better housing, education, and work. They might have more time to spend with their families like people in the movies. What a time to come down out of God's imagination to take my place in the front lines of those who could hope to benefit from the full promise of the U.S. Constitution and have equal rights.

**Daddy, Mother, baby Andrea, me, Billy maternal
grandparents Mama and Papa Harris, Christmas 1949**

Never mind that I came into the world at the Red Cross Hospital for Negroes in segregated Louisville, Kentucky, and that as a girl from a black family, the odds for my future success were low. My parents' hearts were full of enough hope to shield me from the stormy weather that lay outside. In their tight embrace, I must have been one of the most content babies in the world. I was brought home to the upstairs rooms in the house where my father and mother lived with my brother Billy, who was two, on Hale Street in Louisville's West End, the better section of the two areas of the city where Negroes lived.

Mother used to tell me about the man who lived downstairs. He liked to go fishing and would bring home his catches, which Mother, no doubt trying to make a good impression, cleaned and fried. She did this so much that by the time I was old enough to help her in the kitchen, she hated preparing fresh fish. This was sad for me, as her white buffalo, flaky and golden brown, was one of the earliest, scrumptious tastes on my tongue, fried chicken being the first.

By the time my mother's celebrated cooking and baking at Sunday white-tablecloth dinners was a family custom, we were living at 823 South Preston Street in the less desirable East End; but to me it was the Emerald City: Mother was as beautiful as any fairy queen; Daddy, as noble and mighty as any knight; and all the relatives and friends who came in and out of my life were kind. Our house was pleasant to look at too, with its blond woodwork and antique white-enamel-painted mantelpiece and sliding doors. In the front yard, Daddy grew concord grapes and green beans, and in the back, roses that bloomed in the spring in time for my birthday. A long screened-in porch hugged the side of the house, and although I was terrified by the bats that hid behind its forest-green shutters and flew out low over our heads on summer nights, it gave me and Billy and by then my baby sister Andrea a lot of space for play.

Mother had a theatrical flair. She had as much fun as her children, turning the side porch into a playhouse with a bedspread for a curtain, giving me my first taste of live drama and fun with words. She'd also stage programs for us in the front room, using the sliding doors as a slowly opening and closing curtain. One evening my baby sister twirled around as Billy opened the "curtains." In her blue net tutu she looked like the ballerina in the song we heard on the radio, "in her sweet little Alice blue gown;" but the spell was broken when Andrea stumbled and dissolved into tears.

5

As early as I can remember, I was curious about events happening outside our home. Perhaps it was Daddy's coming home with his tan briefcase bulging with papers every afternoon that excited my curiosity. He and Mother would talk about what was happening in the world—about "colored people," about "overseas," about President Truman. A couple of tiny, two-inch square black-and-white photographs of one of my uncles in padded military gear standing on skis against the background of snow-covered mountains, which I later learned were the Alps, lay in a big box that had once contained chocolates. When no one was looking, I'd take that tiny snapshot out and stare at it: *Where were the Alps, and how do you ski?* I'd ask myself. A lot was made of family and friends who had been in the military during the war, like Uncle William, my mother's oldest brother, who was in the army and was stationed at the American embassy in London, at "the court of Saint James," as he was proud of saying. He was awarded two bronze stars for his service. As I got older, Mother talked constantly of how her brothers and sisters' husbands were benefiting from the GI Bill, the government law that helped veterans make up for their time serving in the military.

Fort Knox, which is near Louisville, where all the gold was stored, was frequently mentioned; and as the adults talked, I longed to see it. Gleaming logs were piled high there I thought, like they were in one of Mother's bedtime stories. Mother spoke about appliances and furniture that people had bought at the PX (Post Exchange stores) at which, to her dismay, we couldn't shop because Daddy hadn't been in the service. Everyone, except our family, seemed to have a tall refrigerator, bristling bright as if made of porcelain. We still had an icebox.

I'd watched the man deliver the giant clear chunk on his hunched-over back and ever so slowly release a clamp and hoist the cube into the upper part of the chest. While he did, I'd get a whiff of the pungent metallic smell of the vacant freezer, which I'm reminded of whenever I open an empty vacuum sealed cooler. Not until 1953 did we get a Frigidaire, after getting a television the year before.

Daddy, probably around age thirty-five

My dad's not being in the military was talked about as a handicap, especially as the reason for why he couldn't get a loan to buy a house. All ears all the time as I was, I didn't like hearing him criticized. Sure, he was unique: for one, much older than the other dads; but he did things other dads didn't do. He took us to the hay market to buy fresh fruits and vegetables, then over the bridge to Indiana to the walk-in cold storage freezer to order meat from the side of a cow he owned. He wore a suit and a hat every morning and went off to work as a teacher. Everyone knew Mr. Mudd. He was my champion; I strived to be his.

I'd sit close to him and take in what he said about being ineligible to go to war. Before I was born, he had been "essential" as the principal of a large school in a coal-mining town in Jenkins, Kentucky. Not only was he the head of the most prominent black institution in that town then, but he kept an eye on the students' health; for example, washing their heads with kerosene to kill lice. He was a coal miner as well, having gone down to work in the mines when school was not in session. Such thoughts danced in my head as I was memorizing the answers to questions in my catechism, like, "Why did God make me?" Answer: "To know, love, and serve him." Daddy did all that. But he didn't let being a staunch Catholic keep him from administering to the needs of the Jenkins black community. Although they were mostly non-Catholic, he was their unofficial preacher on Sundays. This gained for him the lifelong title of "Brother Mudd." For a long time, that fact confused me—I felt Daddy's behavior was counter to Catholic teachings—and I didn't understand why he did what he did. But as I came to understand that his valuable work hadn't made him eligible for GI benefits, I saw how it was a curse and a blessing he could never get rid of. Not until the tens of phone calls and written messages of condolence that came when he died years later did I realize how he had improved the lives of so many.

**Coal company town in Jenkins, Kentucky, 1935,
Wikimedia.org, public domain**

When I was four, I knew about President Truman, and like my parents, I was *for* him, because he had continued the work of Franklin Roosevelt, who—both my mom and dad agreed—was great beyond measure. Just how great I wouldn't appreciate until I was an adult, but I quickly discerned that he was up there, like the statues of the angels and saints who surrounded us in our Catholic church, Saint Peter Claver. The story goes that one day Billy and I got into a word spat. Billy said that no one liked me, that I didn't have any friends. My reply—"I *do* have friends: Santa Claus, Jesus, and Harry Truman!"

Mass on Sundays and fish on Fridays was the framework for family life, but while we were strict Catholics, Mother had grown up as an active Methodist. She sang at her church and, unlike Catholic children, read the Bible and knew its stories. While she converted to Catholicism to marry Daddy, promising to raise their children in the church, she held strongly to her native religious customs throughout her life. She'd smile when one of her children panicked after mistakenly eating meat on Friday and take it in stride when she occasionally had to skip Sunday Mass. I would have said it was impossible at the time, but Mother's broad views on religion helped me as I got older.

Mother as a teacher in Jenkins, Kentucky, about age twenty-two

Daddy was a social studies teacher at Jackson Junior High School a couple of blocks from our home on Preston Street. As a teacher in Louisville's Colored School System, he was well-known, and we, as his children, had to be on our p's and q's. Little Mudd was what they called me and my siblings. Woe be it to any of us for misbehaving—we seldom did—for it would have been reported all over the neighborhood. Life was like growing up in a fishbowl, tiny but on view to all.

Our house was full of books and newspapers, and I cannot think of Daddy without a copy of *The Courier-Journal* or *The Louisville Times* at the table before or after a hearty meal. While I buttered my bread, he and mother would talk about topics like Ralph Bunch, the black American diplomat who had received the Nobel Peace Prize for his work in resolving the Arab–Israeli conflict in Palestine in 1950; and the Tennessee Valley Authority, which, they said, saved Louisville in the great flood of 1937. Since current events and what the government was doing were everyday topics, it's no wonder I became a public affairs officer decades later. For though I played with dolls, reveled in tea parties, and had a mind full of make-believe ideas, by the time I was seven, I wanted to be taken seriously.

Relatives and friends pinched my chubby cheeks and grabbed and tickled me, threatening to pull down my panties to expose my birthmark! They'd squeeze my sides to make me laugh, often to the point that I sometimes became nauseous. Soon I got tired of it. Maybe being treated like a living doll made me impatient to grow up. To hurry life along, I made up events that were like things I heard on radio and TV or saw in magazines. For instance, when I was six I began collecting Mary Jane candy wrappers and spreading news of a contest. Whoever sent in the most wrappers to the Mary Jane Company, I announced, would win a doll of that name. Angela Jenkins, my best friend, and others got on board and brought handfuls of the yellow-and-red squares to me each day. We stockpiled them until my book satchel was overflowing and Mother was after me to do something about the stashed bits of paper spilling out of my drawer. Finally I confessed to my friends that there was no real contest. Their reaction, surprising to me even then, was not one of too much disappointment. They seemed to have enjoyed the chase I'd led them on.

Still, I was somewhat ashamed of myself when I went into those childhood escapes. Daddy was always encouraging us to think about the big issues of the world, and I wanted to live up to his expectations. Despite being tall and heavyset, he was a gentle and kind man who never laid a hand on me in anger, except when he spanked me for trying out my new teeth on Billy's shoulder when I was one. After that, I was spared the rod. If I did something wrong, I'd cry profusely. He'd talk to me, listen sympathetically, and say, "Well now you didn't mean to do it, did you?" I'd say no, that I was sorry, would not do it again, and that would end the matter.

Before I knew how lucky I was to be the baby, Andrea came along three years after me; she was like my personal little blonde baby doll. Although I didn't like it that she cried a lot, she was like a film star version of the perfect baby. People fawned and oohed and aahed over her. Our elderly neighbors, the Taylors and the Hamiltons, were the happiest people in the world when Mother let them hold her, and on Valentine's Day, Mother would make a card out of red construction paper and border it with white lace, which she would glue on by hand; she'd cut a hole in the card so that a picture of Andrea's face showed through and give it to them. I had to fight feelings of jealousy. I liked sitting in Andrea's playpen with her under the bright summer sun, she in a wide-brimmed bonnet and me in a straw hat, feeding baby food to her. I'd sneak every other bite of pears and pudding as she looked adoringly at me.

Two years later, when I was five, Mother was in Red Cross Hospital again, preparing to give birth to my second sister, Anita. Granny Mudd, my father's mother, had come from Springfield, Kentucky, to help care for us. Daddy had always liked taking afternoon naps on weekends, and now I could see that he got the habit from his mother, for she liked sleeping during the day too. I hated lying in bed while the sun was shining, and so one afternoon while my grandmother, father, and baby sister Andrea slept on the hot afternoon of July 18 (and Billy secreted himself away), I decided to do something exciting. First, I danced over to the sheer, closed curtains at the window and looked across the street. Mother had told us not to look at what went on over there in the little shack-like tavern where men came and went all day. Beer joint was what she called it, and we were to have nothing to do with it. But I couldn't help wondering about the man in the charcoal suit with the straw basket covered with a pristine napkin, which he carried on his right arm.

So with everyone asleep on that sunny day, I took a good look at him when he came along. He had the usual handkerchief tied around his head, which I found weird but never dared ask about, and the basket. I was hoping I'd see the sandwiches that Mother said were in it. *What were they? Surely more than the baloney or peanut butter and jelly that we ate, since they were special enough to transport so carefully. Perhaps tuna fish with lettuce, eggs, and mayonnaise?* Of course, I never knew because I never got to satisfy my urge to snatch the cloth away. But I could, I thought, as I lay beside Daddy without his undershirt, watching his round stomach heave up and down as he snored, do something else! I opened a bottle of clear-as-water Karo Syrup, which mother had on hand to sweeten the drinking water of the expected baby, and dribbled it on Daddy's skin. I watched with glee as the treacly liquid trickled down the caramel hill of his chest. But my joy was dashed in a minute. The cold seeping liquid startled him, and he woke up! To my relief, while he was not pleased, he didn't punish me. He just went to the bathroom and washed the mess off. I never told anyone about it, and I'm sure he kept it under wraps pretty much too. Billy, on the other hand, as the oldest boy, always had to bear the responsibility for my antics and those of his other sisters, a strong tradition in Southern black families then. While I liked escaping punishment for my actions, I knew it was unfair for Billy to take the blame.

My parents went to great lengths to shield me and my siblings from realities that other children in our segregated neighborhood were learning as a matter of survival about growing up. Most obvious to me as I got older was the care they took in not presenting the world from a color-conscious point of view. That was the lens through which many in our community saw life, natural after centuries of slavery, Jim Crow laws, and customs that kept us in a separate world. Was it better to delay pulling back more of the curtain on the real world? Some say no, that a black child should grow up knowing the harsh environment that awaits her, but I am grateful that my folks kept the curtain closed as long as they did.

From left, family friend; Daddy, William F. Mudd; his youngest brother, Richard "Roscoe" Mudd; Granny (Daddy's mother, Mary Jane Mudd); the groom, Daddy's brother John L. Mudd; and the bride, Lenora Marchbank (Aunt Lee), and her relatives

Born in 1906, the grandson of slaves, Daddy was a giant of his time, a sort of black Horatio Alger character who had pulled himself up as far as he could by the flimsy bootstraps that life afforded him. By the time I came to know him, he was a respected leader and educator with a college degree and postgraduate studies. He had a library of books that went back to the 1920s, and he could go into such details about Franklin Roosevelt and Harry Truman that I thought he had dealt with them personally. But his story was one of struggle and hard labor. He was nineteen when he finished the eighth grade and went to Kentucky State College in Frankfort, a historically black institution. When he'd say that, as a child, I would be embarrassed thinking that he must have been rather slow in school. When I got older, I came to understand that he had had to take six years off, between seventh and eighth grades, to devote more time working on the farm where he and the family helped raise tobacco from sunup to sundown. And there were no schools nearby for Negro children beyond eighth grade. "Sis," he told me, his eyes moistened by the memory, "I got sick of the smell of tobacco." He never smoked and barely tolerated Mother's habit, which she didn't do around him.

At Kentucky State, Daddy went through a course of secondary studies that prepared him to pursue his bachelor's degree. While there, he played football and even coached the team, becoming something of a legend, as I would find out for myself much later. His thirst for knowledge drove him to continue studying, and he went for a master's degree at Howard University in Washington DC. This was in the 1930s, during the Great Depression, when money, food, and work were scarce and Washington was a genteel, segregated Southern town. To supplement his income, he was at various times a chauffeur and cook. He discontinued his studies when he was well past thirty, to accept an offer that he couldn't refuse to be principal of the large consolidated school in Jenkins, Kentucky, in Appalachia. Daddy lost his father when he was hitting his stride as a young professional. That year, 1938, must have been full of sadness for him, for earlier in that same year, he lost his brother Thomas as well.

The oldest child and son of his family, Daddy was left to be father and older brother to his siblings as best as he could, helping support them and his mother. Thus, by the time he settled down with Mother, he had already contributed to the upbringing of seven brothers and sisters. Forty years later when I was struggling at American University to finish my master's, I drew on his strength to power through and complete my studies, for him as much as for myself.

My mother, Julia, was fourteen years younger than my daddy. She met William when she was teaching at the school in Jenkins. With long auburn hair, dark brown eyes, and an oval-shaped face with sharp features, she was a classic beauty. As they said then and now, she could have "passed for white" and more than once was mistaken as such. (One section of her family actually did.) She liked to tell the story of when she sat in the whites-only section of the local theater in her hometown of Norton, Virginia, and got away with it, but she never stopped emphasizing how bad she felt afterward. Her face would widen as if she could see the flames of the fire that had burned down her childhood home in Norton when she was a young woman, explaining why they had moved to Tazewell close by. Dramatic and articulate, she made sure that her children spoke correct English —no uh-huhs and yeahs—and she decorated her musical French, which somehow in her one-room mountain classroom she had soaked up, with gestures and poses as if she were performing on a stage. She sang and hummed, on her own or to the tunes on the radio, continually.

When we got a piano, her long ivory fingers blithely touched the keys, coaxing out tunes like "Autumn Leaves," "Because," and "Some Enchanted Evening." I can't remember when there wasn't music in our home.

Our family amused itself. We were around the heavy, dark mahogany dining table every evening and the conversation was lively. Hearing popular slogans like "I like Ike," which referred to President Eisenhower, I learned my parents' worries about what was happening in the country. "He spends all his time playing golf," Daddy would say of the former general who now was president. Eating with good manners was important. We each had our own Fiesta Ware dinner plate of different colors; mine was canary yellow. For entertainment, we watched TV. While I felt that I watched too much TV, compared to today, it wasn't a lot, just two hours after school most days. *Howdy Doody* and *The Mickey Mouse Club* were my programs. (Eventually, I got a Mouseketeer hat and wore it like Annette, Darlene, and the other kids on the show.)

Sometimes we'd listen to Mother's spellbinding stories: not traditional Brothers Grimm and Hans Christian Andersen tales, which she told us at bedtime, but reminiscences from her childhood: making frosted cakes and wearing pretty dresses luminous with beads and bows; seeing the epochal 1939 film *Gone with the Wind*; talking about Shirley Temple—especially her curls and how to make them, with a brush dipped in sugar water on hair wrapped around a broom stick. Invariably, she'd recall her best friend Clara whom she'd protected from the children who mocked her dark complexion. Daddy's tales were tall and all about his grown-up years, not his childhood: riding down the street in Washington looking at the White House and the Capitol and writing great things on his Royal typewriter. Sometimes, both parents would hint that they'd seen ghosts. Mother, I felt, was making hers up, but Daddy's—who had grown up next to a graveyard—I believed. As I got older, the beguiling TV series *The Twilight Zone* presented by Rod Serling captured my attention. His tales of the supernatural would make our imaginations run wild. Often when I look out of the window of an airplane, I think about the episode with the man perched on the wing.

Living in between heaven and earth was a warm reality for me as a child. Once, some of us at Saint Peter Claver's were convinced that we'd seen a statue of the Blessed Mother shed tears. Other times, I'd conjure up narratives while sitting in the quiet church staring at the somber velvet drape of the confessional. At home, one summer evening we were absorbed in Daddy's telling us a ghost story. The room was darkly lit with jars of candles when a face covered in white loomed at the screened-in window beside me. First, I screamed my head off; then I got mad when I saw it was Billy playing another joke on me! Just the day before, he had tucked a live moth between the pages of a magazine so that when I turned the pages, the winged creature flapped right into my face, almost scaring me to death!

On Saturday mornings, we got to watch as much television as we wanted. Gene Autry, the Lone Ranger, Roy Rodgers, and Dale Evans were my friends. Like many of my generation, I was raised on these TV stock characters and looked to others in shows like *Father Knows Best* and *The Adventures of Ozzie and Harriet* as role models. When I was nine, I had a burning desire to be a cowgirl. That Christmas, I got a red cowgirl hat and a brown suede jacket with tassels like buckskin. In good weather when we played outside, I'd gallop around imagining I was in Dodge City with Matt Dillion and Miss Kitty.

Daddy could come up with fun things to do all the time: When I was very young, one of my favorites was riding on his wide knees to the tune of "Whoop De Whoop," which he sang and blew through his lips, sounding like a horn, moving his legs up and down like a horse on a merry-go-round. *Corny old Daddy! He made up this silly song,* I thought, only learning later that it was indeed a tune from the Jazz Age, probably one of the blues.

We visited our out-of-town relatives in the summer but we went to Springfield frequently since it was closer to Louisville. We got used to going to the outhouse and using slop jars before our relatives installed toilets in their houses. When they did, I asked my cousin Rita over the phone, "How is everyone acting now that they have indoor bathrooms?"

"Crazy . . . everybody's acting crazy," she said.

Mother was famous for the sumptuous spreads she cooked and laid out for visiting relatives: fried chicken was her usual grand main dish, prepared so crispy and flaky in the "new and improved cooking oil" Crisco. Though she, like most Americans, was misled by the false claims of the new substitute for lard, Mother was ahead of her time in taking seriously the bad effects of animal fat and emphasizing balanced eating. Still, our cuisine was southern, which meant fried and fattening. Mashed potatoes with gravy were my favorites. Green beans, which I got used to from the time Daddy picked them off the vine in our garden, we'd have often, seasoned with a chunk of fatty boiling bacon. Crunchy iceberg lettuce with rich, meaty red tomatoes that with a shake of salt tasted like a meal in themselves were constantly on our dinner table. We ate well and observed good manners every day, but when we had "company,"

Mother served these dishes in more special ways: She'd top the tomatoes with dollops of mayonnaise, a new convenience for her, from a jar. She'd arrange the chicken artfully on a platter, making it look like a picture in a magazine. For dessert, she could make any number of sweets, but her piece de resistance was lemon meringue pie, its topping whipped so high and tasting so light that it melted in our mouths. Warmth, laughter, smiles, hugs—all those good feelings tumble down as I think back on those family gatherings.

I loved all my relatives and could look forward to as much good food as a child could desire in their homes, in Springfield, Tazewell, or Columbus. But my favorite was when we visited Daddy's sister Aunt Lucy and her husband Uncle Andy in Ottawa, Illinois, not far from Chicago. In the early fifties, before she had her own four children, Aunt Lucy showered me with attention, doting on me with dresses she made. One was lemon yellow with a coffee-colored ribbon running through the eyelet lace bodice and hem; another was white with blue polka dots. But my favorite present from her was the red lollipop panties trimmed in snow-white lace, with silver jingle bells that dangled from the top of each leg. Running about with my bells tinkling was like wandering out of a storybook whenever I wanted. Going to see Aunt Lucy and Uncle Andy was a great adventure that I always looked forward to and savor to this day.

Aunt Lucy and Uncle Andy

Those summer trips were the brightest times. On our first trip in Daddy's two-seater, "Ole Lizzie," Billy and I had to stretch out on the rear window dashboard for the whole daylong trip. It was unforgettable, not only because it was the first road trip I can remember, but because it was the first time I was called the N-word. On our way to Ottawa, we were stopping to see an airplane that was on display in Chicago. While they had never flown—Daddy never would in his life; Mother only many years later—they were keen on seeing what they could of rapidly developing passenger flights. Daddy parked the car on the sidewalk, and while we were getting out, I heard, "You n——s stay off my grass!" come from a window where a woman leaned out, pointing her fingers at us. As Mother hurried us onto the sidewalk, mumbling under her breath, I was so confused about why someone was condemning us with this hateful word that I couldn't pay attention to what the museum guide was saying about the wooden airplane.

Years later, on another trip, as times had gotten increasingly hard for our family, I was on pins and needles when we visited Aunt Lucy. Weeks before, Mother had drilled us on good table manners. We had been the please-and-thank-you kids all our young lives, but for this trip, possibly to make up for our lack of new clothing or to counter the charity that Mother did not want to accept from my father's family, she had us behaving at charm school level. Yet as soon as we got there, Uncle Andy began telling us that at the dinner table we didn't have to say please and thank-you for each and every request. "If you see something you like, just take it!" he snapped. While I didn't relax my obsequious mannerisms—after all, I had been trained—I did immediately like Uncle Andy all the more for his generosity. I relaxed and settled into enjoying myself. Even when their two-year-old, my cousin Philip, would tickle my toes at night, I wouldn't let it bother me as I had when we'd arrived.

To supplement their income, Uncle Andy and Aunt Lucy raised turkeys. When we'd visit, I was at first afraid of the feathered creatures whom I knew ended up as Thanksgiving dinner, but I got used to trailing Aunt Lucy as she ran after and fed them. Aunt Lucy told me years later that those turkeys had given them so much trouble, that sometimes they had to chase them to the edge of the highway, racing to catch them before they crossed the road. While I didn't like anything that suggested "country," like the putrid smell in their coop, I got more comfortable around the fat powder-feathered birds. Yet unlike our dogs Spot and Limpy and cats Ginger and Silk, the turkeys didn't strike me as having unique personalities.

Years later, Aunt Lucy also told me how Daddy had taken good care of her when she was finding it difficult to work and go to college. He often gave her money and surprised her with a dress so that she could go to her senior prom. She said he was a "fine big brother."

In those days when we were on Preston Street, Mama and Papa Harris, my mother's parents, lived with us when Andrea was a baby. In her hairnet and laced-up leather shoes, Dollie Harris was soft-spoken and kind but always looked old, even though she probably was just in her fifties. For that matter, so did my father's mother Granny, Mary Jane Mudd, appear older. With so much mixed blood on both sides of my family, my grandmothers looked like white women. While I was cautious around Granny Mudd, I felt easier around Mama Harris. She did keep me on edge, however, when one day she saw me pressing my pug nose against the full-view mirror of one of the doors of the six-foot-high Victorian wardrobe.

"Don't do that. You'll make it flatter. You must pinch it every day," she said, showing me how by clutching her own pointed nose between her fingers. That's when I started to think that this centerpiece of my face, which was like Daddy's, not Mother's, was not to be proud of. Later, Mother, who recoiled at racial slights, told me my nose was "just fine." I only needed to throw my shoulders back and stand up straight.

As I got older, I came to understand the advantage that some lighter-skinned blacks thought they had. That my mother was good-looking by Western standards but never considered herself advantaged by the color of her skin had a profound impact on me. Her attitude affected how I perceived other blacks and how I would regard whites and, eventually, other races, nationalities, and ethnic groups. Daddy also wanted us to look beyond color, at least until we got older. JS, one of Daddy's students, often babysat us when our parents went out. I was almost eight when I realized that he, who was like a big brother, was having problems because his schoolmates were bullying him on account of his dark complexion. I hadn't thought much about the darkness of his skin; I hadn't given much, if any, thought to the differences in shades between my mother and father, or between me and Billy for that matter. Amazed that someone as kind as JS could be teased because he had darker skin stuck in my mind like a flag that could pop up in a game. With time I began to see why Mother talked constantly, and sadly, of the taunts that her darker-hued childhood best friend had endured. In her little town of Norton, deep in Appalachia, in the Blue Ridge Mountains, blacks were a small percent of an already small population of no more than 1,300. Exposure to the wider world came slowly to all the inhabitants. Mother seemed to say that she wished she could have absorbed some of her friend's melanin to make her happier and that she didn't at all think of her own light skin as a bonus. On the contrary, it was something she had worked around in order to fit in.

Though not understanding the color consciousness of blacks made me awkward when I entered a predominantly black college years later, it kept me free from the senseless prejudice of those within a minority discriminating against others in the group because of skin color. While she was from a more confining place than Daddy, Mother liked to paint herself as someone from a sophisticated time: probably based on what she'd heard from her brothers and over the radio. She talked about Count Basie and Joe Williams, about riding in a dining car on a train to Philadelphia, and a night of clubbing in some city near the East Coast.

Daddy, in contrast, presented his younger self as earthier—slogging it out as a farmer, doing fine without toilet tissue, using newspaper instead of wax paper to wrap his food. With us he'd sometimes go on back-to-the farm drives to economize. One day he packed sweet potatoes wrapped in the "want ads" section of *The Courier-Journal* for our lunch. Neither Billy and Andrea, nor I ate them. Each of us, acting separately, threw them in the waste can right away, so embarrassed were we to show our classmates that our family not only couldn't afford baloney but also was so uncouth as to use newspaper for food wrap! A string of stories like that flood my mind as I recall those days: A skinny chicken that Daddy bought from which we were supposed to get fresh eggs (but didn't)! We children were told not to pay attention to our father's country binges, and siding with mother, for the most part, I didn't; but I couldn't resist peeking through the window to watch my nonviolent Daddy wring the poor bird's neck. Oh, and the hog's head that he bought for himself—not the rest of us as forbidden by Mother—to eat on New Year's Day; and the cucumber rinds that he pickled and canned over three weeks, which even he couldn't eat—all were a part of his rural upbringing, according to Mother, and we shouldn't imitate him.

Yet, years later, when I was grown-up, Mother would wear the widest and biggest Afro while showing great interest in country music. She said she was country before country was cool. In those days, before I paid attention to the roots of black and bluegrass music, I was like that too:

every Saturday night I'd clapped and sung along with Randy and Cactus, performers on *Hayloft Hoedown*, a local weekly television show.

Of course we were country, proud of our bluegrass roots. The Kentucky Derby was a festival that I looked forward to every year: our family would go to the annual parade, standing for hours watching the festooned floats go by, whooping and cheering the local personalities riding on them. While we never went to the Derby Week square dancing in the streets, I sometimes watched it on TV, and years later I couldn't wait to try it myself when I took a required course in folk and square dancing in college. I could do-si-do with the best of them. We had our own viewing of the majestic "Run for the Roses" horse race in front of our television with mint juleps, made with the essential aromatic sprigs fresh from our garden, and a wee taste of Kentucky bourbon with lots of lemon and sugar over ice.

By the time I was in the kindergarten of the grade school linked to the junior high where Daddy taught, I acted as if I were grown-up. I had to be the big sister, and I couldn't wait to go to school. I wanted to go out into the world like Daddy. He wore a suit, carried a briefcase, and read important-looking big, thick books. I wanted to be treated like a grown-up, and I didn't like the way my kindergarten teacher Mrs. Edwards fawned all over me and my classmates. "Yes, you're my baby," she'd swoon, elegantly coiffed silver hair ringing her face. I wanted her to act like the distinguished teacher my father was. People called him Professor Mudd. I had a hard time accepting corrections for childish acts—I didn't talk back but deeply internalized the criticism—so I made sure I was "a good girl."

In kindergarten we were given peanut butter on a hamburger bun and a carton of milk for a snack. I got into the habit of throwing mine away, for I couldn't bear to eat the dry spread with no jelly like I'd have it at home. More revolting was the milk, which was not as cold as I liked. I also detested that we had to eat this concoction on a brown paper towel, the same ones from the dispenser that we used to dry our hands in the lavatory! What shame I felt when Mrs. Edwards pulled the squashed sandwich, which I had only taken two bites of and thrown away, from the trash can. I was mortified. How could Mr. Mudd's daughter do such a thing? And with the shame went the unspoken insinuation that I hadn't cared about the starving children in China.

Decades later, when I was studying Chinese in Taiwan, my teacher Chen Angel told me about how grateful she and her family were for the food aid that the U.S. Agency for International Development had sent to the island in the fifties. She showed me a photo of her and her sister in shifts made from the sacks of donated grain with "USA" stamped on them.

Making my first communion was as good as it gets, even better than Halloween, which was wonderful for me and my sisters. I'd dressed up as a fairy queen with tiny silver bows that Mother had sewn on a wide net gown. All of my life I have looked for chances to wear fancy long gowns. My first break came when I was as young as four: I got to wear a pale blue dress, white nylon socks, and Mary Jane patent leather shoes and be a flower girl in a Tom Thumb wedding at Aunt Evelyn's gray stone Methodist church across from Catholic Saint Augustine's, one of the three Catholic churches in Louisville then. Though tiny and old fashioned looking inside, I thought our church was the best. Making my First Communion in there when I was just three weeks short of my seventh birthday was the best day of my life up to then.

The smell of crisp fried bacon and sweet cinnamon rolls wafted through the back window of Saint Peter Claver's kitchen, as family and friends gathered around to congratulate me and my grade one classmates after the priest laid the first wafer of the Blessed Sacrament on our tongues. Standing in the churchyard and smelling the food that was to come after breaking my long overnight fast, I could almost taste the smooth, sugary snow-colored icing that laced the sweet rolls, as well as the sheets of rich yellow scrambled eggs. I was wearing a white dress and veil. I looked like the bride that I had begun noticing I was supposed to be one day.

That was spring of 1953, in the "merry month of May." In the preceding weeks, I'd had a lot of time to focus on the heavenly and the pure, for it was the Virgin's month, full of special sermons, hours of kneeling saying the prayers of the rosary, and singing choruses of ringing melodies—not just "Ave Marias" but huge, fulsome songs like "Dear Mary We Crown Thee with Blossoms Today"—which made my spirit soar. As I smiled for posterity while my mother looked down into her trusty Brownie camera to snap my picture, I distinctly remember thinking: *this is as good as it gets. If I smile well enough, wish sincerely enough, keep my hands folded straight enough, I'll go to heaven.* Although it's not always been as carefree as a May Day, I'm glad I stuck around for many more years.

THIS IS A GREAT MYSTERY

3

Sissy

In August 1954, resistance to civil rights patrolled the rocky road my family was on. One afternoon the movers came and cleared out the house; we crammed into Daddy's dark green Buick and headed for our new rental home five blocks away. I was worried that we had lost our cat Ginger forever, as we couldn't find her when we piled into the car. The barbecue stand at the corner, catching lightning bugs in a jar, the nickel I regretted not accepting from Mrs. Harris's grown-up son because he was a stranger—all these times were with me as I left my childhood home.

But the jolt of leaving Preston Street faded quickly, for soon we were unpacking while our familiar furniture was being put in place. And Ginger came back slinking under the fence a few days after we arrived. Lined in gray siding, with a front, side, and backyard, our new place seemed as good as our old one, although the fireplace and woodwork were of a dull, ugly coal color, which scared me. The blond sliding doors of our old brick house were gone too. The new place did, however, have compensations: an upstairs! I had wanted to live in a house with a second floor and was excited about having steps to climb, like in stories I read and saw on TV. Stoically, I accepted that my sister Andrea and I would have to share the one and only room that was upstairs, and harder still, we had to share it with a boy—my brother Billy.

He didn't like this arrangement either, but we had no choice. For us it was literally a step-up! We wouldn't have to convert the dining room into a sleeping space as we had to on one-bedroom Preston Street. In both houses, Mother and Daddy had their own room, which was sacrosanct. A new baby would get to stay in it for a few months, or out-of-town relatives would get to sleep in their bed; but those were the rare exceptions.

In good weather we whiled away the evenings playing cowgirls and cowboys. Even Billy, who didn't play with girls, joined my sisters and me galloping behind the Enro Shirt Factory. We'd mix weeds and water to make a "stew," and I just knew I was in the Wild West. Occasionally we'd find an empty five-foot-tall-and-wide brown cardboard box in the factory's trash pile. While it wasn't the wooden piano crate that Mother told us she and her playmates had when she was a girl, which she said they made into a life-size playhouse, it was close enough. We made it into a console television with a screen and knobs that we drew on with crayons.

Our house wasn't far from the Louisville Slugger factory, where the world-famous baseball bats were made. We were all fans of the favorite American pastime: Jackie Robinson and the Brooklyn Dodgers were our heroes. Though in the future I did not play team sports, in those days I played baseball, batting the ball and running, trying to make a home run. A faint scar on my left knee proves how hard I tried to get to first base.

Even though the Kentucky Street house was in an industrial part of the city, we had lots of open space. We had a deep backyard covered in green grass and in it a swing set that Daddy bought but never got around to nailing down. To get around the hazard of it jumping up and off of the ground and hurling one of us over while we were on it, we'd sit on the bars, one of us on each side, to hold it down. In the swing I'd pump my legs hard going as high as I could, throw my head back, and hoist myself up, closing my eyes, feeling with glee the quiver in my stomach that I knew would give me a fright but which I couldn't resist. For an nth of a second, I felt like I was flying.

Most special was when we would get tired of swinging and pretending that we were out West, we could play in the real house that was at the back of the yard. Daddy rented it out—sublet it—but when it was vacant, we had the incredible luck of using it for our own playhouse. Once a friend came home with me after church to spend time in the house with us, but when the mini cakes I took out of my little oven tasted like pepper, I decided she was weird and didn't invite her to share my toys again.

As the oldest sister, I was called Sissy; giving up being the only girl was a fair trade for having, at that time, two younger sisters as permanent playmates. We'd set our small dinette table with tiny dishes and bake miniature boxes of Betty Crocker cake mix in my petite electric stove. We also played paper dolls, having them live in our foot-and-a-half-high doll house that I'd gotten one Christmas. Sometimes we'd punch paper dolls out of store-bought books, but mostly, we'd use cutout models advertising dresses in the Sunday magazine. And like all American girls, we had our dolls. Mine, growing girls, were like me. My sisters, on the other hand, got dolls that looked younger, like them, rubber baby dolls that drank liquids and peed. My most prized was Sweet Sue, a walking doll, so-called because she had jointed legs that could be moved to make her walk. She was a brunette and wore a pearl satin dress sprinkled with blue flowers. I forbade my sisters to touch my dolls, but Anita has confessed, only in recent years, that she played with Sweet Sue when I was at school! Collectible dolls like bride dolls and those in fancy long costumes were all the rage, and I was often given one or got one as a prize. As they had to be kept on a shelf, I never got to fully enjoy them, though they must have been giving me the message of how I should appear and got me used to how ladies looked in the old days.

"Big girls" was a play we never tired of. As in real life, I'd be the big girl and oldest sister; and Andrea and Anita would be, as they were, the younger ones. Pretending I was sixteen, I'd tell them about my friends who went to the hop and about lipstick and makeup and other bits and pieces I picked up from the teenagers in TV shows. We'd talk about our imaginary boyfriends. Mine was Tom. We'd make up stories about going out on dates. After a while, I got tired of pretending that I had a boyfriend and decided to do something about it: I took a five-foot-long brown paper dry-cleaning bag and drew a life-size boy on it, like a paper doll. But when I cut it out, I was disappointed: He wouldn't sit up as I had intended. He just slunk down and folded up!

An avid reader, as I got older, I was constantly trying my hand at composing—letters, stories, and poems—like my mother. I imitated her interest in dramas, getting my sisters to act in plays and song performances. Once, we rehearsed *When Did You Last See Your Father?* I had found the play in an old volume of a 1920s set of the *Book of Knowledge* encyclopedia, which I had bought for five cents at a parish rummage sale. The play was based on the painting by William Frederick Yeames, done in 1878, showing what might have taken place in a Royalist household during the English Civil War. My sisters were good sports, especially Andrea, who would dutifully fall on her knees when I, as the lead player (of course!), would ask the critical question:

"When did you last see your father?"

"I saw my father last night in a dream," she'd dutifully reply on cue with deep emotion.

And When Did You Last See Your Father? painting by
Frederick Yeames; Wikimedia.org, public domain

In the years ahead, even as we began to feel the squeeze of not enough—like having only fifty cents to spend at the school fair and worrying about money to buy shoes—I didn't consider our family poor.

For one thing, I had the riches of health, except for the usual childhood illnesses, and didn't miss much school due to sickness (or other matters); although I caught many colds. Nonetheless, I was surprised when, living in Gabon in 1994, I discovered that I had survived tuberculosis. The dreaded disease was often talked about in hushed tones in the fifties and sixties. Though I wasn't aware of anyone in my family who had actually contracted it, I recall an unfortunate incident that took place one afternoon in the kitchen of the Kentucky Street house: A dear relative was extremely frail and thin. My baby brother Rodney had been staring at her for a long time as she and Mother talked. Finally, he blurted out, "You know who you look like, Olive Oyl![1] In the rush of embarrassment and scolding that took place afterward, I lost sight of whether or not she had the disease. In 1994,

---

1   From the Popeye cartoon series

an X-ray of my lungs showed a shadow, and an expert in London told me that I had caught the virus as a child but that it had calcified. Sounding like someone in the library of Downton Abbey,[2] he told me how having TB had toughened my resistance: "When those little bugger viruses try to get in your system, they jolly well get the boot!"

I didn't think of our family as poor because I had the bliss of ignorance. While my parents didn't make us think that we were worse off due to discrimination, they did talk about the positive changes that were improving opportunities. Although they didn't speak his name much in those early days, they knew that Martin Luther King was stirring things up in the South, and by the mid-fifties, I began to hear Daddy and my uncles talk about civil disobedience, no doubt in view of what was happening in Montgomery in 1955 with the bus boycott. Blacks in Louisville were also ramping up their public demonstrations against being treated as second-class citizens.

The push was for the right to use public accommodations; Martin Luther King came to speak in Louisville in 1956, and Aunt Evelyn took me and a few other children with her to hear him. While the details are blurry, I do recall being overwhelmed with tears as he spoke, the magnitude of his voice filling the silence in the Protestant church and knowing that I was part of something bigger than myself. Dr. King would come in and out of Louisville many times over the years, once even to the neighborhood where our family lived; but by that time, I had moved away.

Shortly after, I went with Aunt Evelyn and two other kids to buy tickets at the Fontaine Ferry Amusement Park. I hated being told that we couldn't buy tickets when we went to the window. I could see one of the Ferris wheels in the park grounds, and I so wanted to break through the turnstile and get on the ride, but no, as I already knew, we weren't allowed to because the park didn't serve colored people. Although that experience was sad and humiliating, it enriched me because, as my aunt told me, we had to get into places where we were entitled to go, to break down Jim Crow laws that prevented us from getting in.

---

2   *Downton Abbey* is a historical period drama created by Julian Fellowes in the U.K., which aired in the United States on PBS television from 2011 to 2016. Set between 1912 and 1925, it is about an aristocratic family and their domestic staff and how class differences between them changed after the First World War.

The Blue Boar restaurant was another off-limits place often talked about in our home. It was a lovely setting for a meal, with linen tablecloths and smartly dressed wait staff. We could see the inside through its wide picture windows, but we couldn't go in. When it finally did open, as did Fontaine Ferry, to blacks, I had left Louisville. And the harsh reality of both establishments was that as integration took place, they became less attractive to most consumers as "white flight" took over and people of European origin and higher incomes fled to the suburbs.

At home, with my brothers and sisters I had to stand in front of the television and watch Nat King Cole with his limber tongue and slicked-down hair croon "Mona Lisa." *Who was he anyway? And who was Mona Lisa?* I dared not ask during what were obviously sacred times for my parents: Negroes on national television.

Our eyes got big when we saw some of the pictures in the weekly black newspaper, *The Louisville Defender*: photos of heads and frozen body parts in refrigerator freezers on the front page, for instance. My parents seriously depended on getting the latest news on the Negro community from this now modern and highly respected weekly, but all we children could see was the glaring green of the newsprint and the rude contrast of the dark complexions in the photographs. The pictures in *The Courier-Journal* looked better, though I was careful not to share this view with my father. I recall Daddy reading an article about Thurgood Marshall and the Supreme Court decision ending school segregation. Marshall was the NAACP's (National Association for the Advancement of Colored People) lead counsel. Daddy had met him, talked about him and the NAACP all the time, and was fortunate to live to see him appointed the first black justice on the Supreme Court on August 29, 1967. In those days we placed all of our faith in the justice that we thought would be delivered by the highest court. After the 1954 decision, Earl Warren's name—he was the chief justice—was spoken in hushed tones in our home. Mother's family descended from some Warrens, and for a while we wondered whether we were distantly related to the famous chief justice.

We weren't poor because we always had humor and laughter, and that kept my spirits high. Again, it was my parents' stories that captivated me: Mother was the queen of her senior prom in a full-skirted chiffon dress twinkling with silver bows, which brushed the tops of her satin pumps; but then she was the only student in her one-room school in her final year. Daddy was not an ordinary cook when he worked in Washington—he piled mashed potatoes high on the plate like a hill, decorated with red pepper, calling his creation "Red Bird on a White Mountain." We watched the popular comedians on TV: Milton Beryl, Jerry Lewis, Lucy and Desi, Red Skelton, Jack Benny, and, always, Bob Hope. Although depicted in the most racist, stereotypical ways, we didn't see that when we chuckled at the nappy-haired kids in the old Little Rascal films. Keep it light was the mood in our house even when the undertow was roiling, nearly knocking us off our feet.

Perhaps what contributed most to my feeling of not being poor was the confidence that I came from a noble past. As inconceivable as it may sound, my mother's ancestors had lived in bondage to keep their families together, for they were not all of African descent. A number were descended from Indians; many had so much Caucasian blood that they looked it. In that group were ancestors who fought at Bunker Hill during the American Revolution. Daddy's folks had been enslaved not far from the mansion in Bardstown known now as the Old Kentucky Home, where Stephen Foster visited and was inspired to write his iconic songs. That site was the source for the lead character in Harriet Beecher Stowe's groundbreaking novel *Uncle Tom's Cabin*. We children were imbued with a sense that times were changing, that we shouldn't see the world as a war between black and white, and that we would have the opportunities to do things much greater than our parents. My father would have beamed with pride over *Roots*, the book, written by Alex Haley, and the TV film series it spawned, as well as the cultural phenomenon and change it accelerated. As a diplomat, I'd draw on the little that I knew about my parents' roots to talk to overseas audiences about Alex Haley's best seller.

Although the perimeters of my existence were narrow, they were strong, and to me they were wide. They were my family and the Catholic church. The latter, next to my parents, had the single most important influence in my formation. Mass every morning, except Saturdays, was routine; Latin prayers, said in response to the priest as he was conducting the Mass, and the accompanying music, which I sang in the choir, must have lured me to a fascination with languages that I would go on to study.

Within the fold of the church, I had the professional teaching, the kindness, and the generosity of my teachers from elementary through high school—the sisters of Saint Ursula. Nor would I have been able to tap into the deep spiritual brook that was filling up in me had it not been for the soft touch of the Franciscan fathers. Father Angelus, our parish priest when I was beginning school, was a humble man of German birth, who in his brown monk's robe with roped belt hanging down the side looked like pictures of the famous saint of Assisi. Like the birds and the butterflies, we children hovered around him. Saint Francis's prayer that ends with accepting the things one cannot change and having the courage to know the difference reminds me of how Father Angelus talked. And he had a gentle touch: he would give a pat on the head on the playground; softly whisper a sermon; and give a gentle penance. His successors, though not as popular as him, and with their own peculiarities, also hold special places in my heart. One was so obviously fond of drink that when those of us who had sung in the choir would gather around him at a long table after Christmas midnight Mass, standing behind him the boys would hold up empty wine bottles to make us laugh! Later, another parish priest, who looked as unhappy and crabby as I sometimes felt in my teen years, lent me twenty dollars without a long speech. I had circled his house for an hour before mustering the courage to ring his doorbell to ask him for the loan. He told me I should never be ashamed to ask the priest for help.

Sister Alexis, my first-grade teacher, looked like the Mother of Jesus herself, so much so that when I was six, in my reveries, I had a hard time distinguishing her, my mother, and the Mother of Jesus. The dedicated men and women of the church broadened my world by showing me that kindness could come from all people.

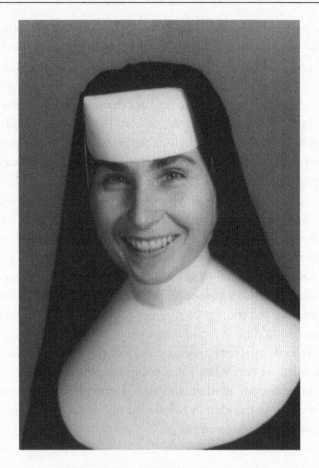

Sister Alexius, first-grade teacher

If a stable, nurturing home life laid the tracks for me to succeed, studying under the Ursuline sisters gave me the best chance to do that. Since grade school I had followed the Ursuline way. Our school, St. Peter Claver's, was one of three elementary schools for blacks in Louisville, and it was run by the sisters of Saint Ursula. Although they were white, they treated us as if our minds and souls would determine our future, barely emphasizing that we were a segregated minority. Their demand for excellence and high achievement jelled well with the mood of my life at home and my evolving personal desire to make something of myself.

Attitudes were poured into my head since I was six by these sisters dedicated to teaching: Freeze when the bell rings—training me to be still. Stay quiet for lengths of time—forcing me to hold my tongue. Be silent and stand when the person in charge enters the room—drilling in me an invaluable lesson for the career I would choose. "Where there is disorder, there is no clear thinking," one nun would say, fidgeting under the neck of her wimple. Her words ring in my mind even now, reminding me to slow down and take a moment to think.

4

All-American Girl

A medium-height, white-haired old man with glasses was the first picture I saw on TV. He was President Truman walking across the White House balcony in the last days of his presidency. That was in the fall of 1952, when I was six, and Daddy was bemoaning the fact that Truman had not run for a second term and the Democrats had lost the White House. The word international kept coming over the airwaves and out of my parents' mouths, and I took it in. Over the next eight years, I saw the frowns on my daddy's face as we watched President Eisenhower shaking hands with serious looking people. I liked seeing the president's wife, Mamie, with her short hair and bangs. But what made the most impression on me were the news and public affairs TV shows I watched with Daddy on Sunday evenings as I got older.

One of these programs was *The Twentieth Century with Walter Cronkite*, which began in 1957 and was narrated by the voice that we came to associate with truth. The half-hour episodes presented events that were significant in the unfolding of the century and told us what they meant in the context of American history, politics, and culture.

Another program I liked was *Harvest of Shame*, presented by Edward R. Murrow, which was about migrant workers who picked fruit. This opened my eyes to dirt-poor poverty and shameful labor practices in the "land of the free." I was comfortable looking at the cigarette-smoking commentator who was in our home on Sunday evenings in black and white. We'd also watch him interview celebrities like Liberace and Marilyn

Monroe on *Person to Person*, and we watched his tide-turning show on McCarthyism in March 1954 on *See It Now*. At that young age, I didn't understand what it was about but knew it was important.

Harvest of Shame imprinted itself more on my mind. Daddy raged at how the disgraceful abuse of migrant workers had long plagued America. He must have been reflecting on his tough experience as a farmworker. Looking back, I am amazed that my parents, who were at the bottom of the ladder socially and economically, made their children aware of those who were much worse off. Far from making me feel as if I had the right to a handout, their attitude made me feel that I must show the world I could do things as well as others and that I must take care of myself and make life better for those less fortunate. Poverty of spirit didn't seep into our home.

Father Angelus had taught us the Christmas carol "*Stille Nacht*" ("Silent Night" in German), my first contact with a spoken foreign language, not like Latin, which we uttered in church but which was no longer used to communicate. I was learning about Europe, not only of the war, but of the horrors of the Holocaust, something my mother often talked about as we were rolling out dough making pies on the kitchen table. The Mudd family's lives were made much more bearable by the help of Jewish people like Mr. Kreitman, who gave us credit at the corner grocery store, and the people who gave us credit at the Lewis Store in downtown Louisville, making it possible for us to have new outfits at Easter, albeit at high interest. Those real stories, with the imaginary ones, the fairy tales that my mother told us, must have made me paint mental landscapes of Europe, long before I dared to think that I would ever cross the Atlantic and see the grand continent. Later, when I lived in Belgium and visited Germany, a lot of the food was familiar. For instance, the *wiener schnitzel* was so like the pork chops Mother had prepared, with rich brown gravy and applesauce. Once in the nineties, on a visit home while I was living in Brussels, Andrea and I stumbled on, of all permutations, an Afro-German restaurant in downtown Louisville, and we had an excellent meal.

I loved school and was keen on every subject, even science (although there wasn't much of it) and the scant bit of geography that was squeezed in. I was consistently at the top of the class. Set to start third grade when we moved to Kentucky Street, the fright of our unwelcome arrival in the neighborhood, which I'll soon talk about, made school a safe haven and made me more determined to burrow into my studies and school life. By fourth grade, I was a champion of words in our small class, where Phillip

Ferris and I would be the last standing in spelling bees. Social studies, though not formally taught, made its way into our classes, and I had a lot to say on political and civil rights issues.

One topic, what to do about the surplus wheat in silos all over America, was constantly cropping up. Was it more moral to throw it overboard into the sea or to send the grains to the needy people in Russia? We all knew that Russia was an enemy of the United States, but wasn't it wrong to throw excess food away when people needed it?

In my first decade of life, the tunes of "Stars and Stripes Forever" and "God Bless America" looped through my head. My brother and I would put our hands over our hearts when the national anthem, "The Star-Spangled Banner," played as the TV signed off on Saturday nights. Thus, it's not surprising that as I learned history, I became consumed with the story of my country, from what we were taught was Columbus's discovery of America to the Declaration of Independence and the Revolution. Caught up in the fervor, I gradually became sad and disappointed as I learned more and more about why there was a civil rights movement and what this meant for me as a Negro, a black person in America.

I kept asking my mother and daddy questions. I couldn't believe that I was not included in the "We" in "We the People," that children like me were not loved, even by our good and honest cherry-tree-cutting-down first president, nor was I sure of what I was hearing about the terror of slavery. When I learned that we had been allowed to rent our home on Kentucky Street to spite people on the block who were against integrating the neighborhood, I was perplexed. *How could it be that I was not supposed to be here to have the life of other American children?* I took being an unwanted member of a minority group hard. I sought to filter out as much of what I was hearing about whites not liking blacks as I could. It was ugly and frightening.

Happy as I was in my young world—and I would not have anyone claim that America was not meant for the likes of me—the crowds on TV yelling, hitting, and siccing dogs on black children trying to go to school were hard to watch. Arkansas was far away, but as I watched those nine try to integrate Central High in Little Rock in 1957, I felt cold and scared that the same inequality was taking place in my hometown. Racial bias was distorting my harmonious life, and I had to take decisive action to clear a race-free space for myself. At a church rummage sale, spotting a two-by-three-foot painting of George Washington that was like the one in the public library on Lampton Street, I slapped down my last two nickels, bought the heavy glass-framed object, hauled it home, and nailed it on the dining room wall. Mother raised her eyebrows but didn't say a word. I thought that this outward show of allegiance would settle the matter of my full entitlement to the rights of an American once and for all.

George Washington, 1825, by Gilbert Stuart; public domain, Wikimedia Commons, Walters Art Museum

A natural teacher, Mother helped at our school, substitute teaching and taking my friends on field trips to local sites: the dairy, where we got to see powdered milk rolling off a machine in a giant gauzy sheet; the pie factory, where racks of hot out-of-the oven fruit pies won me over to the succulence of blueberries and cherries; and WAVE television station, where we shook hands with some of the staff and got to see the *Hayloft Hoedown* set. "Your mom is so pretty," my classmates would say. Since I had already begun to think of myself as not pretty in our Southern culture, where belles reigned, having a mother who was gave me the vicarious chance to be best-looking girl.

Even with our limited exposure to going downtown, when we did go there to shop as Mother insisted during the Christmas holidays, we always got to buy small white paper bags of roasted, salted peanuts and multicolored gumdrops. The chunky squares of chocolate looked delectable too, but our pennies wouldn't stretch that far. Besides, we had a red-and-gold tin of homemade fudge, dark and light, chock-full of nuts made by and sent from Mama Harris in Virginia. We'd sit on Santa's knee and tell him what we wanted for Christmas. We weren't in New York, but Christmas was always like *Miracle on 34th Street*.

While living conditions were not ideal for me and my family in Louisville's East End, I saw myself as an all-American girl, and as I got older I used my imagination to fill in the blanks where I didn't have the experiences. For instance, when my fourth-grade teacher told us that tomorrow would be Fire Prevention Day and she read from a brochure with a fireman's helmet on the cover about what to do to avoid fires, then told us to write an essay on how our families planned to celebrate it, I didn't bat an eyelash. That evening, with gusto I wrote about my family's plans to mark that day: We'd throw out trash and hazardous containers in a safe way, making sure all electric wires were not exposed. We'd practice escaping the house if a blaze was in progress. Best of all, we'd go into the attic and clear it out. Now, this was teasing facts quite a bit, because the attic on East Kentucky Street was a crawl space that I never could enter. Located on the wall opposite the room at the top of the stairs where I slept, a bridge would have had to been laid across the steps to enter it. It was one of the disappointments I'd had when we moved into the house. In my essay about how we would celebrate Fire Prevention Day, I said that we went into the attic and cleared it out!

"Sissy's a liar," Billy told Mother as we bounded into the house filled with the smell of oatmeal cookies after school the next day. My essay had been chosen as the best; Sister gave it a gold star and hung it on the bulletin board. Mother never scolded me for it, and I didn't feel guilty about making up the story. After all, how could it be wrong to write a good essay on something that I'd never heard of anyone celebrating? It's what I knew my family, as good citizens, would have done if we had had a house like those on television.

Life would get difficult for us on East Kentucky Street, but I kept on believing in the American Dream. When I was ten, I won first place in a citywide Catholic Students Mission Crusade oratorical contest. Loud and clear I professed that "of all things in the world, the Catholic church is the most beautiful." What inspired me to speak of the church in such abstract, poetic terms? The inkling I had at the last minute to speak from the heart, like a candidate refusing to speak from a teleprompter in the last days of a campaign. I abandoned my prepared speech and riffed on what I was feeling and then wrote those remarks down. Even while practicing with my teacher as my classmates were making faces trying to distract me, I stayed on message. Winning the CSMC oratorical contest made me feel on top. It launched me on my career of making a living by using words and being actively engaged in what I cared about.

Mother made sure we had a well-rounded meal in the evening. She'd worry out loud, "How am I going to make dinner on one dollar twenty-five cents?" Daddy had given her that to buy food. Somehow she managed, cooking filling, tasty meals: ground meat loaf in rich gravy covered with tomato sauce, sweet onions, green peppers, stewed cabbage, and navy beans. On Fridays we'd have the obligatory fish—tuna on toast topped with condensed mushroom soup, or my favorite tuna croquettes; on Sundays, fried chicken or roast beef. On Saturdays, as poor as we were, for breakfast, pork chops with fried apples and homemade biscuits.

Though Daddy and Mother did not see eye to eye on some things, like his bingo playing and occasional gambling on the horses, they always seemed to put all that they had into improving our family life. When Daddy would win "the big money," he'd bring home gifts for my mom, like miniature boxes of costume jewelry—and once, an intricately carved cedar chest full of chocolates. The romantic symbolism of his gestures made a huge impact on me. When he won the three-hundred-dollar "coverall" (putting chips on all the numbers of the bingo card), he came home and took us out to dinner, ceremoniously announcing that he would be paying off a bill or buying some long-needed item, like new shoes for us kids.

On summer evenings, he'd take us to the airport to watch the planes come in or to the railroad tracks, where we'd watch the trains go by as we ate White Castle hamburgers and sipped orange sodas full of crushed ice.

Just as when I was smaller, as I got older, Daddy continued to help me out when I got into tough situations. He hated to see me unhappy. For example, when I was ten and we got a piano and I started taking the free lessons that came with it, I grew to dread them. The teacher, Miss Frances, was nice enough, but she gave me boring scales to practice, while I wanted to play melodies like Mother did. Once, when Daddy was dropping me at my lesson, he knew that I was not happy about going, and he let me sit in the car while he went to his meeting at the board of education nearby. That became our habit and secret. I never did learn to play the piano.

Like all American kids, we loved ice cream. A long summer day would often end in "going out for ice cream" to the drugstore, where it was hand-dipped into a cone. Other times, Daddy would bring it home in a carton, and sometimes we'd go to a stand and get toasted waffle cups of milky custard and eat them in the car. But my favorite way was to get it scooped up in front of me. I would lick and lick my double dip of chocolate, savoring the crunchy, plain vanilla cone long after Billy had gobbled up his.

We'd go to a drugstore near our house. I always longed to climb up on one of the red-and-silver stools at the soda fountain, where we would order our treats; I wanted to sit down and twirl around. But before we set out for the store, Mother would firmly tell us that we were not allowed to sit at the fountain and that we mustn't try. While she told us that we couldn't because "colored people" were not allowed, my stomach always knotted up, and I wanted to say something, but I couldn't because I knew how much Mother hated what she was telling us. Following her orders, we would silently get our ice cream cones and quickly leave.

Even though we had rehearsed it before going, I was always crestfallen when we went into the store and I couldn't sit at the counter or when, to take another example of how we had to stay out of the way, we had to lie down on the floor of our father's car while he was driving through certain neighborhoods, especially some parks, where Daddy said "colored people aren't allowed." When we moved to East Kentucky Street in August 1954, we were the first black family to live in the all-white, working-class neighborhood, right after the Supreme Court's 1954 decision to desegregate public schools. We moved the week before school began, and that was when my perfect world began to crumble.

The house was near Male High School, which was supposed to begin admitting Negro children, boys, the Tuesday after Labor Day, in the first week of September. A few days before, in the early hours of the morning while relaxing with her beer and cigarette, Mother was startled to see the shadows of tall flames on the wall as she was going upstairs, and that caused her to rouse Daddy. One of his students had already called for help, and the fire engine came, flashing lights, encircling our house and front yard as a small crowd gathered on the sidewalk. The next morning, leaving for my first day of third grade, I saw the burned wood and charred remains in the garbage can and asked what happened. The Ku Klux Klan had burned a cross in our front yard. Confused and afraid, I wondered why anyone would use the symbol of the Crucifixion to scare us from our home.

Standing in the courtroom with my family and uncles, I realized it wasn't like Perry Mason on television at all. I thought I'd get to sit in the chair in the witness stand and answer questions posed by a dashing legal counsel, but the reality was much more matter-of-fact. My father told the story of how we were being harassed because of our race, and he signed some papers. Since the cross burning, life had been one scare after another: A woman waved a newspaper in my brother's face forbidding him to ride his bike in front of her house. I could no longer skate up and down the sidewalk because I would cross in front of the house, which, my parents suspected, was occupied by Klan members. One hot morning the next summer, we found our dog Spot curled up in the corner of the garage whimpering in pain. Daddy took him to the vet and had him "put to sleep." He had been poisoned, probably by the same bigots who didn't want us on the block.

5

Big Girl

I had to grow up. Living where we were not welcome and the increasing size of our family was forcing me to. During most of our days on Kentucky Street, we were four children, a family of six for five years, which was a long time. When Helene came along in 1958 to light up our world, we became a family of seven. Two years later, we were eight when Rodney rolled in, bouncing around like a ball of energy. In 1963, came our jewel of a baby sister, Evelyn, whom we nicknamed Poochie, when I was a senior in high school, completing our family of nine. By then we had moved house twice in one year.

Being in charge of my siblings and helping look after the house had gotten me used to the idea of being responsible for people and important things. But when I finally had to abandon childhood at age eleven, I was not ready. It happened fast: I was unceremoniously co-opted to help Mother play Santa Claus, whom, fantasizer that I was, I still believed in! Three months later, blood was oozing uncontrollably out of me; I was becoming a woman. While I was looking forward to being a teenager and couldn't wait until 1960 when I'd be the magic age of fourteen—new decade and new life for me—as fast as my starry-eyed childhood slipped away, the more tightly I held on to it. Even though I may have reveled in the age of innocence too long, the slowness seems not to have hurt me; on the contrary, it gave me a soft cushion that helped me absorb the shocks of life.

Like a lot of children, along with Billy, I had to look after my sisters and be responsible for the house after school before Mother or Daddy got home. That was when I was ten, and Mother went back to work to help support us. Becoming a latchkey kid cracked the looking glass through which I saw life: having to deal with keeping track of the house keys; giving up television shows to clean the kitchen; and the hardest, staying inside to keep an eye on the little ones when I wanted the freedom of carefree play. I had liked playing big girl, but being one was something else. I began to feel cut off and apprehensive and resented giving up my imaginary escapes.

To prolong the transition, I sought refuge in books and affected a scholarly image. I gave up the life of a cowgirl and spun fantasies based on the lyrics of popular songs—Elvis singing "Love Me Tender," for example, but also Frank Sinatra. I'd sing along to his "Witchcraft" pressing my ear to the tan portable radio I'd received that Christmas. I started reading *Photo Play* to take my mind to other places, like California and dazzling LA.

By eighth grade, already weighing too much but with curves, I looked like the adult that I would become. I tried to project the image of being a joiner, a team player, but I kept my distance in a group by taking the role of leader. I was cautious around adults, because they didn't tell me the whole story about most things to which I needed answers. I had to move on from playing big girls to being one myself.

With my hard landing in preadolescence came a decline in our family's economic status. Money had always been a factor, but since our lives had revolved around our parish church and school, we had been sheltered from the roughest realities of hard times. The situation became worse when my father retired early from teaching, and my rose-colored life turned blue. Of course when we went to Frankfurt, Kentucky, the state capital, to collect his two-thousand-dollar lump sum retirement pay, we thought we were millionaires. In 1957, $2,000 had the buying power of more than $17,000, a considerable sum in those days. At age fifty-one, Daddy probably planned to pay off his debts and make a living in shoe repair. At the state building in Frankfort, Billy and I played on the elevator, riding it up and down while Daddy, Mother, and the younger kids waited for his paperwork to be completed. We all went out for a big meal in a restaurant afterward, and we got new colorful summer clothes that spring. Gas was only about fifty cents a gallon, but to save on spending, trips to see relatives were curtailed, as were extended family get-togethers. We lost touch with relatives and began to feel like poor relations.

Beholden. It's a state that my mother dreaded being in and which she would go to great lengths to hide. For instance, she would make our home and our appearance seem as if nothing were wrong: If the lights were cut off because we could not pay the electric bill, she'd cook in the fireplace, even in July, and she'd help us have fun doing it. We'd use kerosene lamps and pretend we were on a camping trip. That's the time that Anita, the baby then, whom we could not trust to keep a secret, proved us right by blurting out to a friend from our old neighborhood that our lights were cut off. Billy and I had already been worried that someone would find out by noticing the smoke coming out of the chimney in the middle of a July day. Now we were exposed for the poor people that we were becoming but didn't feel like we were.

As we fell on tough times and those trips to the hills of Virginia stopped, I lost contact with Uncle William, who'd always sent me the best Christmas presents and whom my mother depended on as her "big brother." I missed the wonder of going to the movie theater, where he operated the projector; we considered him the owner because he acted like he was, not buying tickets for me and my brother and sisters but taking us in for free and getting us all the cellophane-wrapped candy we could want to snack on. In Virginia, in Tazewell, in Holly Town, in Big Stone Gap, I would see white people who looked like us, and I wanted to ask why this was so, but I knew that I had to keep quiet. In Southwestern Virginia, my mother's family acted as if the civil rights movement was not taking place.

They called themselves "colored," and even years later when "black" came into vogue, they preferred not to be called as such. I thought they were just being narrow-minded and old-fashioned, but I'd later learn, from reading an unpublished family oral history written in 1909, they had good reason: not only did European blood obviously run through our family, but, as I've noted, Pamunkey, Choctaw and Cherokee Indian blood coursed through our veins as well.[3] Even more satisfying was to discover that one of my ancestors had blazed the trails of the West with Edward Beal who, on previous expeditions, had collaborated with the legendary scout Kit Carson.

---

3 An unpublished family history documents the Pamunkey and other Indian connections.

Charles Mudd, many times
great-uncle on my father's
side, fought for the Union

Cynthia Holley Warren, my
great, great, great grandmother
on my mother's side

Re-Elect
KENT MUDD
INDEPENDENT CANDIDATE
for
City Council
"83 Year Resident
of Springfield"
NOVEMBER 8, 1977

Uncle William

Great-Uncle Kent, from Daddy's
side of the family, in the 1980s,
first black elected official in
Washington County, Ky.

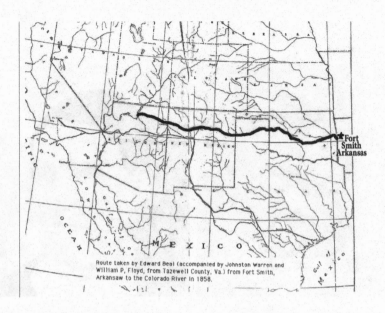

Route taken by Edward Beal (accompanied by Johnston Warren and William P. Floyd, from Tazewell County, Va.) from Fort Smith, Arkansaw to the Colorado River in 1858.

Map of Edward Beal's expedition survey of the Western plains in about 1858; my ancestor, Johnston Warren, was appointed by the then governor of Virginia to aid Beal; with permission of the artist, Rekha Kaula

Hoyt Warren, my maternal great, great-uncle, with his brothers and sisters

As 1959 came and I would be thirteen, a teenager, and was looking forward to high school, our family's sharp descent into poverty pulled the rug from under my feet. Times had been tough, but now I was feeling it. Even when he was a teacher, Daddy didn't make enough to buy a home for our family, but he had taught his children that times were getting better. Now that I knew that times wouldn't get better if changes didn't happen to give blacks more access to the same good life as other Americans, I began looking for a better life outside of my home.

Helping Mother with the housework gave me a lot of time to hold tight to the threads of my younger years and spin dreams for the future. Like the old country tune said, the proper role for children was to "be your mother's little helper . . ." (This song existed before a song of the same name about drugs came out.) The nuns encouraged us as girls in that thinking. Probably my sense of doing things well also made me very good at it. For instance, I got used to washing linen in the bathtub, rubbing each item up and down on a soapy board, before we had a washing machine with a spin dryer. I'd help Mother hang the bleached, spanking clean sheets and other items on the clothesline to flap in the wind. Our furniture, curtains, and rugs were old—Daddy had brought them with him from his mountain home in Eastern Kentucky—but they had to be polished and dusted.

Wishing that we had modern, light, upholstered sofa and chairs, if I'd known how, I would have cursed the shiny pink-and-blue striped fabric covering the seats of the dark wooden framed chairs. Instead, I rubbed their delicate arms and legs, becoming familiar with every crevice. Even though I was by myself while doing these chores, I was embarrassed by the starched yellow couch cover decorated with roses. *Who but our family used a couch cover?* I helped Mother when she washed and starched it once, a major job requiring a deep tub of water, lots of rinsing, the required starching with hot water, and several bouts of wringing the thick cotton with bare hands, not to mention the long hours of ironing. I became a master at pressing the ruffles; with several sprinkles of water and all that starch, their ends stiffly stood out.

The coffee table had a blotch of discolored wood in the corner where someone had spilled, as Mother would say, "alcohol," meaning—I didn't know then—not the kind you rub but the kind you drink. Its dainty curled-up legs, one of which was broken, had to be handled ever so gently lest it toppled over. Polishing and waxing it, I kept my spite for it to myself as I lifted the protective glass cover. Here I would take my time to pause and enjoy looking at the montage of black-and-white photos lying under it. Now that they are lost, I strive to hold on to those glances.

Even though I liked lurking in the living room after cleaning it and sneaking a look through my father's books locked in a four-foot-high case, my forte was cleaning the kitchen. Almost every Saturday morning from ages eleven to fourteen, I had to defrost the refrigerator. Defrosting was a complex operation, but it had to be done so that the ice that had caked in the upper freezer compartment would not build up and interfere with the overall cooling of the insulated box. Auto defrost was unheard of in our house. I'd begin by removing all the food and drinks; I'd pour boiled water into the aluminum ice trays and let them stand for a couple of hours. While the ice was melting, I'd turn my attention to the gas stove—the iron burners, white enamel surface, and the inside of the oven, rubbing and rinsing and pressing as hard as my hands could. By the time I finished the stove, the refrigerator would be clear of frost and ready to have the contents put back. I hated this four-hour Saturday chore, but with Mother hovering around, I had no choice but to do it. What was worse, I had to stay alert and make changes when needed—for example, during hot weather, remembering to keep the food on ice in large pans to keep it from spoiling when it was out of the refrigerator.

The only good thing about this drudgery was that it gave me time each week to listen to *American Bandstand,* hosted by Dick Clark on the radio. Reception was scratchy, since Louisville didn't receive the broadcast directly. It was relayed from an affiliate, and there were pops of weird sounds in between songs, but I didn't care. I'd turn the volume up high and sing along to all the latest hits, picturing the teenage girls and boys dancing. By keeping up with the pop chart, I was living my fantasy of a bobby-soxer. On Saturday nights I'd repeat the strategy for TV, tuning in to *Your Hit Parade*, which, again, since there was no direct broadcast to Louisville viewers, I had to watch two weeks delayed at 11:30 p.m., the transmission so unclear that the picture looked like it was snowing. My sisters had all gone to bed, Billy was doing his own thing, Mother and Daddy were enjoying their beers, and I was falling in love with Pat Boone crooning "April Love" in his white buckskin shoes.

When John "Rodney" was born in 1960, that did throw me off course. I was not ready to deal with another baby and took some time to get used to the idea. I'm not proud to say it, but I was probably resentful of my mother for spoiling my familiar world. One beautiful cherub, Helene, was wonderful, but another, especially a boy, didn't fit in with the calm atmosphere in which I was living my life. With his shiny blond curls and bright complexion, he looked like Goldilocks, and as the second boy that my mother had longed for, after four girls, he was spoiled. When I came home from school, he'd chase me around the house, hitting my feet with a stick, forcing me to climb onto the bed to get out of his reach. He was a holy terror, but Mother didn't seem to take my annoyance seriously. One day, Billy got fed up with the way my sisters would brush Rodney's hair into ponytails, making him look like a doll, and marched him off to the barbershop and got his beautiful locks cut off!

By that time, with Andrea and Anita getting older, Mother stopped depending on me as much to help at home and let me take the time I needed for homework, school activities, and babysitting. That set of circumstances began to create a gap between me and Mother that, I am not proud to say, I did not take the initiative to heal until well into my adulthood. That gap kept me from knowing Rodney, whose life was brutally cut short when he was in his prime.

I was becoming a woman, and my mother was still having babies, and my Dad, my idol, was demoralized as he could not work. In 1958, after he had retired from teaching and was looking for work, I'd sit with him as he combed the want ads looking for a job. We would watch the morning news with its graphic depictions of the numbers of unemployed: little stick figures lined up next to percent signs. He would say that he was just another statistic among those unemployed, and that he didn't take it personally, but not having a job sapped the pride of this man who had worked all his life. I took it personally and couldn't bear to think of him as a stickman on a chart.

My father had been heavily influenced by the great former slave, educator, and founder of Tuskegee Institute, Booker T. Washington. Like the man from Tuskegee, Daddy believed that blacks should acquire skills that they could do with their hands to stay economically independent. He thought he could turn his part-time skill teaching shoe repair in evening trade school into full-time work, but that didn't pan out. My brother and I would help him in the shop, which he ran for the white owner, on one of Louisville's commercial streets. I can still smell the leather and feel the vibration of the machine that buffed the shoes, but I also recall that very few customers came in. It seemed a lonely, strange place for my man of books and briefcase.

In the summer of 1960, after I'd completed eighth grade and just before I started high school, we moved from the house on Kentucky Street. The KKK and the racial harassment had not made it easy living there, but we had many happy times in those seven years. Our neighbors on both sides were wonderful people who had not gone along with those trying to drive us out of the neighborhood: The Harveys, whose house was on the left, often sat on their porch in the swing wearing their country-Western hats, with guitar music blaring on the radio; they were kind. The Stabiles, on the right side, were warm and outgoing. They invited me to be friends with their niece Sue Carol when she came to visit them. We two would spend afternoons sewing cushions and eating mouthwatering Italian delights that Mrs. Stabile would insist I share with her niece. Sue Carole was my first nonblack friend; she was like me, my sisters, and my school friends. I found no difference between us because of race.

We left Kentucky Street to move into a house in the West End, the better section for Louisville's black community, which was a significant 18 percent of the population, on Woodland Avenue. I thought it was our dream house, for even though we were still renting, Mother, who had always longed to have her own home, acted as if it was. She went to a lot of trouble to decorate and make it cozy. I especially remember the bedroom that Andrea and I shared: Mother painted the walls dusky pink, and the bed and chests of drawers cream with a light teal trim. She stayed up late during the night working to make the room picture perfect, putting tiny glass knobs on the drawers so that they would sparkle like crystal and ironing and putting crisp white cotton doilies on the tops of the chests and bedside tables.

As on Kentucky Street, the small attic room at the top of the one-story house was off-limits to us. But Billy would sneak in when the landlord wasn't there, make prank calls on the telephone, and one day let me join him. So glad was I to share in his fun that I didn't dwell on how "bad" our behavior was. He'd dial a number; we'd take turns saying hello in a disguised voice and then slam down the receiver.

That room was kept as a space for the man who owned the house. And since, as we later learned, he and my father had shaken hands on the rental agreement, and not signed a lease, eight months later in March 1961, we were forced to move on short notice when the man asked for his house back. Despite having finally settled in what was for us the American Dream home, we had to move—again. Mother was beside herself with disappointment; Daddy had been too trusting in this fellow black "brother." I was also seeing a two-timer for the first time, for our landlord had another woman and child whom he wanted to move into the house. When she cooked chitlins, something we never ate because Mother said they needed too much cleaning, the pungent, unpleasant smell that permeated the house was overwhelming, and I had to go out in order not to feel nauseous. The low-down morality of the situation stunned us as much as the suddenness of having to move. My parents had tried all of my life to keep us away from such an environment; now we were facing it directly.

In the eight months since we'd moved to our new house, the tough times had rushed up against us. As buying food became a problem, Mother used her enormous range of wits to feed us. She'd soak a bag of navy beans, add a bone or a piece of bacon, a can of tomatoes, whip up corn bread—what Daddy called "Johnny cakes"—and lay out a filling dinner. She would run up a bill with the milkman who stopped by in a truck twice a week. She'd order half-gallon cartons of orange juice and milk and sickeningly sweet white powdered sugar donuts to fill our stomachs for breakfast—all on credit that she negotiated with the milkman.

Our desperate situation became real to me when, for the first time, Thanksgiving of 1960, we didn't have turkey and trimmings for the table. What a change, as we had been used to feasting on the traditional big meal and took it for granted. Fear of not having food was one of the bleakest periods of my life. I don't remember ever really being hungry, but I do recall Mother's wringing of hands and Daddy's vacant stares when they were trying to put together enough resources to feed us.

A few days before Thanksgiving, our neighbors, the Boones, were leaving to spend the holiday out of town. While they were away, one of their friends asked Mother to hold a box containing a cake and give it to the Boones when they returned. Naturally, Mother agreed to this neighborly gesture. The square, eggshell-colored box stood on a corner of the sideboard, and we children stared at it, imagining how delightful it would be to just have a taste of the luscious treat inside. Our desires got so bad that we started sneaking licks of the chocolate icing of the equally flavored cake. We nipped and stared at that confectionary so much that Mother finally decided that we should cut it up, sit down, and eat it properly, and we did.

In the warm afterglow of a stomach full of cake, I began worrying about what Mrs. Boone would say. I had babysat for her children and was proud that she and her husband seemed to think well of me. Now, she'd think I was part of a family that couldn't resist stealing someone's dessert!

As befitting her, Mrs. Boone's reaction was dignified: she didn't make a fuss about what we'd done and continued to ask me to babysit, knowing, I'm sure, that I could use the money. I'm sure there was outside food help around, but my parents were proud. We lived the fiction of a middle class family as stoically as we could. Daddy even went to Columbus, Ohio, to work in shoe repair in a department store and live with my aunt and uncle, but the money spent on long-distance calls and the misery of separation tore at all of us. He came back after six weeks.

I started spending a lot of time babysitting for Aunt Evelyn, who lived in a spacious house on the Ohio River, with a swimming pool and a boat dock. We considered her and Uncle James rich. Aunt Evelyn had constantly asked Mother to give her one of us, because she had only one son, who was now grown-up. "You make such pretty children, Julia," she would say, adding that Mother could easily have babies, while her own fate had not been as kind. While Mother said she would never give any of us away, she did readily let us stay with Aunt Evelyn from time to time, and though they were not related by blood, Aunt Evelyn was like an older sister to Mother; both she and Uncle James were like close relatives to us. Still, I lived with the fear of our family being split apart by the generosity of well-meaning people.

"Aunt Evelyn" in the early 1980s

Years before, on Kentucky Street, I had to spend the night with the late middle-aged woman who sublet the back house from us. I hated having to sleep under her stack of heavy quilts on the sofa with its creaky spring mattress, which rolled out into a bed in her overheated front room, smelling the floral air spray that permeated throughout her little house. Mother and Daddy evidently wanted to show the childless woman that they could be generous with the only wealth they had—their children.

Aunt Evelyn continued to take me to meetings in Protestant churches, thus putting me in the heart of the movement in Louisville. We'd sing songs like "Ain't Gonna Let Nobody Turn Me Around," "Freedom" (to the tune of "Amen" from *Lilies of the Field*, a 1963 film starring Sidney Poitier), and the resounding "We Shall Overcome."

Although Aunt Evelyn paid me only three dollars for ironing all day on Saturdays and gave me little money for taking care of the two young children she had finally adopted, I was grateful for the job. Her trust in me and the second home she gave me were invaluable. During the week, I'd often sleep at her house, and I could eat whatever I wanted from her well-stocked kitchen. She prided herself in entertaining. I helped her arrange lavish parties: with shrimp, stuffed lobster tails, and rice dishes from her Alabama past. Drinks were offered liberally, and I'd wiped streaks out of the various-sized cocktail glasses and got to know about highballs and other mixed drinks. Once, before a do, she had me help her hoist her best Kentucky bourbon up onto a shelf in her bedroom closet. "They're not going to get their hands on these bottles," she declared as I wondered why she would hide her best liquor from her guests.

When the landlord on Woodland asked for his house back, we were forced to move; but this time, even though it was before his illness when he could still work, Daddy did not have time to raise enough money to rent another house. We had to move back to the East End, into the Sheppard Square projects, in a section of Louisville where blacks have lived since slavery: Smoketown. This was the beginning of a downward spiral for my mother. She had sworn that she would never live in public housing, and all of us were in a daze since we were blindsided at having to move on two weeks' notice. The feeling of being thrown out, the poignancy of leaving Mother's artfully painted rooms, and the bleakness of our new digs—dull brownish-yellow cinder blocks and cold, hard gray concrete floors rampant with roaches, which we tried in vain to eradicate—rattled us. After we moved in, Daddy didn't laugh or smile often anymore, and Mother pretty much gave up putting a positive spin on things.

That July when we were getting set to vacate Kentucky Street, I caught a sight of my Mother that showed me what poverty can do. She was standing at the washing machine in a starched, orange floral maternity blouse, her auburn hair swept back in a stately bun, her eyes pleading. That was before Rodney was to be born, when her younger sister from Columbus, Aunt Helen, who was visiting, was scolding her: "You're due in six weeks and haven't been to a doctor!" Mother looked "caught." I was humiliated for her.

Throughout all the instability—the move from Kentucky Street, getting settled and taking the bus to my new girls' high school, then suddenly having to leave our Woodland house and shift to the Sheppard Square projects—I threw myself into my wonderful new world of school life. I tried to be like one of the bobby-soxers in the movies as much as I could, for I was still a dreamer. Going to great lengths to fit in, I made the best of things. After we moved to the projects, Daddy signed us up for public assistance, and we started receiving powdered milk and eggs, flour, canned cheese, peanut butter, and Spam. Billy started working to help out at home, and I increased my babysitting on weekends to take care of my expenses.

Cash assistance for a family of eight was a mere twenty-five dollars a month in Louisville in those days of poor people "living high on the hog off of welfare" as many claimed. As small as that amount was, we were luckier than previous recipients: Foods from the national food surplus, part of that wheat to Russia issue that had worried me in grade school, like peanut butter and flour, had only been incorporated after the Kennedy administration had called for them to replace the unhealthier lard and cornmeal that had gone to indigent families. A neighbor would sell Daddy large, almost-empty drums of ice cream, which we'd eat pretending that the gritty taste did not bother us; we of course knew better. Daddy never declared bankruptcy; he should have but was too proud.

Before that time, in May of 1960, while we were still on Kentucky Street, as eighth grade ended and my fourteenth birthday loomed large on June 5, I felt at the top of my happy heap. I *was* in our little community: I had the good wishes of close friends, my teachers, relatives, and my parents. After a couple of years of inner conflict, stoked by taking part in the civil rights movement, I had less anxiety about people like me not being liked and not having the same chance as others.

The nuns at Saint Peter Claver had emphasized that if students didn't pay attention and learn certain things, we would not be "up to par." I didn't know at the time that we were being insulted to our faces, and neither do I think the sisters meant to do that. I took their advice to heart and held on to it until a sister in high school enlarged on the idea, telling students that settling for average "par" was what many did. "Remember, girls," she'd say, "there's always room at the top."

I never felt the sisters were racially prejudiced, although in hindsight I can see the implicit biases they had. They were, after all, products of the time, from the same population as the society outside the convent. I took their encouraging words to heart and did my best. When I was in sixth grade, my real feelings had been tested: An after-school practice of Stephen Foster songs ended in the first utterance of the N-word I'd heard from a nun. Sister thumped on the piano in frustration, screeching, "Jeanie, Jeanie . . ." She was standing with her foot on the piano pedal, her reedy voice hitting that high note that the boys, on that sun-swept spring day, couldn't or didn't want to reach. We girls were getting it, and

I had been mentally seeing myself in a long hooped dress on the steps of "My Old Kentucky Home." I was into Stephen Foster visiting the pretty, young ladies, who had welcomed him, but the boys would have none of it. After an hour-long attempt to bring us up to par in this drawing room antebellum entertainment, Sister got so frustrated that she said, "You're nothing but a bunch of n——s!" We students left in a united protest, boys and girls together, to tell our parents. While I wanted Sister to get her due in the way of complaints from our parents, I secretly felt sorry for her: the boys *had* acted up!

What I learned in grade school paid off for the rest of my life: such as when, in fifth grade, Sister said in teaching English grammar, "Listen, if you get this now, you'll never have to worry about it again." That made sense to me. I sat up straighter and "got it" then and since.

By the end of the eighth grade, I had developed a deep relationship with God on a personal level. Wishing really hard in my make-believe world had made praying natural; but when harsh realities hovered over my secure globe, I would ask God for help, and he always came through. I'm not saying I got everything I prayed for, but I accepted all that I got as a sign of my pleas being answered. Results came after I made an effort to help myself. Along the way, as I put away childish things, I learned to pray more realistically, without magical thinking. I also learned to ask God for forgiveness. That kept me humble.

With all the singing and celebrations at home and in church, I learned to be grateful and to take the time to acknowledge others' generosity, a good thing, for I would have lots of that. Blacks were feeling that they were going to have a chance for the better life that all Americans wanted. When I was told that I would be going to Ursuline Academy, I breathed a sigh of relief. Although I tried to act as nonchalant as I could, inside I was shouting, "Thank you, God!"

Courtesy of the archives of the Ursuline Sisters of Louisville, Ky.

6

Ursuline Girl

The good thing about moving into the projects was its proximity to Ursuline. From Woodland I had to take a bus. While not a problem, I had to allow ninety minutes to get to my new school on time. From Sheppard Square I could walk or catch a bus and be there in forty-five minutes. Fortunate to attend this all-girls high school on a scholarship, I thought I was the economically poorest in the class (and that even the orphans were better off), but I've come to know since that others were struggling too.

The Sisters of Saint Ursula ran two secondary high schools—the one at Shelby and Chestnut, in town, which I attended, and Sacred Heart on Lexington Avenue, out from the city, where the boulevards were lined with leafy trees and the houses saluted passersby loftily, set back from the pavement. Our school attracted students from working-class families, while the other school was for the well-heeled. I never paid attention to class when I was at Ursuline, nor did my school friends speak to me of it. Besides, I was "beyond class," so to speak, being from a minority. While Ursuline closed its doors long ago, I'm proud to say that my niece, Billy's daughter Alyshia Mudd, went to Sacred Heart. For me, Ursuline was a palace of learning.

Buying the required uniform was out of the question when I was to enter its hallowed halls because the money situation at home was tight. The matter had pressed on my mind all that summer of 1960 as our family was moving and settling into the West End, and I had to be creative to come up with the prescribed garb. I saved as much money as I could from babysitting and ironing and was able to purchase the skirt, blouse, and cardigan from a less expensive outlet than the one designated. For physical education, I dyed the ivory-colored cotton shorts I'd been wearing all summer the required navy blue. I did manage to buy the obligatory clip-on black string tie that all of us seemed to hate. We'd pull the Western-looking bow off as soon as we left the premises.

Keeping me and my sisters and brothers in shoes was a constant concern of Mother and Daddy, but somehow I was able to get new ones: brown and white saddle oxfords with brand new laces and socks that I folded down above my ankles. I pulled my hair back and wore it in a ponytail the first year; for the second year, I got it cut and wore it in the popular bouffant style. I'd wash my blouse every night and dry it in front of the fan or on the heater. When the collar frayed, I detached it and turned it over and sewed it back on by hand. I also washed my skirt and cardigan as needed. While I'd sometimes be self-conscious about the increasing shininess and length of the sweater—in those days synthetics couldn't stand much washing and drip-drying—I pretty much managed this system for all four years, once or twice buying a new blouse. I was okay, clean and neat. And none of my classmates ever made me feel that there was anything wrong with my appearance.

With Catholic Students Mission Crusade team: from left, Linda
Lane, Mary Beth Walsh, Pat Hellman, me, Hilda Ford, Judy Gay

With debate teammates Linda Lege, Margaret Thompson, and Kate Wilder; all photos courtesy of the archives, Ursuline Sisters, Louisville, Ky.

Ursuline Academy, which opened in 1859 and closed in 1972, is listed as a historic site on the national register of the Department of Interior as an example of late nineteenth-century religious and educational structures designed by regional architects. Built of dark red brick with limestone trim in the Romanesque Revival style, the gateway imposed its presence as I looked up at it. Going under its arch entering school each morning, I felt calm and peaceful. All distracting thoughts were shunted to the back of my mind in this quiet haven where concentrating on learning was the thing to do. The stained glass chapel windows were a delight to my eyes, and the nuns sweeping about silently with great dignity keeping everything in order made it a refuge from the threat of disorder outside. How terrible it is in these days of revelations about the hard times some have had in Catholic schools—and it is right that members of religious orders be brought to justice—but my memories of the Sisters of Saint Ursula are of their kindness, caring, and dedication to excellence. Ursuline Academy gave me the grace and certainty that I needed to have the confidence to explore what I wanted to do in life.

The education was classical—Latin, French, world history, biology, chemistry, algebra, and geometry. Since fourth grade my favorite subject had been English. Now in high school I could spend time with the poets—the British: Longfellow, Tennyson, Browning, and, of course, Shakespeare, to name a few. I lost myself in the worlds of the American writers Hawthorne, Melville, Twain, and Louisa May Alcott, and the poets Emily Dickinson, Carl Sandburg, and Robert Frost, and became familiar with others. I absorbed English grammar just as thirstily: the logic of diagraming sentences was comforting; conjugating verbs was fun; identifying parts of speech gave my world order.

French vied with English as my favorite subject. Taught by a Belgian, it was my first extended contact with someone from a foreign country, from Europe, a connection that would spur me across seas and shores throughout my life.

I made friends easily and enjoyed being in their close-knit circle. Behind those walls we seldom spotted a member of the opposite sex, and when we did, we made such fools of ourselves giggling and whispering that it's a wonder any man—maintenance or otherwise—ever came on the premises. Active in clubs, singing, drama, and student government since my first year, I joined the debate team in my final year when one was being formed. I was eager to hone my public speaking skills, and since my father had debated in college, I wanted to follow in his footsteps. An added incentive was our coach Skip April, who was not only dynamic but very good-looking. He was a student at Bellarmine College, which was then only for men. Before his arrival for our weekly debate class, girls would crowd the coatroom and primp, applying lipstick, hair spray, and perfumes to look good for him. When the team was chosen, I was among them, but I'm sure it was not for my looks. Though pleased to be selected, I was not surprised. I was used to public speaking since I was ten and felt it was a part of my destiny.

In those early days of Medicare, our team debated the pros and cons of guaranteeing health care for all. That issue led me to set out on a life of reading broadly and deeply on America's economic and social history of poverty, making a lasting impression. I came to appreciate the changes brought about by Franklin Roosevelt, and I got a better idea of what my parents had said to me about his social welfare policies. Since my parents hadn't stressed how slavery was linked to being poor, I came to see my family's situation in the larger context of America's story. And as I built on my knowledge in high school, that and my parents' continued commitment to the rightness of this country ensured that I grew up relatively bitter-free even in dire economic conditions.

Adhering to the strict lines of behavior UA required wasn't a problem because I had no social life outside of my family and community. Within Ursuline's environment I was free to build castles in my mind, of wonderful things like traveling to England and France. And despite the school's forbidden fruit atmosphere—chastity and purity had to constantly be monitored—I could follow sixties pop culture. Like my classmates, I was enraptured by the Beatles, seeing them for the first time on Ed Sullivan's TV show.

Paradoxically, as much of a dreamer as I was, I didn't brood about not having a boyfriend. Being at home with my siblings or at school with my friends brought out my nurturing skills, and in return I got all the physical affection I needed. Besides, girls in my neighborhood whom I had thought were carefree teenagers only years before were now pushing baby strollers. One of my classmates was planning to marry immediately after graduation, and I couldn't see why: *Why would she not want to put her education to good use, at least for a while?* I spent a lot of time thinking about the issue, wondering if I was lacking in something because I didn't want to get married right away, especially since I didn't even have a boyfriend and had never dated. What really made me weigh the pros and cons of finding someone and getting married soon was an offhand remark that Mother made one day as we were polishing the living room furniture yet again. Much to my surprise, without any warning she let me know that she was not happy having opted for the traditional role of wife and mother. Fifteen years later, she would tell me about having to give up her dream of acting on the stage when her mother wouldn't let her attend a summer drama camp in upstate New York all expenses paid. An unchaperoned girl didn't do those things in her day. Hurt and puzzled by her outburst, I began to seriously think about a life of working.

In 1962, when I was sixteen and in my second year of high school, something happened that altered my world forever: Daddy was driving me to the Corpus Christi procession where I was going to meet my high school classmates. The event was taking place at Churchill Downs, where the famous derby horse race was held. I'd been there with Daddy a few times when he took us for the last run of the day when admission to enter was free. I was looking forward to returning to the historic place and circumventing the track like the crowned thoroughbreds. And as I seldom had a reason to get dressed up and my friends hadn't seen me wear anything but a school uniform, I wanted to show off. I had taken time to make myself look good, wearing high heels and a beige spring coat that, though much too heavy for the hot June temperature, I wore because it flattered me.

In those days when blacks and whites stayed apart, I didn't hang out with the girls I went to school with; and summers were particularly hard because I couldn't find jobs in stores and shops like they could. Even the popular volunteer stint as a Candy Striper in a hospital was off-limits to people like me, so going to the Corpus Christi procession, sponsored by the Archdiocese of Louisville, was a rare chance to be with my schoolmates at the start of summer vacation.

On that day, Sunday, June 24, 1962, I thought I'd be breaking the mold, but all at once the car slowed, and from my seat in the back, I saw Daddy's head slump. At first, I didn't panic because I was with Daddy, who always had everything under control. After a minute or so of silence, I heard him whisper, "Sis," slurring his words, "I'm going to stop here for a while . . ." Then his voice trailed off. I sat in the silent car off of the two-lane road, looking at the still trees, which weren't moving in the humid heat of summer's first days. Finally, Daddy said that he believed he had had a stroke. Although I had heard of the condition, I didn't know what it meant. We sat for what seemed like an hour. With no cell phones in those days and no 911, it never occurred to me to get out of the car and scream for help. Blacks didn't do that. I could picture my friends wondering where I was, and I hated not being with them. I was disappointed that I had to miss out—again. But when Daddy very slowly started the car and, staying in the right lane, drove at what seemed like a creeping pace of about twenty miles an hour, I began to realize the enormity of the problem.

I appreciated the skill of his driving and the tenderness he was showing me by trying not to have an accident. As he maneuvered us home, I was overcome with shame of my selfishness. From that moment I vowed to do what I could to make life easier for him as he went through his debilitating illness from which he never recovered. He, the man of letters, lost his ability to read. That he still had his sight was a blessing but made his condition all the more frustrating, because while he could see the words, he could not remember their meaning.

One day in the fall of my senior year, one of my teachers cornered me in front of the frosted glass doors leading to a side exit, backing me against them: "Don't you want to become one of us? Why don't you join us?" she asked, standing so close that I could see her teeth and the pink of her mouth as her stiff collar lifted up toward my face. I knew the Catholic tradition of one child of a large family "going to Christ," and I had spent hours reflecting on doing so. But all the sisters I wanted to be like were of European origin; the ones who were of color were working as nurses or in the kitchens of convents, and they were not Ursulines. I could see myself as a teaching nun, but that didn't seem possible, and most importantly, I didn't feel called to the religious life—didn't have a vocation. I felt bad that I had to tell Sister that I didn't want to join the convent when she pressed me on the matter. I was embarrassed for her because she seemed in a hurry for an answer.

Although I hadn't told anyone, I had already found what I wanted to do. I was not yet sixteen when I saw a photo of two young women in a magazine, in black sheath dresses, hair pulled back off their faces, smiling and looking very attractive in front of the American embassy in Paris. The caption said they were in the U.S. Foreign Service. Having been interested in international and current affairs for a long time, I knew immediately that I wanted to be like them and work at an embassy. Since I wanted to go to college, whatever it was that you could do in the Foreign Service with a college degree, I wanted to do. Not long after, I came across the name of Georgetown University's School of Foreign Service, and though I eventually went to American University's School of International Service, back then, the idea of getting an MSFS, a master of science in the Foreign Service from Georgetown, struck me as the right next step toward my goal. I enjoyed telling everyone that I was going to get an MSFS. That sounded slightly off-color and stopped them from asking me any more questions about what I'd do after graduation!

As I said, I didn't have a boyfriend. Not having a "steady" was causing me to miss out on what I thought was the life of a "typical teenager." In the absence of a real romance, I read fiction with strong romantic themes— for example, a novel about the Christian Lygia and the non-Christian patrician Marcus, *Quo Vadis*, set in ancient Rome. I read the over 550-page book once and was starting to read it again when Mother caught me huddled on the floor beside the bed one afternoon and told me not to waste my time. I felt like Mary in the Bible story of Mary and Martha. I wanted a contemplative life, but Mother wanted me to get out more and have more experiences.

In the touchy-feely community I grew up in, I was used to hugs and kisses, boys pulling my pigtails, and having my brothers' friends and male cousins around. This atmosphere helped me get used to the opposite sex. Ironically, the more the nuns warned us about sex, the more I thought about having a boyfriend. I painted a day when I would have a guy I could be proud of. I blush when I share it, but I projected onto every priest who wore a suit, leading our annual retreat or talking to our class, my thoughts about life with "the perfect one."

What with studies, homework, activities, helping at home, and babysitting, the closest I came to dating in high school was going to my senior prom, which my mother insisted I attend when I was chickening out at the last minute. I had good reasons: getting the formal wear together seemed too overwhelming, and since I had been stood up on my first date, I wasn't sanguine about succeeding in getting an escort to the prom.

Being stood up on my first date had a lot to do with my lack of confidence in finding a mate. Our youth club at Saint Peter Claver had organized a Valentine's Day dance when I was sixteen. I thought of the event as the perfect time to celebrate that sweet number by going to the dance with my first date. I invited a boy in my brother's class. He was two years older than me and from a well-respected family whose oldest son was in a seminary training to be a priest. I thought of the oldest brother as a knight in shining armor from a heavenly family. That made his younger brother the next best person to have for a first date! When the younger brother didn't show up on the big night to pick me up to go to the dance, I was devastated, until Mother shook me out of my tears, saying forcefully, "You don't ever want to go to pieces over a boy." Looking as smart as I could in a straight black jumper with a long-sleeve pink satin blouse, I went to the dance alone. Despite my hesitations, I had a good time with my friends from grade school days, like Bobby Jackson and Maggie Porter.

That's why going to the senior prom over a year later was fraught with anxiety. After I was set to go with a friend of Billy's whom I'd known growing up, at the eleventh hour I was traded. That's right, exchanged like a bag of marbles. When my intended date told me he had arranged for me to go with another person, I was livid! I didn't like being treated like a commodity, but as my new escort could afford the corsage and the breakfast after the ball, after the lengths mother went through—she pawned a precious necklace and other treasures to pay for my dress— and not wanting to miss out being with my classmates, I gave in. Freddie Flemister turned into the prince who took me to my ball. I had the time of my life in a long pearl and silver gown, with a violet orchid corsage on my wrist, swaying to the music of Henry Mancini in a hotel ballroom decorated with masks and symbols of "charades." That was the theme of the prom, prompted by the film of the same name, starring Audrey Hepburn and Cary Grant.

That night of the prom, I felt like the daughter of a king, but back in my first year at Ursuline I had been made to feel like a queen: A competition to sell magazine subscriptions to raise money for the school was held. The person who had the highest sales for the day would be named "Queen for a Day" just like on the TV show. I was elated when I won (due to Uncle William's buying a large number of subscriptions). I can still see myself with the sparkling silver crown on my head and carrying a bouquet of roses. That experience helped me reach out to accept the smiles and kind gestures of my new friends and change from seeing myself as a girl living in the projects to one who was lucky to venture out of them and make new friends. They weren't black, and while I'd never been to school with whites, I jumped on board the four-year trip through Ursuline. I gave myself permission to go on the ride.

Another time, Mary Jane Raible, who was in my class, and I became soul mates when we were both at the church where President Kennedy attended Mass while he was in Louisville on October 13 and 14, 1962, stumping for the Democrats in the midterm congressional elections which would take place that November. The Saturday evening before, my sister Anita, who was eleven, and I had gone on a long trek by bus to the airport to see the president arrive. Emboldened by our fantastic success in seeing him in person, we decided to make it over to the fairgrounds close by to get a better look. Beating incredible odds, since there was no sidewalk, we walked on an island in the middle of the expressway in the dark, traffic roaring down the lanes on both sides, headlights glaring in our faces, and made it to the fairgrounds. Seeing President Kennedy ride around sitting on top of the backseat of his open convertible (like he would that horrible day in Dallas a year later) made us determined to see him close-up when he was to come to Sunday Mass at Mary Magdalene's, near where we lived the next morning.

We woke up very early so we'd be in front of the church to see "our Catholic president," and we did! A photograph showing little Anita in the crowd of hands reaching out to President Kennedy as he exited church was carried in the next day's *Louisville Times,* October 15 evening edition. Not caught on camera was me pleading, "Mr. President, Mr. President . . . !" as his eyes met mine, and he grabbed my hand too. I didn't wash it for the rest of the day! And I'm glad I held on to that golden moment, for that glimpse of Camelot would turn to days of Hades just over a year later.

Anita, younger sister, before shaking hands with President Kennedy during his visit to Louisville in 1962; with permission of *The Courier-Journal*

In the same week during which John F. Kennedy visited Louisville, the Cuban Missile Crisis happened, from October 16 to 28. Praying that the nuclear weapons wouldn't arrive in Havana and blow up the south coast of the United States during those fearful days brought me and my classmates closer together. Hours of kneeling in the chapel and talking in class as we imagined the ships bringing the weapons across the oceans was intense. We all wanted America to stay safe and free.

Nonetheless, my thoughts about Fidel Castro were conflicted: Years before, when he came into power, I'd seen him on *The Ed Sullivan Show* in his revolutionary uniform. For a brief while, he seemed to be presented as an example of a heroic, democratic revolutionary seeking support in America. But as Cubans began to flee to Florida, and after the failure of the Bay of Pigs invasion, and now with the missile crisis, it was clear that he was the villain who wanted war, while President Kennedy was the champion of peace.

Those months would prove to be the last days of a precious time for me and for America. After seeing my first live performance of a Shakespearean play, *Macbeth*, I felt like I was in the tragedy the Bard had dramatized. With my classmates, I watched the play performed by Louisville's leading theater company at Mercy Academy, just a few streets from Ursuline. The play had just finished when a sister came out in front of the somber curtain, startling us with the news that President Kennedy had been shot and the prognosis didn't look good, putting me and everyone I saw in a daze, as if the world had turned upside down. After the cast had taken its bow, the sister told us what we already feared: that our beloved president had died.

A group of us walked back to school and stayed together with Sister Jeanette, comforting one another. Now there was no time to escape to my make-believe world. I had to go on within the hellish reality that was marching toward me. Like Bill Clinton, also from lowly circumstances, and who had met JFK while in high school and had been inspired by him, I was motivated by our thirty-fifth president to see myself as a contributor and not a victim: "Ask not what your country can do for you—ask what you can do for your country." Those words of President Kennedy's inaugural address gave me permission to see the power I had to do something for America.

Being in UA's orderly environment helped me resolve all kinds of "hang-ups," like getting over the complex I had about my wide nose. In biology class one day during my sophomore year, we were discussing genes. I asked: if I had plastic surgery on my nose, would my children inherit my more aquiline feature? All my friends and teacher Sister Hildegarde looked astonished. "*Boue* (my French nickname), why would you want to change your nose?" Linda asked, putting her arm around my back. Then in unison the class told me my nose was fine the way it was, that they liked it and I shouldn't change it. Since then, I have never wanted to.

Some days after school I'd go "hang out" with my friends at the candy store around the corner. I had never been allowed to sit down in drugstores, so when Margaret took me there, I almost burst with joy: jars of vividly colored gumdrops, stacks of brownies and cookies, chunks of fudge were in glass jars, and batches of peanut brittle in cellophane were on the shelves. We sat at a table in front of the soda fountain, making me feel that I was finally entering a forbidden world. The tall dark-haired man of European origin who waited on our group served me Cherry Coke and potato chips as he did my friends. I was doing what other American teenagers did!

One day after leaving the candy store, Margaret and I were crossing the street as a dark-skinned boy looked into our faces as he ran passed. When we got to the other side, we saw a woman with grayish-blonde hair lying in a puddle of water that was turning red with the blood coming out of an open split in her head. Her groceries lay helter-skelter, cans rolling on the sidewalk as her limp arm rested against the brown paper bag torn open on her abdomen. As the police came, we were overwhelmed by what we had viewed and spent time walking around and talking about it before we went to our homes. We knew that the boy we had seen crossing the street was the person who had knocked the woman over and killed her.

In time, we were interviewed by the police separately and had to identify people in lineups, and also individually. We both had uncomfortable feelings when we discovered whom they found guilty. Comparing notes, we found that the convicted boy was not the same one who passed us as we crossed the street! In trying to put me at ease when I expressed my uncertainty to him, as my mother and father stood beside me, a lawyer told me not to be concerned, that the boy they had convicted had done a lot of bad things. I have never felt right about that; I know that studies have proved that eyewitnesses tend to get identifications wrong, but at seventeen, I could see clearly, especially close-up. Being black made all dark-skinned boys vulnerable to being found guilty of a crime even if they hadn't done it.

I had been active in school events and was even elected president of my senior class. The camaraderie of my friends and the changes coming for blacks buoyed my spirit and determination. After the March on Washington in August 1963 and Martin Luther King's "I Have a Dream" speech, I was burning with more desire to keep on; sure that day would come soon when we'd all be "free at last." Civil rights waves rushed up and rolled all across the United States: demonstrations, marches, and meetings happened almost every day. In March 1964, the NAACP in Kentucky organized a March on Frankfort, the state capital, to demand passage of a public accommodations law. Ten thousand rallied; Martin Luther King addressed the crowd, and celebrities, such as Jackie Robinson, took part. In order to go, I had to miss school, breaking my perfect attendance record, which I hated doing, but was necessary to take part. Try as I had, I was dismayed that I hadn't gotten any of my classmates to come with me, or so I thought. As they felt when the March on Washington took place seven months before, people were afraid that the event would turn violent, and although the Washington demonstration was peaceful, people were still apprehensive about people of color gathering in large groups. When I saw Cecelia Stultz get out of a van and get on the bus taking us to Frankfort and sit next to me to go to the event, I wanted to cry. Marching and singing, we made our way down the narrow streets of the black neighborhoods, to the steps of the commonwealth's imposing capitol.

Courtesy of the archives, Ursuline Sisters of Louisville

As close as my friends and I were and as happy and enriching as my high school was, it was separate from my home life. I never invited my friends to Sheppard Square, and they did not invite me to their homes. That's the way Louisville was—very segregated, if not legally, then certainly by custom. Whites lived in their world, and blacks in theirs, except for one notable exception: Linda took me to her home, and I met her kind, tall father and other members of her family, including her twin brother, whom I'd heard a lot about. We sat chatting around their dining table, and I thought that their home felt very much like mine.

Life was awkward. With small children at home and Daddy disabled, none of my family ever came to see me perform in school activities, except on the last day when I graduated. Not having my folks to cheer me on was hard, but I swallowed my urge for self-pity and took comfort in the freedom I had to participate in evening programs. I told myself that I was helping Mother by not making her feel bad because she couldn't come to my activities. Besides, by mixing with my classmates and their families, I got used to being with more people outside my community on my own. That was a head start for being the only member of a group among different circles in the future.

In August 1963, some friends from Saint Peter Claver's youth group and I went to see Johnny Mathis perform at a large venue on the outskirts of the city. Gushingly handsome and touching my heart with his ringing renditions of "Chances Are," "The Twelfth of Never," and other top-of-the-chart hits, Johnny swept me away for two enchanted hours. In the jam-packed hall, I swooned like girls at an Elvis concert to his honeyed voice. Imagine my surprise when I, who seldom went anywhere or met anyone new, famous or otherwise in those days, ran into Mohammed Ali on the performance hall floor as I rushed toward the backstage to get Johnny's autograph! "You're a Mudd, aren't you," he declared more than asked, blocking my way. I was used to people spotting me as a Mudd, but Cassius Clay—we still called him that—was a rising star, and *he was saying hello to me*. He said what I knew, that my Uncle Johnny (John L. Mudd) had taught him at Central High School. Fresh from a win in London, having achieved an Olympic Gold Medal three years before, in August 1960, he was a top contender for boxing's heavyweight championship, which he would win at the end of the year 1963. When we met that night, I got the impression that he was happy to have someone recognize him in the sea of screaming girls swarming around another idol.

The next summer, 1964, as in previous years, I tried to find a regular job, for now I needed money for all the extras not covered by a generous scholarship I had accepted to attend college in Baltimore. Billy was working full-time, and opportunities were opening up, but I couldn't find a job. Stores and supermarkets where girls I went to school with worked didn't yet hire blacks, and in the Catch-22 of the unemployed, I couldn't get a job because I didn't have one, other than babysitting and housekeeping. Finally, I swallowed my pride and answered an ad for someone to assist in the care of a senior citizen. As luck and my bus-riding experience would have it, the address was in the upscale area of Louisville near the Ursuline Mother House. I eagerly rang the front door bell of the colonial brick that bright summer morning. After introducing myself to the stout woman who answered, I froze in my tracks as she told me, "Go to the back door."

Since integration was taking place all over Louisville—parks were opening up, blacks were being served at certain restaurants, we could go to white movie theaters—I thought it strange that she should ask me to go to the rear entrance. But I took a minute to calm down and found the courage to do as told. I went to the back door like my ancestors during slave times and like those who had menial jobs were still doing. I was a disaster as a caregiver for the woman's invalid mother (who was sweet). I only lasted long enough to get two weeks' pay. That and stashes of five and ten dollar bills were rolled in plastic and penned inside my long leg panty girdle as I dressed to leave for college. On arriving in Baltimore, Mother told me when I telephoned that the woman I'd worked for had called and asked me to return to the job. Hearing that made me feel good and Mother proud. "She's gone away to college," Mother, who never could resist a dramatic gesture, had trilled.

In addition to being recruited to attend Morgan State College in Baltimore on a debate scholarship, I was offered scholarships to two other historically black colleges (HBCUs) in the Deep South. I was also warmly encouraged, with a scholarship, to go to Bellarmine, the Catholic men's college in Louisville that was opening its doors to blacks and women. Although I was grateful and immensely proud to be invited to the two other black schools as well as Bellarmine, after growing up in Louisville, I didn't want to go farther South, and I wanted to get away from Louisville. Mother, who never tried to force her ideas on me, was outspoken on the importance of getting away and going to Morgan.

Perhaps she, who was so full of talent and ideas, wanted her daughter to have a life that she couldn't have. Over twenty years she had given birth to seven children, and although she had enjoyed teaching—she was probably the first African American to teach in Louisville's Catholic schools—she had to give it up when she was pregnant. I was confident that I could make a family, but I wanted to realize my vision of having a professional life as well. When I boarded the train for Baltimore, with all the cash inside my underclothes, I was afraid to move from my seat for the entire twenty-three hours of the journey. My guardian angel must have nudged me when I somehow found the nerve to get off in Baltimore.

Becoming

"*What we think, we become.*"

BUDDHA

7

Historically Black College Coed

D.O.W. Holmes Hall, courtesy of Morgan State University

As I stepped out of the taxi at the grand entrance of Morgan, on the outskirts of Baltimore on Cold Spring Road, I drank in the view: Neo-Gothic rooftops pointing skyward, manicured green grounds, and a clock beckoning me from the top of the main building. This would be my ivory tower. I straightened my spine, threw back my shoulders, and walked ahead. Destination: Tubman House. Bright sun seared the pavement. Wringing wet from the heat, black pumps and sheer stockings squeezing my feet, the legs of my panty girdle compressing my thighs and waist, after what was by then a day of travel, I was exhausted. As I pushed against the weight of the front door, I sensed a new world awaited me on the other side and took my time going in.

The main lounge was scattered with chairs and an odd assortment of beige and brown floor rugs, confusing me. I was expecting something more formal with a front desk. But then the director, with a name like "Miss Walker," tall, pink and powdered in a purple dress, with raven hair slicked back in a tight bun, came to greet me. Stern and stylish, she looked spectacular, a woman of color who was like someone in a film. Her bright red lips formed a broad smile as she said, "The little girl from Kentucky!" That scared me, but I braced myself for the oddities that lay ahead. As she showed me to my room on the second floor, I clammed up and didn't know what to say. Two iron beds and a bare cold floor with a washbasin and mirror in the corner made me feel like I was in a jail cell. I had never lived away from home without family, and though I could not begin to think of this new place as home, I faced the fact that, as rough as it looked, this was where I would stay for the next year.

One half hour at a time, then day by day, I took the newness in until I got used to it. I listened, asked questions, and said hello to all who reached out to me. Although I still felt out of place, by the end of the first week I had a circle of acquaintances and was on the way to making friends.

I was fortunate to have Crystal Moore from New Castle, Delaware, as my roommate; we were in room 217 of Tubman House. Outgoing and kind, she had a face capped in a sheen of dark curls that reminded me of girls I knew back home. We got along from the start and helped each other settle in. We were like sisters during that first year; she even took me home with her six months later for Easter of 1965, introducing me to the Northern United States. How strange and overwhelming it was to realize for the first time that slavery had taken place in the North, all along the East Coast, including the dot on the map that was Delaware. Crystal took me to the first slave auction block I'd ever seen, in Wilmington.[4] At Morgan, we locked ourselves in the room one late afternoon a few weeks later to teach ourselves to smoke cigarettes. Everyone was doing it, and we were going to keep up with the crowd. After a few seconds of puffing and coughing, I was scared stiff when hot ash fell on my thighs, and I stopped once and for all, never smoking again.

Tony and Paulette, both from Baltimore City, lived across the hall, and we quickly struck up a rapport. Both went out of their way to make me feel welcome, giving me advice and sharing food their families brought them from home. Tony took me under her wings along with other girls who did not have dates that autumn and led us back and forth across the gym floor at my first college dance, and only the second big dance, in my life. "Circulate," she commanded, as if she were a charm school teacher; and back and forth we went, until, suddenly, I was swept up in the arms of a kind-looking young man in a dark chocolate brown suit. Before I knew it, we were slow dancing. I was going to *make it* after all!

Sherry Nixon from the Bronx, New York City, lived next door. I had declared that I was going to major in English. As Sherry had also chosen this subject, we instantly became friends, remaining so until the too early end of her life in 2008. Freckled-face Cathy—we called her Chatty Cathy, teasing that she looked like the popular children's doll—came over from Harper House, the dormitory connected to ours. Charlene, from Cape Cod, Massachusetts, came over too. She kept everyone in stitches with her Donald Duck impersonations. Once while I was taking a shower, someone stole my towel, and I, who loathed revealing my unclothed body, had to scamper down the hall to my room, naked and dripping wet.

In those early days at Morgan, my mates and I were constantly hungry. We spent a lot of time talking about food and secretly preparing and sharing it. Fast food—McDonald's and the like—hadn't come on the scene, so we had to depend on our wits. A food truck pulled into the parking lot near the

---

4   According to the online Encyclopedia of Greater Philadelphia "Slavery and the Slave Trade," by James Gigantino, Asst. Prof. of History, University of Arkansas, slave labor was integral to the region. New Sweden Colonists whose settlement from 1838 to 1855 centered on present-day Wilmington, Delaware, near Philadelphia, imported some of the first African slaves in the mid to late seventeenth century. As my DNA estimates that I am 27.3 percent Scandinavian, mostly Swedish, I wonder if I am descended from those slaves in Wilmington.

dorm most nights doing a brisk business, selling, among its mouthwatering choices, steak submarines packed with onions and oozing mayonnaise and mustard, and thick salty French fries. I couldn't afford these indulgences, but Sherry, who had a medical condition requiring that she eat constantly, bought from the truck and offered to share with me, though usually I wouldn't accept and would only have a taste. I contented myself with rolls and sandwiches saved from the cafeteria, which I'd have with cocoa or tea I'd make in my hot pot. Everyone liked the tuna salad I whipped up when we'd pool vittles in a late-night feast. With crunchy saltine crackers, it made a hearty snack.

Cooking wasn't allowed in the rooms. Except for the toaster oven in the basement study hall kitchen, there were no appliances or hot plates for warming food; microwaves weren't yet in wide use, and the study hall was a good distance from my room. It was then that I realized that one sometimes has to break the rules to keep going, something I hadn't learned to do before without a lot of guilt. On cold winter nights with hours of study ahead, I had to break the rule of not preparing food in the room to stem the cravings. My friends and I would inevitably get caught by Miss Walker. We'd rush to stash our loot away as she'd come down the hall, keys clanging, and search the room to find the fixings on the windowsill: "No cooking in the rooms!" she'd pronounce as if sentencing us to life. We'd listen standing stiffly at attention and promise not to do it again, knowing full well we would.

During that first year, going to dinner at the cafeteria with my dorm friends was an introduction to college culture. Not used to mixing in an all-black, coed, predominantly Protestant environment, I needed to learn how. Skepticism about the food was the "in" thing, but for me, the steaming plates and sit-down meals were comforting. My friends warned me about eating too much "mystery meat," the ground makings of the giant meat patties that the cafeteria served, and in those days before the use of antibiotics when the poultry industry was not yet mass producing, the chicken pieces looked huge. Rumor had it that the food was injected with saltpeter to curb students' sexual urges and that this affected the taste. I'd take whatever my meal ticket allowed and pile it high with mashed potatoes and gravy on the side, with a vegetable, drink, and cake or ice cream.

The meals were all right with me. But, wanting to fit in, I let my friends, who had money to buy food from other sources, influence me, and like them, I started giving it away. Or, rather, trading it with the football players who sat at the table next to ours. I hadn't figured out at the start that we were flirting with members of the exalted Morgan State Bears football team. We'd swap our food for their ice cream and milk, as they had a higher meal allowance and liked to share their extra food with us, which inevitably got us to talk to them. While my many new friends wanted to strike up romantic relationships with the players, I wasn't as interested. I had had enough of football to last me a while, what with Daddy's stories of gridiron glories when he was at Kentucky State, games on TV, and the rough-and-tumble of playing tackle with Billy when we were children. And I didn't yet have my mind on finding a boyfriend right away. Wisely, however, I kept my thoughts to myself and went along with the food fun.

Fortunate to have a full scholarship and a grant sufficient to cover my room and board, I did have to go without something to eat for an extended period once. For a couple of days the funds for the second semester hadn't gone through the administration office, and my meal ticket was cut off. I carried on as if nothing was wrong; I must have nibbled on stored items and a few dollars remaining from the cash I'd brought with me from home. That of course couldn't go on, and on a Friday afternoon, as I was passing a bakery near the campus. I went in and found myself fumbling in my purse for loose change to buy golden-crusted bread rolls. After I had selected two, as the flaxen-haired lady behind the counter was putting them in a chalk-colored sack, I was counting my pennies when I saw that I didn't have the fourteen cents needed. A sinking feeling came over me. I felt like the Little Match Girl. In my mother's countless retelling of this Grimm fairy tale: the poor orphan would press her nose against the window of the home where she watched a family feasting at Christmas dinner. Now here I was in college in Baltimore, embarrassed to have let myself be in such a predicament, when the lady reached under the glass and put more rolls in the bag and handed it to me. "Please," she said. "You've heard of a baker's dozen?" That food got me through the rest of the day and gave me the courage to speak up for myself on Monday morning to get my meal ticket reinstated. That lady's kindness and generosity was a memory I often retrieved later when I felt downhearted. Her random act of kindness helped me maintain my faith in the goodness of human beings.

As much as I could, I settled into the unpredictability of living in the dormitory. I never did get used to the silliness and ruckus that went on. I had to bite my lip to get through most of it. I was just too focused to take it seriously. Not only did I have to stay alert to someone pulling the prank of taking my towel, but I had to be ready for the worst explosions of madness during the night.

Once, while studying with Sherry and Eleanor, my friend who like me was, as the Easterners would say, "from the South,"[5] from Virginia, we were pulling an all-nighter writing up summaries of the poems we had covered in our introduction to English literature class. We were to have done this as the course proceeded but had procrastinated. Who could write a summary of the heart leaping up "when I behold a rainbow in the sky"?[6] At the last minute, we had to power through the night and write up tens of poems, half of the four-inch-thick textbook's contents, to turn in the next morning. Suddenly someone knocked on the study room door and told us that the boys from Baldwin House across the footbridge had phoned: "We're coming over to see your panties!"

What on earth? I thought. In my robe and slippers, I followed some girls down to the corner of the hallway and peeked out of the open window at the boys in their jockey shorts, some adorned with red, yellow, and green feather headdresses, sprinting across the bridge whooping like wild animals. My study pals and I locked ourselves in for the whole night during the melee. Another time, the raid was more organized—Miss Walker probably had something to do with that. We opened our rooms in the spring for a visit from the young men again. As I had been dreading someone going into my drawer and taking out my undies, I had made sure that they were stacked and ready for viewing, although I was concerned that someone would remark on their plainness; I didn't have silky lingerie, not even for display. The afternoon rolled along, and the young men were quite courtly in glancing at the contents of my open drawer and looking around my corner of the room until one of them lifted my fluffy pink-and-white bunny rabbit, an Easter gift from my sisters, from my bed. He had exposed the hole I had burned into my patchwork quilt bedspread. I was mortified.

---

5 Maryland, like Kentucky and Virginia, was a slave-holding state, making it strange that my friends and I did not think of it as "the South." Like me, my friends considered the cotton-belt states "the South." Maryland and Kentucky, though slave-holding, were border states; they didn't secede from the Union.

6 From the poem by William Wordsworth (1770–1850), "My Heart Leaps Up"

That hole had caused me grief. For the first time in my life, I had done something so bad and publicly disgraceful that I lay on my bed for an entire afternoon crying and berating myself. The handmade multicolored cotton quilt was a going-away present from a relative. I had spread it proudly on my metal-framed bed to lighten up my part of Tubman House; I'd gotten compliments on it. Using electric irons in the rooms was forbidden, but not wanting to venture to the cold basement one day, I ignored the rule and laid my blouse on the quilt to press the wrinkles out. I got distracted and let the steaming appliance rest too long on the fabric; then suddenly a ring of smoke went up, and I was lucky the clothing and bedding didn't erupt in flames. I just couldn't understand how I had done something so stupid. I whose worst punishment in school was for having said the first part of the *Pater Noster*, the *Our Father/Lord's Prayer*, with the priest out loud in Latin! I whined and prostrated myself on the bed afterward until at last some girls got me to see that mistakes happen to everyone. That was probably the first time I stopped taking myself so seriously.

Laughing and playing along with the nonsense helped me get along with all the girls; I wanted to fit in. The constant prank that caused those of us who wanted to study or sleep was the fire drill. *Ding, ding, ding,* would pull me from my slumber just as I was falling asleep. Throwing on coats and shoes, we'd scamper out to the back lawn; those in charge would call the roll and count our numbers, and after waiting for the firemen to tell our director that we could return, we'd try to get back to sleep while girls who had sneaked out in the middle of the night stole their way back in. This regular event was a scheme cooked up by those girls, for they were staying out beyond the 6:00 p.m. curfew. The next day I'd be tired and anxious from this recurring "emergency" and resented the inevitable inconvenience. Of course the curfew was too early and unrealistic. Most, if not all, of us were used to being out past dark before we started living at Tubman House.

Other times, good and happy times, but still somewhat unsettling, were the sudden bursts of dormmates into our room and out of our window onto the roof, after dark on fall and spring nights when the fraternities would serenade us: the cool Kappas in their casual zippered jackets and hooligan flat hats singing, "Dear Kappa Alpha Psi;" the intellectual Alphas (Daddy was an Alpha Phi Alpha), in dapper coats and ties, would sometimes throw flowers; and the coolest, "baddest" Qs, Omega Psi Phi members, snaking out their dance formations below. We knew they were dangerous and loved the temptation. But the romance of the unannounced serenade soon became a bother, since our room was the throughway.

When we weren't in, the door could easily be opened by kicking out the bottom metal vent so that giggling girls could wriggle through and barrel out of our window onto the roof. This became a constant worry when I was set to finish a project or get to bed so I'd be fresh for my next morning's eight o'clock class. After two years of campus living, the second in Truth House, I moved to a room in Morgan Park on Hermosa Avenue, walking distance from the college. I stayed there with a gracious young family for my last two, junior and senior, years. Not a moment too soon, if what I later heard was true: "The dorms are like casinos," someone told me. Still, by forcing me to face an unfamiliar culture, campus living was a brisk immersion in how to get along with people whose lifestyles were different from mine.

8

Wider World

When I entered Morgan, I was an awkward, self-conscious, skirt-and-blouse, scared-of-her-shadow girl who didn't know much about living life outside of the protection of the Catholic church. For all the good preparation that twelve years of parochial schooling had shaped me for, it left me best fitted for remaining in a round space. I'd be secure and comfortable but cut off from what was happening in other parts of America and the world. Falling asleep after those noisy nights on campus, I'd see those women in the magazine in front of the American embassy in Paris and tell myself that I must find a way to join the Foreign Service and be like them. How and when, I did not know. I only knew that I would do my best to make this dream a reality.

In the meantime, I still had a lot to learn about living in this new frontier. I had to learn to think outside the box. Eighteen years of close-knit family care and guidance had drilled in me that I must take care of my person and respect myself, but it hadn't prepared me for the choices I would have to make in the social and sexual revolutions that were exploding in 1964. Fortunately, hours of self-reflection, in prayer and in periods of enforced silence in Catholic school, had trained me to take stock of myself, particularly during trying times. At Morgan, I'd count my blessings. Having been a scholar, class leader, debater, and active in youth groups, I was confident. Living through poverty had given me a deep knowledge of how to make it through tough times. Not having it all was having it all. This was the priceless coming-of-age gift my parents gave me.

During my first week at Morgan, in September 1964, I went to the welcoming convocation along with 926 other students in the freshman class. From the podium, President Jenkins told us to shake hands with the persons seated to our left and right, which we did with exaggerated energy and nervous laughter. Then one could have heard a potato chip drop as he said, "Two of you will not be here in four years." *How could he make such a prediction?* I wondered. Surely it was one of those usual dos and don'ts that are not to be taken literally. But four years later, when members of our class marched up to the stage to receive our diplomas, I saw that he had almost nailed it. As a state college founded for the education of freed slaves, as I was to discover, Morgan was much easier to get into than it was to get out of with a degree.

Morgan State is now a university and remains a proud HBCU. In high school, I had been one of a handful of African Americans and often the only one in a class or activity. Now I was one among many. In high school, in a segregated city, but with white girls who lived in an equally confined, albeit wider, environment I had been loved and made to feel comfortable. When I got to Morgan, an expressly black college, I had to get used to living and studying among people who were racially like me.

So how did I make the transition from all girls, all Catholic, to predominantly black and secular? Being outgoing, even though I was shy, helped. Knowing what it was like to be an outsider also had prepared me. I took every opportunity to get to know people, not just those who were like people I had grown up with, but those who carried themselves well, held their heads high in the black middle class; those in suits and ties; those in high heels, as well as those in workers' uniforms; those who dressed up for Sunday chapel; and those who, like me, wore the same dress to Mass and didn't wear a hat. And to make my circle even wider, I got to touch base with students from other countries.

In Louisville, "foreign" had meant German, French, and Italian. I had not thought about the people of African descent who lived south of the border as being foreign—or for that matter, as being American. Except for the films of sisters working in foreign missions, which I was excited to see, especially one with nuns in a canoe somewhere, we didn't talk much about other countries. All those years I was with the mission crusade, it never dawned on me to ask about missions.[7]

Thus I was intrigued to meet students from other countries, like the ebony-colored, glossy, long-haired girl from what used to be British Guiana; a friendly and soft-spoken guy from Honduras who looked like he could have been related to me; and Shirley, a sophisticated twenty-four-year-old from Liberia. She was acquainted with that country's president, William Tubman, called "the father of modern Liberia." Once, I was telling her about feeling guilty because I had missed the bus that would have taken me to where I would join others in a civil rights protest. She obviously also hadn't gone, and standing with her hands on her hips, she gloated: "Child . . . why should I waste my time for freedom for you blacks in America? In my country we have had our freedom for a long time!" Having only recently learned while at Morgan that Liberia was founded by British and American slaves fleeing bondage in the United States, I didn't know enough to discuss her country and the challenges of its democracy. I didn't know much about Africa or about the slave trade. Shirley once took me with her to the ambassador's residence in Washington, which opened my eyes to how well the top ranking diplomat in an embassy lived.

I thought of Africa as an idyll, and I had been drawn to it by way of my fascination with England. That was why the charm of what sounded to me like a British accent and the swagger of a lavender-shirted young man from Nigeria attracted me. The strong scent of his eau de cologne preceded him. We had chatted on the quad, and while he was not easy to say no to, I hadn't led him on. Yet he persisted in trying to get me to go out with him, even calling me when I was in Louisville in the summer. His letter came smelling of perfume, declaring his affections on light purple-colored stationery, so hot and sensuous that it could have burned up in the sweltering August heat.

Being at Morgan, I had to learn the ways of Northeasterners. I had to say, for example, "soda" instead of "pop"; get used to over a thousand and one ways people ate crabs and other delicacies of coastal cultures. This took some effort. Fish on Friday was a habit for Catholics like me who couldn't eat meat on that day. No one at home talked about clam chowder like they did in Baltimore and up North when I traveled to my friends' homes. I had

---

7   One of three parishes for African Americans, Saint Peter Claver Catholic church was considered a mission by the Louisville Archdiocese.

---

no idea of the Eastern Shore, knowing only the bridge that crossed over the Ohio River from Louisville to Southern Indiana.

Although Baltimore had been settled by Catholics, it is not surprising that in view of slavery's practice of separating families, most of the students and faculty did not profess faith in the Church of Rome. That is an ugly story but not one for this book. Suffice it to say that the church was complicit in slavery like other institutions. Getting used to operating in a non-Catholic atmosphere was a steep hurdle to cross. Learning to mix with non-Catholics when I had been taught to avoid them was a riddle I had to crack to get along with people in the wider world. Since first grade I had been taught to avoid the damned "occasion of sin," especially when mixing with members of the opposite sex. As I ventured into the unknown world of non-Catholics, I found that they were like me. I came to appreciate the example Mother and all my Protestant relatives on her side of the family had shown me of how good people in other religions could be. Going to worship with my non-Catholic friends when I visited their homes was inspiring. I could not have made it through Morgan without their hospitality—Ernestine's huge family Thanksgiving, for example. Her missionary aunt and uncle had kissed the ground when they returned from West Africa the week before. In that day when blacks were rediscovering Africa, I was struck by how happy her relatives were to return to America.

My first debate partner, whom I'll call Cynthia, was a Pentecostal. With long brunette broomstick curls, wide glasses on a sharp nose, and a sandstone complexion, she looked like she was twelve years old, like Charlie Brown's girlfriend. But she had the wisdom of someone much older and was brilliant, made straight As. Her righteous sense of justice was powerful. When I sought her advice on a professor who gave me a left-hand compliment—he had criticized me for not majoring in his subject—she said, "Tell him he doesn't have a license on scholarship." As I got to know more people from other less orthodox denominations, I saw that "Holy Rollers" could be the most generous people. Their music and worship service made me more comfortable than the newly instituted folk singing of the Sunday Mass I attended. This was the paradox of my life: born into a minority group whose outlook was shaped by a minority religion in a society controlled by a majority population. I used to say, only half-jokingly, that if you're going to be black in America, better to have been born Baptist.

Fast-forward a few years, when I was at the home of a well-to-do young Indian woman in New Delhi, and her diamond-necklaced mother said to me, "I bet if you'd sing, you'd shake this room." Yes, I thought, with *"Kyrie Eleison"* ("Lord have mercy") from the Mass in Latin), not *"He's Got the Whole World in His Hands,"* as you suppose.

Not only was I not steeped in the spirituals of my African American ancestors, but, as I have shown, while transitioning to college I had to get used to the revised practices of the Catholic church, which were taking effect after the changes of Vatican II.[8] I was supposed to forget the music and the Latin that had held my hand as a child and while growing up. At Morgan I went to Sunday Mass in a small room off the cafeteria and sang from a book of songs in English accompanied by guitars, while my Protestant classmates attended a service in the splendid college chapel, listening to the soulful raptures of the Morgan Choir, then highly regarded, now world renowned.

Yet religion, though a strange route in my new world, was not the only new one. The strangest was getting used to being in a mixed-sex environment, coming from a female-only school and a family of more sisters than brothers. The priests who joined us on Sundays—one played the guitar for the service—were outgoing; we students sometimes cooked and ate with them after a religious discussion during the week. When one of the guitar-strumming young clerics, in his black suit and religious collar, seemed to delight in telling me that he was soon leaving the seminary, I didn't want to listen to him and rushed out of the room. All the mystery and ritual were changing too fast for me, the foundation of my safe, stable world crumbling beneath my feet.

Being on the Morgan debate team helped me take in the differences of my new surroundings; and since I was often in the company of one of my male debate partners, I didn't miss not having a steady boyfriend. A male classmate, I'll call him Larry, well over six feet tall, lanky, and light-complexioned, used to go around with me for several months. One day a classmate said to me, "Somebody said you two were brother and sister. Someone else thought you were "together." I was at a loss for words, for

---

8   Vatican II, the Second Vatican Ecumenical Council, 1962–1965, focused on the Catholic church and modern life. Many changes, including ending the use of Latin, making services more informal, and encouraging Catholics to respect and understand other Christians, resulted from it.

Larry and I were just friends. In those days I didn't know how to flirt or if I *was* flirting. Once, when I lived off-campus, as I lay on my bed with my legs resting apart, my roommate told me to be careful about doing that. The thought that I was making a play for her left me speechless, but others had gently let me know that I couldn't take another girl's hand or hug her, like we did at Ursuline. Adjusting to a coed world took effort.

By November of my first year, I was feeling at ease in campus life and in my classes. We were debating the topic of search and seizure—whether or not law enforcement could search suspects without a warrant. A recent Supreme Court decision had upheld the rights of a black man, Mallory, in ruling that he had been illegally searched after being accused of rape. A day student with a similar-sounding name sat behind me in a late-evening political science class. He did his best to get my attention and had some good lines. "Pretty brown eyes," was one that got me. I had been teased about my yellowish, hazel eyes when I was in grade school and didn't like it. Mother had tried to convince me that having what the kids called "cat eyes" wasn't a bad thing, but it took this smooth guy's baritone voice to make me feel that my peepers were special. Still, I acted as nonchalant as I could at age eighteen, under the spell of an older man in his mid-twenties. At the last class before Thanksgiving Thursday, he asked me to go out with him on Friday, and I said yes and agreed to wait for his call around lunchtime when he would pick me up.

Friday came and went, and he never called, never showed up. Deflated and alone in the dorm that first major holiday away from home, I had been stood up, just like my first date. I was stunned, silent, and hurt, until I saw the headline in the paper—"Rapes Woman . . ."—with my potential lover boy's photograph. Cynthia sat with me the following Monday as we talked about the close call. "That could have been you, Judy."

9

More than Academic

When I heard about students being tracked in public schools, I cringed because it reminded me of the race-based practices that kept Jim Crow alive. Yet, according to acceptable educational norms, I was to discover students at Morgan were tracked in the first year—that is, put into some courses according to ability. That was when my dedication to the language of Shakespeare paid off. I was put in the top section of fifty English classes. So renowned was the department for its high standards in graduating students with a degree in the language of Britannia that people would say, "You are either crazy or very smart," to those who chose to major in the subject. Being immediately put into the top section was great for my confidence and proof of the effort I had invested in paying attention to my teachers in grade and secondary schools. Books and written work had been the landscape of my growing up; I knew I was right to pursue English as a major.

At the same time, I had come from an environment pulsating in political and social discussion. Change was in the air. I had tasted it and still wanted to pursue my unrevealed desire for a nontraditional diplomatic career. *How would I find a way to get to my goal at Morgan, where paths to professions were clearly mapped out and everyone assumed I'd be a teacher?* I didn't know but decided not to worry about it for a while. English was my strong point, and I would excel in it while learning as much as I could about history, politics, and economics. I'd do this through debating and the face-to-face contacts that it would bring, and by taking courses in other subjects. No one had to convince me of the value of a liberal arts education.

First, I had to get used to the teachers. Except for kindergarten, I had been taught by women in long black dresses with veils and stiff white guimpe fanning out from their necks. Now distinguished men and women in suits and ties looked out at me. Perhaps one of the greatest unknowns is how tough African American professors could be. Having made it as one of the small group of people of color to be credentialed to teach at college level, they spared no one from their exacting standards. At Morgan we used to say that their attitude was "I've got mine. You get yours."

Nothing was given to a student. Grades were earned, except in a few cases, on sheer merit. From day one I learned that as special as I thought I was, I had to prove it by consistently turning in good work, contributing to discussion, and, most of all, making a high mark on the final exam. Gone was the comfortable aloofness of the Ursuline nuns I was used to. Now I had to be at ease with the unique styles of a variety of instructors and professors who looked like me. All of my previous teachers had been Caucasian; now, except for two, they were of various shades of brown, black, and beige. With the nuns I was a girl, but in college, an adult: Miss Mudd.

Sitting at the feet of Morgan's great teachers did a lot to integrate me into my own race and to make me appreciate how accomplished African Americans had been, continued to be, and could become. This was a megadose of self-esteem for someone from a narrow background. By appealing to our sense of excellence, the professors and instructors showed that they had confidence in our intellectual capacities. This approach motivated me and my classmates to work as hard as we could, push ourselves to do more, and do our best and better.

My teachers and mentors were giants with the faith of saints. Just recalling their names makes me realize how fortunate I was to be under their tutelage. Most of them had lived through and were influenced by the Harlem Renaissance, that explosion of 1920s black creative thought. In English, there were Waters Turpin, who had broken new ground as a novelist; and Philip Butcher, who had done definitive work on *Othello* and was a leading black scholar of American literature. He had a lot to say about Mark Twain and got me to see *Huckleberry Finn* as a revolutionary narrative on racism, writing on one of my essays, "There's some good writing here." His encouragement made me soar. Ulysses Grant Lee (his real name) got me to appreciate literary criticism and a few years later told me something that boosted my spirits at a time when I most needed it. I'll share that later. Iva Jones knew all about Victorian literature, had taught in England, and was so elegant and had such beautiful diction that she became my role model. Ruth Sheffey, who also taught literature, wouldn't let us get away with half efforts. It was she who motivated us to stay up all night and write annotations of the poems she had covered in class. And for grammar, Robert Jones, whose explanations of the Germanic origins of English clarified much about how the language evolved. Jean Turpin (Mrs. Waters Turpin) also taught grammar. She gave me invaluable advice when, at the end of my senior year, she found out I was going to India on a Fulbright scholarship. "Take time when you're there to see other places. Don't hurry back," she said, cornering me on the stairs one day.

She embodied the ideal HBCU educator. Since most of her students would be schoolteachers, she gave advice about giving pupils more than what was in the books: "When you see that boy student with his dirty collar, tell him how he can wipe it clean without washing the whole shirt." I was touched by this. I had had to keep my one blouse fresh in high school. "Don't let them get away with turning in sloppy work. Close the door and *teach* them." We students laughed about her manner and how she wore tennis shoes with tailored wool suits and silk blouses, but we admired and respected her.

For French there was Mrs. Law, from New Orleans, who would not permit "any of that Louisiana French." She gave me high marks for an oral presentation, "Le Pont de Londres" (London Bridge), even though my props collapsed and I felt my talk was turning into a comedy routine. And there was the legendary Sandye McIntyre, the outstanding professor of French. He had studied at the Sorbonne in Paris and always spoke the language of Voltaire to his students and made us use only it in speaking to him—in his class or on the street we had to use the language of *La France*, or else we would have to reach in our pockets and pay a fine of twenty-five cents!

As in high school, French held sway over me in college; I took a number of courses in it, including two in literature, and made it through the intermediate level in speaking and grammar. I liked it so well that it became, along with speech, my minor subject. Still, I never could become a camp follower and act more French than the French the way one of the best students in the language did, wearing a beret and pouting with pursed lips.

To me that seemed phony. I later learned that I'd been wrong: imitating native speakers is the best way to learn a language.

A certain professor, who taught history, had spent some time at Bluefield State College in West Virginia. When I told him that my mother had gone there for her teacher training, he took a special interest in me despite his reputation for not being approachable—and for not awarding As. Although I worked assiduously, I did not get an A in his course; I got a B+, which seemed worse, as if he had toyed with giving me the top mark but couldn't. Rumor had it that he had narrowly escaped being lynched, which was why, though it made no sense, he didn't give anyone an A.

Later, I supposed that more than one of my instructors might well have fled a lynching and other atrocities. I'd recall Daddy's anecdote about my brother Billy touching a woman on a bus in Louisville when he was a tot and the woman turning around and looking at Daddy as if he'd done it. Daddy was too sensitive to elaborate on the implications, but he repeated the tale so many times that I came to appreciate the tight wire that he had to walk in order not to provoke a racial incident.

Thomas Cripps, white and a groundbreaker on the history of African Americans, was also one of my professors. Getting in his class had been very difficult, as it filled up quickly, but what a treat it was: he made the black past come alive. I wasn't surprised that later, as stories on the history of African Americans gained popularity in the media, his cutting-edge book on the history of blacks in cinema, *Slow Fade to Black*, came out in 1977.

Others taught and guided me: I was fortunate to be taken under the wings of famous historian Benjamin Quarles, author of a long list of seminal works. His *The Negro in the Making of America*, to note only one, broke new ground in raising awareness of blacks as agents of change in U.S. history. His wife, Dr. Ruth Brett, directed the counseling center where, as part of a work study program made possible by the War on Poverty, I got a job, my first semiprofessional one, in the second semester of my sophomore year. Drs. Quarles and Brett were most generous to me.

They hired me to stay with their preteenage daughter Pam when they went out in the evenings. This was an easy way to make extra money, and I enjoyed being with her, as it was like being with one of my younger sisters. I even washed and set her mane of lustrous golden-brown hair. (Yes, she was black.) I sometimes shared meals with the family, sitting at their table talking with them about campus goings-on. While they were careful not to make me think that I could expect favors from them, they readily gave me advice. Both of these stately people were revered at the college. Having them as mentors was a rock-solid reinforcement that made me certain I could climb high.

Of course, as in most groups, there were cliques; when I let it be known that I was going to pursue a Foreign Service career, Dr. Quarles and Dr. Brett were encouraging. Still, I naively assumed that their support would carry over to the political science department, and I was wrong. I thought that as a debater, I had demonstrated effective combining of knowledge in English and speech and social sciences to make Morgan proud. But when I applied for a political science scholarship, that department wouldn't support me, and I found myself in a strange, kind of tug-of-war situation between the English and political science departments. In applying for the political science scholarship I had inadvertently appeared disloyal to my department. While I felt bad about being rejected by poly sci., I realized that I had to give more attention to those who thought highly of me in the English Department, an early lesson in public relations.

Economics put me in a tighter corner. The introductory course in macroeconomics taught by a white professor in an evening class excited me. I had long wanted to make sense of what I had heard about the economy since high school on television. Statistics were about real people, and poverty had a human face, like that of my family. I wanted to understand terms like "structural unemployment" and "inflationary spiral," which I had bandied about in debates. The instructor was engaging and clear. I met his high marks each time, in assignments, in discussion, and on tests. Yet he seemed to harbor some kind of hostility toward me. He was constantly toying with me when I said something. Why was I, who didn't have a math background, interested in economics, and why was I doing so well in it? He'd never known an English major who could get an A on his final exam.

Thus, when the night came and I answered ten out of ten questions, which were multiple choices and required following a formula to arrive at the correct answers, he was surprised that I had gotten an A. He would let me know, if I waited until he'd checked, how many I'd gotten correct— nine or all ten. In a defiant act of self-respect, I told him, "It's okay, ninety or one hundred, it's still an A!" I didn't want to give him the satisfaction of knowing that I cared.

"But, won't you be taking the course next semester?" he asked, almost pleading.

"No," I said, hating that I wouldn't be able to continue in the subject that I was still keen on, because I didn't want to put myself through what I had just endured in his classes. "I was just taking it because I wanted to know about it," I matter-of-factly told him. "I don't need it to graduate." I can still see his gaping mouth and hand brushing back his ash blond hair from his eyes as I walked away.

Speech was my natural subject. I chose to go to Morgan because it wanted me most based on my success in public speaking. Professor Harold Chin, who recruited me from Louisville and persuaded me to come on a full D. O. W. Holmes debate scholarship, was my godfather in the true sense of the word. Without his encouragement and counsel, I probably wouldn't have gone to Morgan, gotten to know the Washington DC area, gotten used to living there and thus not have caught the brass ring that swung me into the arena that would fulfill my dreams.

Harold Chin gave me the chance, not only exposing me to all forms of public speaking, making me competitive in debating and in giving extemporaneous talks, but also giving me opportunities to travel and discover the Eastern United States and the Midwest. And like a good godfather, he saw that I was taken care of. He was the person who called the administrative office and got my meal ticket reinstated when I was counting pennies to buy bakery rolls. Mr. Chin wasn't Chinese, as I overheard some wonder when we were at other colleges. (And later I'd know Chinese people with the same-sounding name.) Long an educator, he was a widower whose concern for his daughter, who was my age and studying at Mount Holyoke, the number one of the so-called Seven Sisters Colleges, for women, was touching. I was never afraid to go to him for advice and took to heart all that he offered.

Debating gave me confidence. As it had enlarged my world during high school, in college it was a prestigious position that I took great pride in being a part of. Among the many travel opportunities it gave me was the chance to go to Louisville for a tournament at Bellarmine. Although of all our trips, I liked most the ones to New York where we participated in matches at Columbia and New York Universities.

We once stayed at the Plaza Hotel in NYC; and as the only girl, I got to stay in a luxurious room all to myself. I took as much advantage of this legendary hotel as I could, rejoicing in the fine furnishings: the bathroom with its gold-toned faucets and thick cotton towels. As if to the manner born, I feasted on meals wheeled into my room on a table complete with silver, china, and a stiff white cloth, served by a waiter in smart attire with a linen napkin over his arm. I would come in contact with such refinement in my travels in my future Foreign Service career, but the scrambled eggs and bacon at the Plaza always seemed the best.

Another of the perks of being on the debate team was having our own room in the Morgan library. This not only gave team members lots of prestige but was a quiet place for reading as well as working on debate arguments. The audio room was especially ideal for spending time with my new boyfriend since it was adjacent to music-listening booths. We could select and listen to long playing records that I was not familiar with. He would guide me through them on these long cost-free dates, and in this gentle way I fell in love with him and with classical music. The romantic strains of Chopin's piano preludes and Tchaikovsky's concertos and symphonies took me to the Old World of beauty, grace, and creativity, developing in me an unquenchable taste for past centuries that would feed my spirit and soothe my soul.

When my dorm neighbor Sherry suggested that we go to a live concert, we plunked down $1.25 for seats at the Lyric Theater in Baltimore to see that city's orchestra perform Tchaikovsky's Concerto in B Flat Minor. The dramatic flourish of the opening melody, like many pieces by the Russian composer, was familiar in popular tunes; I knew it as the theme for a weekly TV program. Sitting with my friend in the library, each of us listening to a recording of the concerto with headphones, had been enchanting. But when Sherry and I went to hear it live, sitting so high in the auditorium with our cheap tickets that our heads almost touched the ceiling, it was transcending.

Since grade school, I continued to use my feet and voice to raise consciousness on the unequal treatment of my race. One such occasion was in 1967, when our debate team presented an excerpt of the play *In White America* by Martin Duberman. With the support of the college, we went to a convention in Cleveland attended by hundreds of college students from all over the USA. Its aim was to increase understanding among the wide range of students taking part in answer to the continuing race riots flaring up across the nation. Of course, that was a vague and impossible goal to achieve in one week, but I was excited to go to Cleveland, a forward-moving city where I'd never been.

Cleveland had just elected the first black mayor in the nation, Carl Stokes, and I was psyched about being in a city where changes brought about by the 1964 and 1965 Civil Rights Acts on public accommodations and voting rights, respectively, were taking place. Popular culture was transforming behavior, mores, dress, and attitudes. When we got to Cleveland, we saw some incredible sights. For instance, as we made our way through the cavernous lobby of the Marriott Hotel, I saw a couple in the corner in *flagrante delicto*—out in the open—showing me a real example of that popular sixties slogan: "Make love, not war!" I braced myself for seeing things I had not and was not disappointed.

Our contribution to the rally was the play, which explored the wrenched plight of enslaved African Americans over two centuries, based on historical records. Told through a series of monologues and vignettes, *In White America* was a first of its kind to win a Broadway award, and while the history of slavery in America is now well-known, in the sixties people didn't know much about its long narrative. The play required no scenery or props, save for a few additions to what we were wearing, such as a black Stetson hat worn by one of our group in his role of a "Dixiecrat" senator. When he said "boys" with a pronounced Southern drawl, it brought the house down! Our performance went over well, attracting lots of applause and shouts of "yes." At the end, I was left of center stage in my role of a young black girl during the desegregation of Little Rock's Central High School in 1957, uttering the closing lines:

> Mother looked as if she had been crying, and I wanted to
> tell her I was all right.
> But I couldn't speak. She put her arms around me and I
> cried[9]

Concentrating under the glare of bright lights in the packed room, I went deep inside myself to shed genuine tears, leading the chain reaction of many in the audience, who cried too. While I was proud of my performance, I had mixed feelings about making a spectacle out of the serious plight of my race, perhaps because the role came easily to me. And seeing myself on the closed-circuit TV monitor, I thought I looked silly: there I was, beige-skinned with blonde highlights in my hair, wearing a fur-trimmed mustard-yellow coat—not the look the role suggested. No one knew that

---

9   *In White America*, a documentary play by Martin Duberman, Houghton Mifflin Company, Boston Riverside Press, Cambridge, 1964.

I'd had the coat for four years. We hadn't anticipated being on TV and that we should have worn muted, plain clothes for the right effect. But then we were not serious amateur actors. Morgan was known for its leading Ira Aldridge Players; I'm sure they would have sworn that they didn't know us!

Our entry into this event had been through the debate team and with the help of a member from Baltimore who was active in his church's Christian worship program as a youth minister. The pamphlet that invited colleges to participate had said, "Sing, dance, or do your own thing," and doing the one-act play was our thing. Silhouetted in my mind is the picture of a tall, broad, long-haired Burl Ives–looking young man who came up to me at the end and put his sturdy arms around me, wet with tears. Though somewhat startled in this crush of limbs and hair, I found the grace to appreciate that through his action, he was saying, "I get it. I now know what you all have gone through." His tight embrace seemed to be asking me for forgiveness. I told him it was okay. Such consciousness-raising was quite common and very important to whites and blacks opening up to each other in those days.

Of all the music, displays, and performances at the Cleveland event, I got the most out of the small group discussions. Along the way, I had struck up a friendship with a girl who, with her long chestnut hair and slim figure, looked like the popular movie star Twiggy and kept following me around. I couldn't believe it when she told me she hadn't known any black people before, but as I got to know her, I could see that she was telling the truth. We went to discussions together, and as we got better acquainted, I realized that she was too naïve for her own good. A group of youths who reminded me of boys I knew back home sat on the floor with us in our group discussions, telling everyone about how hard life was in the ghetto. While the projects in Louisville did not compare to those of bigger cities like Cleveland, I knew the "hood," and these boys, who struck me as still in high school, were "laying it on thick" to tease the girl. My friend had started giving them money when she heard about their hard lives. I had to advise her to stop. She just couldn't throw money at a situation to fix it. Times were changing. American democracy was finally on the road to consolidation.

How proud I was to fly Eastern Airlines into Louisville Sandiford Field during my junior year with the debate coach, his assistant, and three teammates for the debate at Bellarmine College. As a child I'd watched the planes come and go with my brother and sisters from that same airport, hoping one day I'd get to fly on one of them.

Although our family's usual amusement had been watching the trains go by, seeing the planes take off was better; it was a step into the modern world. The flight from Baltimore to Louisville was my first flight ever. Assistant Coach Patsy Stevens sat next to me. She went on all out-of-town trips with me in those days when a female student at an HBCU required a chaperone. Of course Mr. Chin and three male debate teammates went with us. At the tournament, we had a mind-blowing time sparring verbally with debaters from Ohio, Indiana, and Michigan, and I proudly pointed out landmarks in my hometown to my friends from Baltimore.

I visited my family and told them about the tournament and what I was doing, enjoying showing off as a college girl. That was in spring 1967, and I was increasingly confident; I had been working for a year and could buy clothes to enjoy dressing and looking good. I had been home the previous summer and again that Christmas, making this all-expense-paid trip a bonus in my improving circumstances.

That Christmas, Mother and I had lunched at Walgreens during the holidays. I wore a spring-green dress that hugged my shapely figure. Since bobbing my long treasured but hard-to-manage soft hair, I had let it grow to my shoulders and was wearing it close to my head. From across the table in the booth, Mother told me, "You are a pretty woman." She and I held on to the moment, the only time we had gone out together alone since I could remember, both of us knowing that this was the first time that she had told me I was pretty. Her word had always been that I was "striking." I didn't want to be striking; I wanted to be pretty, and now the prettiest mother of them all was telling me that I was.

When I left Louisville that April with the debate team, I hadn't invited them in to meet my family; and for this, my sister later told me, Mother had been very upset. I carried that guilt with me for years and wish I could have done it differently, but the truth was I didn't think Mother wanted my Baltimore friends to come into our home. As a child I was used to friends and relatives coming to our home, but in the years since our family had fallen on hard times, guests stopped coming. We had nothing to be ashamed of; our house was always neat and clean, but putting food on the table was a daily feat, and friends and relatives probably didn't want to put more of a demand on us.

There were exceptions, however: a cousin came to live with us for a semester while he attended Bellarmine. We loved having him around to watch *The Mickey Mouse Club* with us. He would wear his silky burgundy dressing gown to play the priest at our reenactment of the daily Mass. Nonetheless, as I had never invited my high school mates to my home, I wasn't in the habit of asking friends to drop by. That's why I hadn't invited my college debate team in. Poverty can make a person act poor even when she is rich in nonmaterial ways.

Going home was always hard after I settled at Morgan, and when I did, it was never the same as when I had left it that first time. During my second Christmas back, in 1965, I felt like I was losing my moorings as I prepared to return to Baltimore. In a classic melodramatic scene, me with my arms around his neck and sinking down to his knees as I told him goodbye, Daddy broke down sobbing and begged me to stay. Still choked up, he said something so bizarre that it touched me to the core: why didn't I stay and study beauty culture, become a hairdresser, and make my life in Louisville? Now, I had great respect for Mrs. Seals, our neighborhood friend who had opened her own hair salon. She said I had motivated her to do it since she had done my hair for my First Communion. Still, everyone knew that I was headed for a profession which would take advantage of my education. When Daddy said what he did, I was flabbergasted and let burst a torrent of tears, making the whole occasion sad. *Give up my dream of going into the Foreign Service? Didn't he know I wanted to be like him?*

That's when Mother, who seldom told me what to do, interfered: "Stop it, Mudd! You're upsetting Sissy, and she's got to travel." For the first time, I saw her as stronger than Daddy. She was expressing a preference for what I should do. She would go on to show me unselfishly that she wanted me to realize my dreams. They were, it seemed, no longer just Daddy's; they were hers.

Two years later, at the start of my senior year in college, in September 1967, after a visit home weeks before, I suddenly had to return. I had seen Daddy when he was in General Hospital after yet another attack. Over the years, he had steadily gotten worse since his first stroke in 1962, and that last time I saw him, his cocoa-colored face was red with sadness. I hated seeing him feeling so hopeless, and was embarrassed for him when I witnessed the shabby treatment he got at the hospital. He was sitting up in bed, his gown open, exposing his private parts; no one had taken the time to cover him up. Hugging him when I came to visit, I arranged his gown and kissed him goodbye for what would be the last time.

When I had to return when I lost him, a heavy curtain came down, but his funeral turned out to be an uplifting celebration of a man who had touched hundreds. His life of happy playing-by-the-rules and faith in the future as a teacher, community leader, preacher, son, brother, husband, and father brought condolences from tens of people our family had never met. Born in 1906, he had lived two-thirds of his life by the time I was born and came to know him, so he never really belonged to me and my siblings. His example of overcoming the lowest odds and making a great man of himself stirred the wind beneath my wings. True to his entire life, Daddy's last act was so like him, rounding out his time on earth doing the best he could but always with a surprise. He left this world on the day he was born, September 22, 1967. He had just turned sixty-one.

When I returned to Morgan, I settled back into my routine. I was having a hard time getting the courage to persevere in the swimming course, a requirement for graduation that I had put off completing until my final year. I felt the pressure and was afraid that I would fail. But two of the guys from my debate team came to my rescue. They practiced with me in the pool in the evening, egging me on, and praised how well I floated. As I was plump, it was easy to be buoyant in water, but I accepted their encouragement and learned to swim. The instructor, tall and handsome with wavy wet hair and sweeping mustache, spared me nothing. Going the length of the Olympic-size pool was forbidding. I'd get past the shallow end and begin to panic because I knew I couldn't touch the bottom. "Take a deep breath, Miss Mudd, and continue your journey!" His command still echoes in my ears.

The women's movement was taking place the same time as the civil rights movement. As a black woman, I was used to the idea of having to work and take care of myself and had contradictory feelings about women claiming that their inequality was the same as for blacks. After all of the years of study and making good grades, more than one of my high school friends had chosen to get married after high school. Ursuline had taught us that being a good Catholic mother was the reason behind our education, and of course my mother had raised me and my siblings and had been a caring mate to my father. It would take a few more years for me to sort out the route I really wanted. I wanted to go into a profession, be a Foreign Service officer, but in the back of my mind I wanted a family and a home too. Daddy had often spoken of the day when he'd come to my house on Sunday; he'd sit at my table and eat the fried chicken I had prepared.

Thus I was only an observer of the women's movement and concentrated on its superficial details. For example, how women dressed and the styles they followed absorbed my attention. Girls from the big cities did not dress like the women in Louisville. Many of my new classmates dressed much more like grown women than girls as I had in my Ursuline uniform. Many of the girls from New York and Philadelphia adorned themselves alluringly with wigs and padded add-ons to make them appear more endowed, like they had stepped out of an ad from the back of *Jet* magazine. "There go the hair pieces!" the general sciences lecturer, in his rolled-up short sleeved shirt and bottleneck glasses, would shout when he turned the electric fans on to wake up those in our afternoon lab class who had been dozing.

Not daring to compete with the sophisticates, I spiffed up my "all-American" look, and I did enjoy the wink that a certain young man gave me in English class. The low light of the canteen, where I sipped on hot Dr. Pepper, was the place to be seen. I did my best to "hang out," even though I wasn't and have never been one for small talk. New trends like short-cropped all-natural Afro hairdos and dashiki shirts on men were breaking out all over campus as we went through the churning change of the sixties.

Although I viewed Morgan as my sanctuary of learning, as I got comfortable, gained recognition, and became more observant, I noticed that issues of the inner city existed right on campus. I didn't have to live in the city to experience them. One case that I noticed had to do with the tendency of some rather older young people to spend time on campus but not be officially enrolled. I knew one of these people, a young man with a highfalutin-sounding name, not unheard of among some blacks whose names can be sundry and artful: "Wilshire" was obsequious in his courtesy to me and my friends, always addressing me as "Miss Mudd" as he would have done for the teachers, and he forever could be seen in a tweed overcoat that hung down to his ankles, a suit and tie underneath.

When that morning after staying up all night locked in the study room during the panty raid I explained to him that we were supposed to hand in annotations of all the poems we had read that semester, he protested in his intellectual accent, "I had no idea!" While I rolled my bleary eyes at my equally tired classmates, I felt a little sorry for him. Could he have been *genuinely confused?* Needless to say, Wilshire didn't make it through that class, but he did *show us*: a few months later when we saw a picture of him in the daily paper in a military uniform at the side of a senior officer presenting him an award. He was already an army hero, and we had not yet graduated.

As I learned that cheating went on at Morgan, I found it hard to accept. In my rigid Catholic upbringing, I had no tolerance for it and, therefore, no chance to consider why someone would do it. Everything was black-and-white to me, literally as well as figuratively. Passing off someone else's work as if it were my own would have been stealing. Like many children, I had been drilled in correct behavior, but when I had asked the hard questions as I got older, I had encountered such disappointment from the person I was asking that I had, for the most part, learned not to ask the wrong questions. Still, as I knew more and gained more confidence growing up, I couldn't stop searching for answers, and that could make people think differently of me, maybe not like me as much.

At Ursuline when I was class president, I had asked the priest who conducted our weekly religion class about reincarnation; his response was icy disapproval of the question with no effort to answer. Yes, I did know that such thinking was heretical, but it needed an explanation. My friend Linda reminds me that at Ursuline I once asked a question implying that it was all right for a divorced mother with many children to remarry for the sake of her children and was scolded by Sister for taking such a sinful view. Finally, I was told that I should be ashamed for suggesting it since I was class president! Another time, at a career fair (set up to expose students to careers, especially to a life in the convent), I stood up and asked the woman who worked in real estate, wearing the business suit and navy blue stylish hat, if she thought working detracted from her femininity. That got a big nervous laugh, but of course my teachers didn't appreciate the question. Yet I was glad I asked it, for I was trying to find out about how women who went into other professions felt. Being a goody-goody had cut me off from learning a lot about practical matters.

Mostly I stuck to doing well in my studies by keeping controversial questions inside and unanswered. I could memorize and regurgitate as well as the best of my schoolmates. Years of catechism, and religious as well as classical studies had trained me for that. I parlayed this skill into lapping up whole blocks of texts in subjects clear and unclear and would borrow on my memory in discussions, on written work citing sources, and on exams. If I had given up and taken the work of someone else, that would have been stealing from myself.

Morgan, too, upheld the honor code. This was decades before the popular use of computers, the Internet, and photocopying. Yet grappling with appropriating work that was not my own and other inevitable realities of competitive situations was a struggle. My first hassle had been when I had lain on the bed and cried all day after burning that hole in the bedspread. After my dormmates got me to see that I was carrying the self-flagellation too far, I had accepted the situation and decided to hide the evidence under the bunny rabbit. The next bout was much more difficult.

One of my political science professors who taught a course I was taking on American foreign policy—I'll call him Dr. Gould—was running for public office in Baltimore, natural for a political scientist, although new for me coming from segregated Louisville, where Daddy's working at the local precinct on voting day was the closest I'd come to knowing a black taking part in a campaign. What did cause me pause was that the professor pressured his students, most of whom were football players who depended on his grade to pass the course, to engage in political activities for him. While I wanted to get a taste of working at the grassroots level in an election, I resisted Dr. Gould's efforts to compel me to, because I didn't like being forced to do so and I didn't want to get caught in town with no transportation back to the campus late at night. He wouldn't take no for an answer and pestered me openly in class, adopting a whining voice, making the others, mostly boys, chuckle and make snide comments under their breath. Sitting through this was uncomfortable, but I had no choice but to endure it. Since I sat in the first row, it was easy for him to taunt me. After he accepted that I wouldn't work on his campaign, he'd start in on asking me, "Judy, when are you going to give me some brown sugar . . ."

This was not as embarrassing as it was silly and very unbecoming of a college professor. He looked very much like my father, who would have never behaved that way, but Daddy often asked for "sugar," a kiss, so I knew the meaning. One day a classmate, Gloria, and I were comparing notes about the professor's bizarre behavior. Someone else had told me that she had seen him carry a girl who had fainted across the campus. "Are you pregnant?" he had exclaimed for all on the campus green to hear, Gloria told me. She was preparing to meet Dr. Gould in his office to talk about her academic work. She was worried not only about passing his course but also about being alone with him. A time before, she told me, he asked her for brown sugar. When she told him outright that she couldn't do that, that it was silly, he then went over to his shelf and took down a white paper Dixie Cup and showed her: "See, I have my own!"

Funny, yes. But not so when he gave me a B+ for a final grade and, according to my grades on tests and papers, I merited an A. My then debate partner Herbert Sledge (one judge wrote, "Stop your sledgehammer techniques," on his critiques) gave me the bad news one Saturday morning when we were in the debate room at the library. He had just viewed the grades posted outside Dr. Gould's office. When I heard this, my blood began to boil, and I was angry. "How could he do this? It must have been because I didn't work on his campaign," I shouted.

"It's 'cause you wouldn't give him any brown sugar," Herbert said. Although my debate partner and I were constantly in competition for best debater, I felt his note of sympathy for me. I should have been grateful for it, but it made me even madder, hating having him feel sorry for me. All weekend I rehearsed what I would say to Dr. Gould when I'd catch him in front of his office Monday afternoon. When I did, he showed me my exam and said, "Well, Judy, you got this answer wrong," pointing to one of ten questions. The question had to do with organizing an international meeting. "What contingency plans do organizers make when the conference site is not available for those arriving to attend a conference?" That's when his policy of cheating turned back to bite him.

I read the essay question and answered quickly: I recognized the question from the so-called practice test he'd passed out weeks before. I told him that I had responded to it on the practice exam in the same way I had on the final. To that, he said "You know, Judy, I never read those things." Well, I told him, he had checked my reply as acceptable and I had given the same reply on the exam. I told him that in my duties in the Student Advisory Center I had noticed that mistakes about grades were made all the time. Before he could say brown sugar, he changed the grade to an A!

While that was no fun, it had not been as unpleasant as another time that was much more serious, for it was in my core subject of English: Shakespeare, no less. And the professor—let's call him Dr. Thomas— was a distinguished scholar, or so he was reputed to be. In his class we probed Shakespeare deeply. All English classes were formal, but his were Victorian if not medieval in their strict manner. Gray at the temples and balding, he was considered an authority in his field, but experts are not necessarily good teachers, as I was to discover. One day he gave the class a pop quiz to see if we had read certain works that he had covered. More used to essay questions on English tests, I was surprised by his approach, which seemed unscholarly, as other teachers in the department didn't use pop quizzes. Still, I struggled with the true-or-false queries, finding them hard to answer until the twenty minutes was up.

Then came the most excruciating part, the time when I wanted to crawl under the desk, the time when I was so embarrassed and so alone that I wanted to disappear in the midst of the silent class of students, most of whom I didn't know, for they were almost all day students, who, it seemed, had sailed through the exercise. I could see this when, to save time, Dr. Thomas called out the correct answers to the questions so that the students could correct their tests, then shout the results to him so he could record them.

When my turn came, I was speechless: "Miss Mudd." Dead silence. "Miss Mudd." More silence. I hung my head and sank in my seat as the tears welled in my contorted face. After several minutes, Dr. Thomas's wall of stone crumbled, and his voice softened. "Come sit here, Miss Mudd," he said, patting the chair beside his desk. I slinked over and into it; fortunately, it was near me in the front row. "Now you got that right . . . and that right . . .," he whispered as if he were talking to a dim-witted child. "Now you passed," he said as he inked in some hocus-pocus notes on the page, saving me from God knows what fate I would have inflicted on myself.

My friend Bradford (not his real name) told me later that the test had been passed around for many weeks, at least in the city, where he lived. He didn't know if it had circulated on campus. Since I had not been looking for it, I hadn't seen a copy before the class, as I was not in the habit of seeking advanced copies of tests.

The last quarter of Morgan was the crucible I had to endure to succeed, like the hero in a long journey. I'd had hard times before, but that time was like crossing a ring of fire. It pulls at the heartstrings, but love got me through: love of myself with all my foibles, love of my family, and love of another, my first love. Like me, Francis was an English major, and while he respected and encouraged me, he wasn't beguiled or overwhelmed by my intelligence, which made us a good match. He had pulled me out of the corner—literally, before we fell in love—during my second year. I was in the habit of sitting on the side of the cafeteria while I ate lunch. One day he came over to me and said with a wide smile and big dancing eyes, "Why do you always sit over here? It's like you're afraid of everyone." Waving his arms on each side, he motioned, "See all these people talking and laughing? Come sit in the middle at this table with us." I wanted to tell him to mind his own business, but I couldn't, because I knew he was right. I wanted to be at the crowded table. I just needed permission. Francis was the one who had lifted the rabbit from the quilt when the boys were visiting our dorm rooms, which was how we met. A romantic like me, he presented me a pair of heart-shaped rhinestone earrings lying on red velvet in a miniature box in the shape of a piano sparkling like diamonds for Valentine's Day. By that spring of 1966, we were a steady couple, and let's just say that I got my first case of full-blown hay fever by being in my own version of *Splendor in the Grass*![10]

Around the time I started going out with Francis, many things began coming up roses. Having struggled during my first year and a half at Morgan, living frugally on a scholarship and unsure of funds for traveling home for the holidays, by that spring I was working in the counseling center and my financial situation was more stable. By the fall of 1966, I started getting checks of $75 from the recently passed Social Security benefits for children of the disabled. Not expecting the assistance, I was overjoyed, but I didn't know what to do with the money when the checks started coming, for a while daily, then retroactively. Used to living on a tight budget, I was overwhelmed by my change in circumstances. I had come a long way from scrounging for pennies at the bakery to possibilities of taking advantage of more things. I crammed the checks into the bottom drawer of the chest in the room on Hermosa Avenue, like some genius scientist who couldn't be bothered with money![11]

English had most of my attention: the English countryside, poets Robert and Elizabeth Barrett Browning's love story, her home on Wimple Street from which Robert had swept her away, and their days in sunny Italy. I was also making progress in French, reading in the language now, Flaubert's *Madame Bovary*, for example. And I was getting to know world literature too, Russian, for example, reading the classics of Dostoevsky, Tolstoy, and Stendhal. So consumed was I by Stendhal's *The Red and the Black* that I bought a bright red doubled-breasted coat with shiny brass

---

10 "Splendor in the Grass," from a poem by William Wordsworth, made into a film of the same name in 1961, was a romantic summer drama starring Natalie Wood and Warren Beatty.

11 I have in mind the great African American scientist (and former slave) George Washington Carver, who discovered more uses for peanuts and plants than he could bother to patent. He is rumored to have stashed checks away without cashing them for a long time.

buttons, which I wore with black pants and accessories. As my stash of checks grew, I began envisioning a summer trip to Europe based on an ad I'd read that promised five days, three cities—London, Paris, Rome—for $350. Just a few weeks before, this vision had been a daydream; now I could afford it.

10

Searing Sixty-Eight

The trip to Europe was not to be. By April 1967, I was offered a paid internship at the Peace Corps' main office in Washington for the summer. I leaped at the opportunity, using my windfall of money to move to Washington. While I did have a short pang of doubt—I so wanted to go to Europe—accepting the salaried internship was my first chance to work in the field where I'd been building castles in my mind for years. It's a good thing I did. That experience and those in the months following toughened me for the blasts that lay ahead.

Peace Corps was still a young agency. Staff members could remember those get-it-done days when the Democrats had finally returned to Washington after eight years of a Republican administration, sitting on the floor at their typewriters, sending volunteers to developing countries to show that Americans believed in co-existence. Before being elected senator, John Kennedy had remarked at Michigan University on October 14, 1960, that he thought the idea of a corps of Americans going overseas to promote peace with the United States could become a reality. After becoming president, he put his brother-in-law Sargent Shriver in charge of the new agency. By working for the Peace Corps, I was supporting the late president's dream while embarking on an international career.

Senator Kennedy had also said in those remarks at Michigan University, "How many of you are willing to work in the Foreign Service and spend your lives traveling around the world? On your willingness to do that, not merely to serve one year or two years in the service, but on your willingness to contribute a part of your life to this country, I think will depend [sic] the answer [to] whether a free society can compete." At age sixteen, I had taken his suggestions to heart.

When I interned at Peace Corps, Penney White was my supervisor in the Office of Near East, North Africa, and South Asia (NANESA) in the division of Returned Volunteers. My main task was to research and write a report on volunteers (PCVs) returning from India. I also had to deliver and pick up passports from the Indian and other foreign missions on Massachusetts Avenue and streets on Washington's Embassy Row. What better way to learn how to get around DC than hopping in and out of cabs on messenger runs! And what better way to soak up the reality of international affairs than to do work on matters directly related to them? Within a decade I'd be meeting Indians in their country, but in 1967 I had no idea that the Peace Corps gig was preparing me for that. By working on nuts-and-bolts details, I got involved with the practicalities of the career I was interested in. While I'd later study the subject formally and get an advanced degree in it, in those days I came to realize that effective relations, cross-cultural or otherwise, relied on personal contact. This forced me to push further out of my shell to develop better social skills.

I got used to mixing with other college interns from all over the United States, all of European ancestry but from a variety of backgrounds, from various colleges and universities. My new girlfriends wore miniskirts, so I shortened my hemline. They grabbed meals from the luncheonette on the corner, so I did too. We picnicked in Lafayette Park across from the White House, not far from our Twentieth Street Northwest office.

Francis came to DC, and we went out several times. As he knew the sections of the city where blacks lived pretty well, he was relaxed in showing me his favorite places for music and food. As I was living far from the center of the city, in Northwest Washington, off of Georgia Avenue, near Silver Spring Maryland, the logistics of getting into the city on the bus were complicated, but we didn't mind. Of the most special times was when he took me to the Cellar Door, a small jazz club in Washington's Georgetown, to see the fabulous Nina Simone. And one Sunday afternoon we went to the Howard Theatre. Audiences in front of its historic stage didn't let bad acts remain on stage. Like a gong show, performers pleased or were booed off the stage. I applauded the first and best live rhythm and blues artists I'd seen or ever heard. That doesn't say much, however, for while growing up I was not encouraged to listen to the black radio station and had come to know R&B only when songs crossed over to the popular music chart. In Wahington, I was discovering these golden deposits of black culture.

Tucking into the reports of the Peace Corps volunteers who were finishing their tours in India opened up a vista that pulled me in. I was fascinated learning about Asia, which existed only as what I'd seen in short film clips on TV, and the one time I met an Asian, from Cambodia, at a Catholic mission rally at Notre Dame University. The United States had gone to war with Japan, but while I got some sense of Europe as I grew up, I got no clear sense of the Land of the Rising Sun. *Why are the Japanese men in news reels wearing top hats?* I wondered.

As I had no knowledge of India then and no feeling one way or the other for the volunteers' opinions, I studied their comments objectively, taking them at face value. Their reports on their tours were mostly negative: high marks for the Indian people but low rankings for the situations the Peace Corps had put them in. They felt demoralized because the Indians with whom they worked seemed not to give them the respect they thought they deserved. They felt that this was because they had only generalist BA degrees and not specialist PhDs. In a country where people have had to claw their way to the top through caste, class, a colonial past, and a system of examinations, it is not surprising that the citizens expected to work with Americans who were experienced, but in 1967, I didn't think like that. I sided with the volunteers.

American goodwill, though charming, was not enough in a country that was scraping to feed and care for millions after a long, painstaking struggle for independence gained only twenty years before, in 1947. The Peace Corps Volunteers, on the other hand, thought that by taking two years of their lives and bringing their American zeal to India, they could motivate their host country coworkers to think more kindly of the United States. What they failed to recognize was that for India the United States was a new partner. When Indians spoke of Western ways, they mostly meant Great Britain, not the United States. Moreover, not limited by Cold War loyalties, they were open to Russia for the better deal in foreign aid that the communist nation was offering them. Until the late 1980s, India and America were like two runners aiming toward the same peaceful coexistence cross line but yards apart.

Understanding the geopolitical context in which they had been placed seemed to be unclear. So disillusioned were some of the volunteers that they just gave up; others slogged through their stays without feeling that they had contributed much. Many appreciated the goodwill that they had engendered but were unhappy that their host country didn't feel that friendly feelings were enough. As I read the volunteers' final reports, I noted the hardships under which they lived—many had contracted amebic dysentery, and several felt isolated. This land of hardship was the last place I wanted to visit.

To investigate the basis of their criticisms, I read through files and official records to understand just what the United States policy on PCVs was. As the intern, I had no trouble getting access to the documents. As is now well-known, interns can be given a wide berth when they're working for the USG. I went through cabinets of classified files, discovering that Hubert Humphrey, not John F. Kennedy, had the original idea of creating the Peace Corps. I also found out that the debate over recruiting specialists versus generalists had been an ongoing one in the executive branch. After combing through all of these reports, I wrote my report *Peace Corps: India's Stumbling Block* in which I put forth my findings. More than just a ripple, the report swooshed as it landed on desks. At first, everyone in NANESA claimed to love it. I was congratulated for my outstanding work. Then someone actually read what I'd said. He judged that I had included too much classified information to justify what the volunteers had said about the Indian preference for experts over goodwill ambassadors. "She just took all the negative parts to justify the reports." Of course I begged to differ, but I'd made my point. Like a hot potato, the report was removed to the desk of a cooler head and classified for limited use. Using it was so restricted that I couldn't even take a copy with me as proof of my achievement. Heads could have rolled if no one had put the lid on the revelations in my paper, but I didn't feel bad about it. I was proud because I knew I had uncovered the facts. History has born me out. Today, Peace Corps sends specialists to assist countries around the world, and handling of classified information continues to emblazon the headlines.

In 1968, the daily news was about the Vietnam War and civil rights. Caught in the tumult, the tensions, and the fervor of the future opening up for blacks, I secretly wanted to get away from it all. In a carefree moment, I suggested to Francis that we marry and have three kids right away. "But we have to finish grad school!" he had said—as if to say, "Are you out of your mind?" I felt I could have done it, but after throwing out the initial dare, I have to admit that I was glad he had pulled away from it. That gave me permission to move on toward my goal.

The news in 1968 riveted me nearly every week, sometimes every day, so much happened—the Tet Offensive, Kent State, and the rise of Black Power. Martin Luther King's assassination on April 4 drained the energy out of me and everyone I knew; Robert Kennedy's gunning down on June 5, the early morning after the night of my college graduation, numbed me. Everything was falling apart.

In the sixties so much had changed: ideas, for instance, which carried a whole new way of thinking about America. The Beat Generation and "beatnik" had cued me to the way America was taking new shape, but that was on the coast and "artsy" for me when I was still living in Louisville. Now, though, I couldn't ignore thinking about "flower children." Were they serious or just pretending? But when "hallucinating" and "psychedelic" fell on my ears, they perked up. Drug addiction (and of course alcohol) had long been the scourge of my community, and I couldn't see anything idealistic about "tripping." Yet I knew someone who claimed that he had tried LSD and achieved new heights of understanding with it.

I did not think of myself as a part of the counterculture. Far from it, I wanted to preserve and build on the quality of life in the only culture and country I had. For that reason, I wasn't antiwar per se. Friends, young black men, were going off to Vietnam, and I didn't want to think that they were going there to die. Having confidence in President Johnson, I believed the lies that were being told about U.S. progress in Vietnam, until, like so many, I heard Walter Cronkite say that America was losing the fight. By then, I must admit, I didn't want to give much attention to Dr. King's antiwar admonishments. His "Ain't gonna study war no more" speech had not been widely broadcast, but blacks, like my father when he was alive, felt that this effective leader of nonviolence should stick to civil rights and not venture into foreign affairs. By spring 1968, things were happening so fast that I had to act as if I were wearing blinders around my eyes to focus on completing my requirements to graduate. When we were forced to remain in our residences by a 4:00 p.m. curfew for all students following Dr. King's murder, I sat on my bed staring at the television, watching Washington DC go up in flames and, simultaneously, the mayhem that began to take place in Baltimore and across the nation.

A few fellow students I thought considered me one of them proved not to think so when the old color-conscious issue flared up in my last months at Morgan. I had grown up with this thinking and ran from it like the plague whenever I encountered it: victims of discrimination pressing their feet down on others like them based on skin color. At a time when students were taking over administration buildings all over the country, some radical students had seized control of Morgan's student center and for a short while took on the role of dictating what they deemed was proper for a predominantly black college to teach.

The Black Is Beautiful Movement was growing—my friend, whom I'll call Barbara, sported a short Afro hairdo; and the Black Panthers' rousing spokesman Stokely Carmichael had kept us busy questioning the limits of Dr. King's nonviolence and the certainties of violence. I wasn't sure. I had been up and down the East Coast, even staying in Harlem and inner-city Newark, after the riots there in 1967, enough to know that there would be a "fire next time."[12]

Yet I still believed in the power of right over might and was afraid that physical force would destroy what blacks had amassed and conserved, as modest as it was, despite slavery and Jim Crow.

While I would sit and remain silent during such rousing meetings, when once some of the radicals said that a white man like Thomas Cripps shouldn't be allowed to teach black history, I could not help but raise my hand to stand up to reply. Professor Cripps was the most interesting teacher of black history Morgan had then. Everyone knew that. But as I started to speak, I felt Francis tugging my arm. I leaned over to hear him tell me to sit down. He was afraid that I might get insulted, because, he softly said, as I had light skin, the leaders may have felt I didn't have the right to speak. Stunned and hurt as I was, for I was a true Morgan student, I was more confused. *Didn't they know that we all were in this together?* This incident made me see how some who have been treated unjustly mimic the behavior of their oppressors. Such folly! I was as black as the darkest person there. Color was a false indicator.

When Dr. King was assassinated, I drew on all the strength I could summon to get through the two remaining months. Of one thing I was sure: I had to get away. I would go abroad. I had applied for an assignment with the Peace Corps, but I had also staked my claim on a Fulbright teaching

---

12 *The Fire Next Time,* by James Baldwin, 1963

assistantship to work and study in India. Strange that I should have aimed for India after deciding that I did not like that South Asian country. But when the opportunity to bid on the Fulbright came, I "schooled" myself in India's history and current events. I was especially captivated by the life of one of that country's famous poets, Sarojini Naidu, and that changed my mind. Perhaps I wouldn't like it, but I wanted to find out about the world's biggest democracy for myself. As he had done and would continue to do for many Morgan students, Mr. McIntyre shepherded me through the Fulbright application process, thus having significant influence on my life and doing a great deal to steer me into the lane where I needed to be to merge into the Foreign Service.

'68 FULBRIGHT AWARDS
Afro-American (1893-1988); Jun 15, 1968; ProQuest Historical Newspapers: The Baltimore Afro-American
pg. B5

'68 FULBRIGHT AWARDS

Fulbright grants to study abroad have been awarded four Morgan State College students for the 1968-69 school year, while one student, who has already received a French Government grant has been designated as an alternate for a Fulbright Travel Award.

In four years June graduates have received 16 Fulbright grants. One of the new awards is a renewal to a '67 graduate.

The Fulbright awards are among the prestige grants for Morgan seniors and faculty announced in the preliminary report by Mrs. Mary Ann Franklin, assistant dean of the college.

Included

Also included on the list are 1 Woodrow Wilson Fellowship, 1 Woodrow Wilson Designate, 1 Woodrow Wilson Honorable Mention, 1 Danforth Honorable Mention and 1 Shell Merit Award.

Scholarships to students and faculty members total about $115,000. Not included in this figure are tuition and fee grants which are extra.

Among the colleges and universities offering graduate school fellowships and scholarships as of May 10 are Howard University Medical School, Howard Dental School, University of Wisconsin, Ohio State University, University of Pennsylvania, Northwestern University, Atlanta University, Cornell, University of Chicago, University of Michigan, Drexel Institute;

Rutgers University, Bryn Mawr, Purdue, University of Gaudalajara (Mexico), National Institute of Mental Health, U.S. Army Specialist School, New York University, University of Indiana, Kent State University, West Chester State, Yale University, Morgan State, Columbia University, William and Mary College;

Lehigh University, Boston University, Drew University, University of New Hampshire, York University (Canada), University of Maryland, University of Pittsburgh, Western Reserve, and the Johns Hopkins University.

Recipients

Receiving Fulbrights are Burney Hollis, Baltimore, and Miss Judith Mudd, Louisville, Ky., both to India; Miss Florence Shipman, Baltimore, to Germany; Miss Mildred Jennings, Houston, Tex., a renewal of her 1967 grant to India; and Miss Maria Campbell (alternate), Baltimore, to France. (She has already received a French Government Grant and has been designated an alternate for a Fulbright Travel Grant.) Sandye McIntyre, assistant professor of foreign languages, who studied in France on a Fruibright, is adviser at Morgan.

TO STUDY ABROAD — Three of the five Morgan State College graduating seniors who will study abroad in the '68-'69 school year are shown with their advisor, Sandye McIntyre (right). At left are Burney Hollis, Baltimore and Miss Judith Mudd, Louisville, Ky., Miss Maria Campbell (center), Baltimore, an alternate.

What an embarrassment of riches! One day, I was invited to join the Peace Corps, and the next, awarded the Fulbright. As I could not say no to the opportunity to build on my budding knowledge of India, I gratefully accepted the scholarship. I did, however, regret not being able to live in French-speaking Tunisia where the Peace Corps would have taken me.

It would have been lovely to have had the time to savor my achievements and take time to bid farewell to my friends at Morgan, but everything was moving so fast. Like a song that keeps replaying, I have retraced that unforgettable final night over and over in my mind. How come I was caught in the crossfire, so to speak? Why was my night of nights so overshadowed? On June 5 in Los Angeles (June 4 in Baltimore) Bobby Kennedy was shot. It was the evening of my college graduation and the eve of my twenty-second birthday. He would die twenty-six hours later. Francis and I were going through the motions of having fun at an after-graduation party. The sorrow and fear that clutched me and those around me threatened to bring our once in a lifetime highs down to hopeless lows.

Daddy had died the September before and wasn't able to see me receive my diploma and prestigious international award, but Mother and Andrea came to see me graduate cum laude. Sometimes I think I'm a duplicitous person and that this is my main character fault. Although Francis and I were planning a future together, I couldn't wait to get away from the United States, for it seemed that all my childhood dreams in my beloved country were an unending nightmare. I had to leave America to love it.

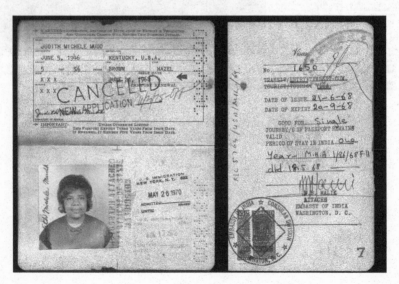

11

Kashmir: Stranger in Paradise

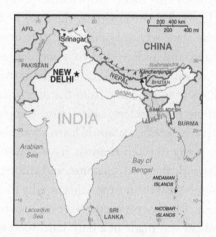

**Public domain, courtesy of the World Factbook,
Central Intelligence Agency**

People pressed, gripped, and yelled as we made it through the airport
with our luggage and into a taxi. Hut-like buildings, shacks, then, suddenly,
grand structures in gray stone, one surrounded by low-hanging branches of
a tree bending and brushing its high walls—these were my first glimpses of
India. This strange land would test my resolve to experience an unknown
culture. I didn't know it at the time, but for me, this new yet ancient land
would take me in as literally part of a family. My classmate from Morgan,
Burney Hollis, had traveled with me on a grant for the same program. We

made our way to Fulbright House, though not without falling prey to the typical scam played on tourists of being overcharged by the taxi driver. Still, we didn't complain. Having missed the official welcoming delegation due to our late arrival—we had a problem getting visas at the last minute and were stranded in New York—we were lucky to make it through the airport and into town on our own. For me it was all a big adventure.

Later that day, we were on a plane headed for Srinagar, in the state of Jammu and Kashmir, for orientation the next morning. A better place to spend the first days in an unknown country one couldn't have asked for, but we were too young and out of our comfort zone to appreciate it. I knew little about Kashmir except its dramatic snowcapped views and mountainous landscape. My college courses hadn't taken me into the epochal history of the subcontinent, let alone the earth-shattering consequences of the British relinquishment of its empire for Indian independence and the creation of Pakistan from the colony that had been Britain's "jewel in the crown."

Now we were in the Vale of Kashmir, the most beautiful part of the divided, autonomous state whose boundaries were and still are bitterly contested by Pakistan and India—and to some degree, by China. We stayed in a houseboat on Nigeen Lake, an idyllic setting reminiscent of when Britons went there to get away from the overwhelming heat of the plains, with our fellow Fulbrighters. Our arrival completed the group of eighteen. In the next two weeks, we would learn about India and the places where we would be going to teach English, have a crash course in Hindi, and get comfortable with the food, customs, and culture.

Living in a houseboat was an experience totally different for me and for most of the others. I had never even been on a boat before. Moored on the lake, our houseboat was made of a dark hardwood with finely carved paneling. Ample bedrooms with Western comforts promised to make us feel more at home. The kitchen, run by a cook and helpers, was behind a wide dining room with an oval table covered with a white tablecloth. Chairs and divans with colorful cushions and small antique tables made up the sitting room; and there were two large bathrooms, for men and women, with spaces for bathing. Western-style toilets were in separate rooms.

The problem with the vacation-like setting was that everyone was sick after the first one or two meals. During the night, participants were retching and running in and out of the toilets to the extent that the late get-togethers, where I thought I'd get to know the others, were like nights in an asylum. Delhi Belly, the uncontrollable voiding of all bodily fluids from every orifice, which comes from harmful bacteria or parasites most easily consumed in untreated water, had ruled out all fun. We seemed to all have it at various times. Fortunately, I didn't get the worst, dysentery, but I was sick enough, out of circulation for two or three days. After checking, our group leaders found that the helpers responsible for the water had boiled it as required but had pumped it from the lake, not from the tank containing the potable supply.

Because some of us didn't feel our best, rather than relaxing, the orientation was like a forced march that had to be endured despite our dehydration, cramps, and frequent runs to relieve ourselves. Still, all the must-sees were kept on our agenda: countless shrines, one an enormous structure to Shiva and others to the gods in the wide Hindu pantheon; a Muslim mosque; and the Shalimar Gardens, which a Persian emperor, Jahangir, claimed to be paradise on earth. We rode in *shikaras,* boats that, when I would visit Venice twenty-five years later, I'd notice were similar to gondolas, except that *shikaras* were partly covered by a roof.

We listened to lectures on India, sitting under leafy trees in our classroom on the verdant grounds of the Government College of Engineering and Technology. We were taught Hindi too, but I retained little. This young woman who only a month before figured out the meaning of words based on Latin and French was now supposed to suddenly adjust her way of learning to a tongue that is recorded in a never-before-seen script—and written *under* the line, not on the line as in English! All I could do was smile and feign attention.

As the two weeks went by, I tried hard to show enthusiasm for the new tastes, sights, sounds, and smells, but I was struggling to keep up. India was an assault on the senses: open sewers, cows and sheep running around in some areas, and hordes of downtrodden people pressing forward here and there, a few of them begging for money. I heard the unfamiliar sounds of languages that did not fall on my ears like American English at all. More than anything, the rectitude of the pastel-shirted men and neat *sari-* or *salwar kameez*–wearing women going about their lives with intent and purpose threatened me. It not only exposed my ignorance of the subcontinent but also made me feel I was in a mystery that I was not at all sure I would be able to unravel.

Most enervating was the increasing sense of being unprepared for the whole experience of India that lay before me. In Shalimar Gardens, for instance, I had been numb, having never seen or thought of gardens like these. Terraced and elegant in marble and foliage, they were a feast for my eyes, yet taking in the vision was difficult. I only knew my father's vegetable garden from my early childhood—and those of relatives in the country. Now I was being told to imagine what a Moghul emperor had said about his garden fifteen hundred years ago. Picturing life before the fifties was hard. I was still struggling, by way of literature, to get a feeling for what it must have been like in America in the nineteenth century. How could I think the way they thought in earlier times? I had my doubts about my abilities. Besides, I was having trouble getting used to the food. In time, I would crave the spicy flavors and the assorted textures of North India, but during that orientation I was thinking only of fried chicken picnics at Chickasaw Park in Louisville. That was my garden, not this ornate place that may as well have been Disneyland. I hadn't been there either.

Just in time, Mercy and Fortune took me by the hand and told me to keep calm, listen, and mind my manners. *Offer thoughtful comments but resist offhand remarks. Above all, don't make a fool of yourself. You'll know more than you did when you started.*

One day, when I was feeling better after my days of throwing up, I was taking a good look at the interior of the girls' college we were touring. The students, with their bright smiling faces and kohl-rimmed eyes, wore their hair neatly behind their ears and were dressed in *salwar kameezes*: long, close-to-the-body dresses and tight pants hugging their legs. These were the original leggings that are now so popular in the West. The female students were all gaping at Burney, whispering about him, and he—tall, bronze, and brilliant—was graciously walking through it all. They glowed as they gazed at him as if he was a celebrity.

Beatle mania was spreading in India. The group had visited the country a few months before, in February 1968, and the press had reported when certain members of the famous group came and went in and out of Indian ashrams. Also, the trend of swooning over male idols was, I was discovering, international, not just something that had started, for me, with Elvis. I didn't know that the Indian film industry was just as influential and as old as Hollywood; I hadn't even known that the Indian film industry existed. Did the college girls think Burney was a South Indian film star?

As I became more familiar with our houseboat and its surroundings and made new friends, I began to enjoy the unique beauty of Kashmir— the dappled beauty of the flowers, the delicacy of the birds. One day I sat with a friend looking at cloth, trinkets, and handicrafts that a turban-and-shawl-wrapped man was trying to get us to buy. Just then a dollop of bird poop splattered on my right shoulder, and I let out a small shriek and started to cry. "It's nothing to be afraid of," the man gently told me. "It's just nature." That *wallah's* (seller) words, the first of tens of such encounters I would have with Indians over the next decade and a half, changed my life, because they encouraged me to think in a different way. His words gave me permission to give India a chance.

12

Delhi: Lectures and Lime Juice

Me with my fellow Fulbright tutors at the United States–India
Educational Foundation, New Delhi, July 1968, courtesy of USIEF

Porridge never tasted so good. The rich goat milk and pearls of grain
went down my stomach soothing and comforting it; the slice of butter on

top faded slowly, melting in with the coarse crystals of sugar caressing the hot cereal. That, with some slices of toast spread with jam, and coffee with hot milk set me up for the day. Two hours earlier, at 6:00 a.m., I had been annoyed when the bearer shouted *chai (tea)* and left it on a tray in front of my door, waking me up. But the strong tea with the steaming milk I added plus two plain biscuits (cookies), the bearer had placed on the side of the cup, encouraged me to get up. A brisk bath, taken with two buckets of water that had been laid in, one hot and one cold, with a cup for scooping it over my body, was already a part of my routine since arriving in this country where the plumbing was proving to be very unlike what I was used to. Habits from my frugal childhood kicked in, and I quickly adapted to the new way of bathing, which was like the sponge baths I'd taken at home on cold winter nights while growing up.

After dressing and breakfasting, I went with the group for more orientation on what to expect in the year of tutoring English in an Indian university. We were staying at the YMCA Hostel, in a commercial area in the middle of New Delhi. Comfortable, clean, and cool with ceiling fans and vented blinds at the windows that allowed a cross breeze to blow in, my room was a restful retreat. Its no-frills design cleared my head and opened my mind, which was what I needed after the ornate Raj style of the houseboat, which overwhelmed me. Our group was there for the next ten days. In addition to listening to talks on Indian culture and appropriate behavior—never use your left hand to eat, how women and men were often separated in public spaces, cleaning fruits and vegetables and boiling water—we were getting our assignments of where we would be sent to teach for the year. I was in no hurry to get this news, as I was curious to know more about India now that I was in Delhi. Rested and recovered, I took advantage of every outing—sightseeing, shopping, dining, and getting to know members of our group.

We'd go off on organized tours as well as impromptu "take a looks" that a few would arrange. Once some of us jumped in a scooter rickshaw (a petti cab) heading for the state emporium, which was still new then, near Connaught Place, a shopping and commercial center built by the British in 1933, not far from where we were staying. After looking around, taking in the delicate handwork and myriad motifs, I bought a handsome black bronze vase with thinly carved inlaid decoration and a lacquered ebony-and-green, yellow oval-shaped papier-maché box that I still display in my home.

In the midst of choosing what I would buy, the thought struck me: *This is communism.* For someone who had grown up during the Cold War and was used to "duck and cover," getting under the desk at school in drills for a possible nuclear attack, this was a pivotal realization. The "Iron Curtain," "Five-Year Plans," and images of stern soldiers with guns marched through my head. But I was taking it in stride, as all the Indian clerks and customers in the store reminded me of people shopping in America. I felt no jolt of fear or force. I just noted the dissimilarities: The difference between this shop and capitalist America was the division of labor. In America I'd take an item off a shelf or point to one from behind the counter, and an assistant would ring it up on the cash register and put it in a bag; I'd pay for it and be on my way. At the Cottage Industries of India Emporium, I had to indicate what I wanted, and an assistant would select it. Then I had to get in one line to pay and stand in another to collect the purchase. As there were other people in the queue, the whole transaction took more time, and there was interaction with more people. I would find that this wasn't so in small shops and in the bazaar, for Indians can be as capitalist, maybe more so, than Americans. There it was every man or woman pushing toward the vendor to buy first and a torrent of words going back and forth in the negotiation over price. The government of India espoused a form of social democracy back then, but it was never Soviet-style communism, contrary to widely held views in the United States at the time.

Getting into Indian dress was going to help me feel more comfortable among the local population, a woman at the Fulbright office advised me, and so I bought two readymade *kurta pajama* sets (like *salwar kameezes*, these were loose-fitting pants with dress-length tops), one in a mustard yellow and black cotton weave that was stunning and looked good on me. The other, pale blue linen with a white embroidered design on the front and three-quarter-length sleeves, did not suit my increasingly golden tanned complexion, but that didn't matter as much to me then. At least my legs were covered; this would stop people from staring.

From the first day of arrival in this world's second most populous country, someone was always watching me, and while I didn't like it, I accepted it because I knew I could do nothing about it. But it got on a lot of my friends' nerves as they were also being surveilled. What was more annoying were the ubiquitous clusters of mothers and children in rags; individuals in deformed states asking for *paisa* (money) on the streets; musicians, with a monkey or a snake, doing tricks for tips; holy men promising good things for a few coins; and countless more puzzling sights. From the start I felt I had a leg up on my groupmates. Many of them felt bad because they could not do anything about the poverty, and seeing it made them very uncomfortable.

While my heart fluttered when I saw poor people, and I hated how the beggars continually nagged and how I couldn't get away from them— they were everywhere—I didn't feel guilty about their miserable lot. Rather, I took it all in, watching people act like I'd never seen before. This detachment, which may sound heartless, probably helped me live in and learn about India. When I did finally leave India, I remember being mocked by a beggar on a railway platform: *"Paisa nehi,"* she imitated me, even using my Kentucky twang as I kept telling her, "No money." By that time my Hindi was good, but in times of stress we tend to intone in our native language. In India even the beggars were proud.

During those days of getting to know more about this exotic land, I was all eyes and ears and suspended judgment: I got in line; traveled on buses; and stayed with the group dutifully, seeing one sight after the other. In time, after many years in India, I would know those places like the back of my hand, acting as tour guide to first-time Americans, but in July 1968, I was a tourist beholding, for the first time, structures that had symbolized the British Empire—India Gate, Rajpath, Rashtrapati Bhavan—sun burning my nose, sweat trickling down my back, and my new *chappals* (sandals) cutting between my toes. No matter that the sites didn't mean much to me, as I had no context. I viewed, listened, and trudged on. I did enjoy the Red Fort, the sixteenth-century red sandstone creation of Shahjahan, the same emperor who built the Taj Mahal (which our group didn't visit), and the sound and light show that was put on to dramatize life under the rule of the Moghuls. But mostly what I saw of Indian life on the streets was much more captivating: motorcycle taxis (scooter rickshaws); bicycles; hand-pulled wagons with only two wheels; men on the streets doing all kinds of things, like selling green packets of paan for chewing, like tobacco; flower vendors hawking rings of fragrant white jasmine for women's hair; and various huddles of city dwellers eating, trading, talking—life itself.

During breaks I'd sip *nimbu pani*, lime juice in water, which soothed the stomach and aided digestion. I'd only graze over the food served at lunch; my body was too overheated to eat. Like the local people, I'd sneak a nap in the middle of the day, when the temperature was the hottest, over one hundred degrees Fahrenheit often. In the evenings we'd sample the variety of restaurants in Connaught Place. When we went to Narula's, well-known for its Chinese food, I was too timid to admit that I couldn't use chopsticks and struggled to do so, barely getting enough into my mouth. I'd never had Chinese food before. In Louisville, that cuisine was not around when I was growing up; and in Baltimore I didn't spend much on unfamiliar food, even if it was around. So I got my first taste of East Asian food in New Delhi.

The "new" part of the city was recent, having been carved out of Delhi district in 1911 when the capital of British India was moved from Calcutta. Old Delhi, on the other hand, pulsated with 24/7 activity; it was where we needed to go to glimpse real India. Going there the first time was, like much in the subcontinent, overwhelming. Everything was happening: yellow, red, and blue colors danced in the materials of what people wore in front of my eyes. Stinking sewage, often not far away, choked my breathing, while ribbons of sweet smells wafted from a vendor's cart in front of me. I wanted to taste these hard-to-resist delights, but I had to take my new experiences in small chunks and didn't sample the street food. Controlling myself until evening fell, I went with my friends to the famous Moti Mahal's. There I savored dishes that sent me to heaven when they touched my tongue: tandoori and butter chicken and crispy *naan* (flatbread) for sopping up the sauces.

Baby Boomer that I was, it was not until I was in New Delhi that I attended my first pot party. Some of our group were sitting around on the floor in someone's room at the Y and started to smoke. When dark-haired Gary (not his real name) passed the pipe to me, I told him and everyone that I had never smoked marijuana and didn't want to try, but asked if I could stay at the party just the same. He said sure, and no one made a fuss about it. The buzz was about how the Beatles had spent long evenings imbibing during their stay in India. I'd later learn about hashish-laced cups of milk that Indian men would drink under the moon in certain Hindu rituals. I loved my friends that night for not making a big deal out of my not smoking.

This was after we'd just got our assignments of where we would be teaching for the year, and we were very excited. Those who had been in India before, for short times, regaled us with their anecdotes about not eating the holy bread when they were in Indian temples (they said it sometimes contained cow dung!), about wading in the holy Ganges River, things like that. Scenes of all types ran through my mind. I couldn't imagine the new life that lay before me, and while I was somewhat apprehensive, I was now chomping at the bit to get on with it.

The next morning, I was in the sunny lobby chatting with the Fulbright staff about my assignment to Nagpur, in Maharashtra state. Culture shock was starting to crawl up my back. I didn't take to India at first: the contrast between what I had seen in America and what I was seeing in this new country was too great and I could not immediately warm to it, but I was going to give it a try. In no way would I deny myself this unique opportunity. Living in India was getting easier: Delhi was better than Kashmir; Nagpur, although one of the hottest cities and not one of the places travelers seek out, couldn't be so bad.

Burney had to leave on short notice, a big shock for me. For a moment, the thought of being truly alone with no link to my immediate past gripped me. But then I looked at Sharmaji and my new friends, and I felt a part of a hard-to-get-in club of adventurers discovering a new world in one of the oldest cultures on earth.

Sightseeing in Delhi, Humayun's Tomb

13

Fulbright in Nagpur

Public domain, CIA World Factbook

Nothing in the going there gave me a clue to how a year in Nagpur would transform my life. To say I had misgivings about liking it is below understatement. From what I had sampled in India so far, I dreaded the idea of living in this past-its-day city: the food, the flies, the language, the heat, the cacophonous music, and the hordes. On the other hand, a Fulbright was not something to be tossed away; it could help me get to my dream of working in the Foreign Service, and out of respect for Morgan and all the others who like me had won a chance to see more of the world through the program, I would stick it out.

Nagpur was a hot topic. Steamy oven temperatures greeted me as I stepped off the train. Delhi's thermometers rested around 100 degrees daily, and the humidity and the heat wore me down at first. One afternoon in those first days when the mercury was over 120 degrees Fahrenheit and I was hailing a rickshaw to take me to my teaching job, the driver, wearing shorts with a rough cotton turban wrapped around his head to shield him from the sun, asked casually, "Where do you want to go, baby?" I thought he was trying to be fresh, and I wasn't in the mood, to say the least! It turned out he was just being friendly. "Baby" is a term for a girl; he could see I was young and was giving me a compliment. Good that I held my tongue; I was lucky that he was willing to take me anywhere in the deadly heat. As the saying goes, only mad dogs and Englishmen—and I added "Americans"—go out in the noonday sun; the local inhabitants stayed inside until sundown.

That sleepy city was centuries away from how Nagpur seems to be today when I read about it on the Web. Like much of India, it thrives with modern conveniences and tourist enticements. When I arrived in July of 1968, I braced myself for a year of the strange and unexpected. I couldn't see how living there would enrich my life, except as an accomplishment on my resume; I was to be proven very wrong. I didn't know this part of the Indian heartland would nest in a space forever pulsating through my life, forming the basis for mastering the art of living across cultures around the world.

During the British Raj, Nagpur was a center of military activity and the site of a Gandhi *ashram*, a social and spiritual center, but by 1968, it had lost its appeal. Situated in the state of Maharashtra, smack in the middle of the Indian peninsula, like many places in that country, Nagpur had a culture and a history of its own, known and appreciated by those from that place but not as much by outsiders. I found out recently on the Internet that a "zero stone" put there by the British attests to the accuracy of its geographical distinction. In 2002, over three decades since I lived there, the city celebrated three hundred years of establishment, but the land that it occupies goes back to 3000 BCE. In 1968, after already living for twenty-two years in the rhythm of four contrasting seasons in the Southeastern United States, my body had to quickly adjust to Nagpur's tropical climate, with its oppressive heat and the downpours of torrential monsoon rain. How could I know that I'd get used to such dramatic weather, that I'd live in the tropics in the future, even preferring it?

Nagpur American friends: Ellen and Missi, my Fulbright flatmates in local dress; with Tom, Peace Corps, and Phil, USAID, in topis

The train ride from Delhi was full of unseen sights and sounds. Unlike my journey from Louisville to Baltimore four years earlier, I was not afraid. I passed the time by paying attention to the unusual landscape—sometimes parched, then green, now rocky—and the panoply of styles of dress: women in striking silk and plain *khadi* (rough homespun cotton), print *saris, kurta pajamas*, and *salwar kameezes*, their heads veiled and unveiled, splotches of vermillion on the foreheads of those who were married. Hair was mostly worn pressed down, radiant and neat with coconut oil; no confusing that lingering smell I'd get a whiff of all the time. The variety of snacks sold on the train and carried by passengers reeled my senses, and speaking with porters and fellow travelers in simple Hindi—*aacha* (good), *bahut aacha* (very good), *shukrya* (thank you)—I tried out my language skills.

What a warm embrace it was to be met by the small group of Americans in Indian dress at the station. Missi (Mildred Jennings), also from Morgan, who had come a year before, stood smiling and welcoming me. Petite, her head covered by the end of a yellow-and-white *sari* to shade her from the sun, she was warm yet formidable. Two Peace Corps volunteers—one unusually tall, blond, and thin, the other of medium height, with a floppy, wide-brimmed hat pulled over his head and his legs straddling a bicycle—offered me their hands and saw that my luggage got to the flat (apartment) where I was to stay in the center of the city near Saddar Bazaar. Nothing seemed familiar.

Missi, who was from a large Texas family, presided over the house. Her absolute, unquestionable authority was apparent. We were both assertive black American women, but I lost no time dismissing that little quiver that I'd sometimes get when confronting a potential rival and immediately folded the idea of her helping me into my thinking. I'd need all the help I could get! If a young woman from Morgan was already there and had figured out what worked and what didn't, I wasn't going to waste time questioning her on how she thought things should be done. Besides, it would be wonderful to have a black sister to talk to and confide in. Missi never proved me wrong, bore my shortcomings with patience, and showed me respect while pointing out a better way to do many things. She was always a first-class act.

I cannot say this for my other housemate at the time. Tall, with long red hair and a wide forehead, Kathleen (not her real name) reminded me of Jackie Kennedy, with the same wide-set big eyes and thick brows. However, she was, like Missi, studying sitar with the teacher, *Guruji*, who came to our house to give private lessons. I liked her, at first, and found her way of speaking interesting: the Boston "aah" and the Kennedyesque "r" were charming. I didn't think anything of her haughty manner—I was used to such behavior— but I would change my mind about it.

My meat-and-potatoes-eating habit was not helpful in a place with an entirely different cuisine. Eventually I'd get used to it, but that took time. No American fast-food chains like McDonald's or Kentucky Fried Chicken existed in India then. Had it not been for the peanuts and the sumptuous fruits, and lots of Indian-style Coca-Cola—Campa Cola—I probably would have gotten sick from malnutrition. The cola, of course, was bad for me and contributed to my increasing weight gain, but I didn't care about that then. Eventually we had to dispense with the services of the cook (whom I'll call Savita), when we all fell ill with stomach trouble; I had to work hard not to feel sorry for her. Hardship, misery, and depravation seemed to lurk everywhere.

For instance, during that first month, Kathleen had to monitor an intravenous tube for the young daughter of a poor woman who was in the hospital. The body odors of the patients in the paupers' ward were hard to tolerate when I went there to do the little I could, and the fatal look on the faces of the young girl's relatives made me want to cry. The belief was that people went to a hospital only when they expected to die. I was even sadder when I found that the reason for the high mortality rate in the hospitals was the poor sanitation. Bowls of yellowish-brown fluid lay on the sills of opened windows. Amazingly, the girl did pull through, but the misery and depravation I was witnessing all around me in Nagpur started getting to me. I had to steel myself to live with it. This presented a moral conflict: having grown up as one of the dispossessed, I had to fight feeling like a sham in not dwelling on the dire conditions that I was in the midst of. Hardest were the emaciated children and the lame and deformed I'd see on the streets.

Water, which in America I took for granted as readily available from the tap, took on a whole new meaning. Our helper would boil it in a big aluminum kettle and let it cool afterward before pouring it into a round unglazed earthenware pot. Taking a dipper, I could help myself to cups of the naturally chilled life substance, but Missi kept reminding us to be on guard about the condition of the bottom of the jar. One day I realized what she meant: a wormlike creature had begun to live in the pit of the vessel, and from then on I took care to be more alert to the water preparation. Bathing was done from a bucket with a cup, no showers or sit-down baths; and while we kept toilet tissue, our Indian-style latrine, in the floor with places for putting the feet, taught me the logic of using the left hand and cup to take care of this most personal need. The ritual significance of water was something that I would continue to learn about. Malaria was a constant threat, but although I was a meal for the mosquitoes, I took pills and was fortunate not to get the dreadful disease.

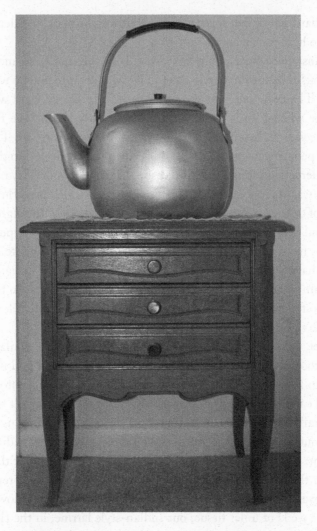

Rama, the housekeeper, looked like a saint. So gracefully did she go about her menial tasks that I felt I was in the presence of a holy person. She glided across the floor in her bare feet, soundlessly sweeping it with a wide straw broom, sprinkling it with water, picking up rubbish and disposing of it, her face a portrait of calm. In the month I had been in India, I had seen countless women who could be described as looking like her. But it was in her deportment, her carriage, and her posture that she distinguished herself. I felt her power. Her smile was compassionate; and she was shy with me—not because she couldn't speak my language and I hers, for she spoke Marathi—but probably because she could sense that I had no idea of the courageous life she was living under unbearable odds. "Missi Bai,"

as Rama called my roommate, *bai* meaning sister, knew Rama's story, and those two had good rapport.

Near the end of our nine-month stay in Nagpur, Rama insisted on the three of us who roomed together coming to her house to meet her husband, welcoming us under her roof. Indians, I'd find out, were like that. They'd invite you into their home no matter how modest it was and serve you whatever they could. They didn't show off. They were just practicing appropriate behavior toward an outsider. Rama welcomed us to her hut in a congested slum of Nagpur. Her husband was a stump of a man lying on his back, flies swarming over him, his children taking turns swatting them away. He had no legs, was paralyzed, and couldn't speak, as he had been wounded in the India–Pakistan War of 1965. Having never been that close to someone in that state of poverty and pain, I felt my insides churning and had to struggle to contain myself and appear happy as Rama's guest. Over our objections, Rama purchased ice cream bars for each of us, paying more than a rupee a piece. We thought of a rupee as a dollar (although officially it was worth less), and since we paid Rama twenty rupees a month,[13] the standard rate, she was spending a lot on us. As much as we tried, she would not be dissuaded from giving us the treat. Such was her sense of how to be a host to her guests—her employers—no matter if they may have appeared to her as pampered American girls.

Shakuntala, ten years old, and Ramdas, twelve, Rama's children, also worked in our house for pay. Looking back, it seems scandalous to have had children working for me, but at the time, it was a system that I walked into; I never thought of contesting it. The family had worked for the American Fulbrighters for years and depended on that support to survive. Shakuntala often wore a matching blouse and pants made of a shiny pink material. Her smile filled her face, and her dark, wide-set eyes exposed a broad forehead, and hair tied back with bright rose-pink ribbons.

Ramdas was like a young adolescent boy anywhere: hair brushed back, away from his forehead, wide black exciting eyes that confidently asked, "What do you want?" or "I already know how to do this." He wore short

---

13 In 1968, the official rate was 7.5 rupees to the dollar; however, one could buy dollars at the higher rate of 10 to 1. Thus, Rama's 20 rupees was worth about $200. One could buy a lot with 20 rupees; for example, my Friday restaurant meal, cloth for a *sari* and the fee for having it made, transport and a ticket to the cinema.

pants and a cotton shirt. Even though working, he was enrolled in a local school that provided free education through the government, a part of the social democracy of post independent India, which was greatly influenced by Mahatma Gandhi, who was dedicated to uplifting the plight of those from the lowest castes. Although caste was outlawed with independence in 1947, the trend continued when I was there—and still goes on, under various covers. Shakuntala, it's a shame to write, was not in school, for as a girl, her life was seen as one of being soon married off into another family. Ramdas became my steady helper and fix-it wise guy, until the day came when I woke up to his game about which I'll soon tell you.

Both he and his sister wore *chappals* that were like flip-flops or, as was customary inside the house, no shoes at all. Eating, sleeping, relaxing—all were done on the floor in most Indian homes. While we slept in beds and sat in chairs at a table to eat meals, we did more things on the floor than we did in America and appreciated having it clean. Like most homes, ours did not have modern air-conditioning; ceiling fans, open windows, and clean floors kept the inside cool.

Rama and Ramdas

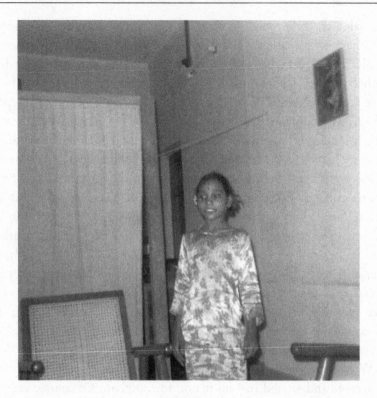

Shakuntala

Peace Corps figured large in my year in Nagpur. Having worked at its Washington headquarters and read about volunteers' experiences in India, I was now meeting them in their environment and knowing some of what they had gone through. Still, getting to know a young man I'll call Mike, one of the PCVs who met me at the train on his bike, kept me humble and showed me that there was so much more to know about their work in India. He had used his mechanical know-how and passion for cycling to invent a gadget for bikes that was being used in his village. Just as importantly, he had contributed substantially to poultry-farming techniques, his assigned project. India was not yet food sufficient in 1968, so Mike made a tangible contribution to saving people from hunger.

Mike came to our parties but was too busy to hang out at our place as other volunteers did, so while I didn't get to know him personally, being in his presence made me feel I was a part of an ongoing, goal-focused group. Still, not good at hanging out, I had since college days evolved a formula for getting through social situations: being a good listener and observer. In the career I was aiming for, mixing socially was a skill I would need.

Six feet, four inches tall and so skinny that it hurt to look at him, another guy, let's call him Bill from Arkansas, had a hard time in his Peace Corps village. The usual complaint that I'd read in those reports of returned volunteers, about the villagers not respecting them for their work, had made his tour hard. As was the case for many volunteers, amebic dysentery had dealt the final blow to any hope of improving his situation. He was waiting for the end of his tour and, in the meantime, spent time with us in Nagpur, becoming, with another PCV, our social director of sorts, telling us how to get along better than they had. "You girls can fly," he'd say, stressing the "y" so that it sounded like "eye" in his Southern drawl. When talking about the amount of money we got per month, one thousand rupees, he would compare it to the five hundred rupees they got, emphasizing how much better we could live. The PCVs talked to us a lot about spending money on a comfortable mattress to avoid the pain they had experienced sleeping on thinner mat-like bedding on the floor. "You girls can *buy*!" Mike would declare.

With Fulbright and Peace Corps, we were all getting more money than the average Indian and had no reason to complain. Of course, we were young, and in America or India, how we spent our money was a concern; but it was also a learning experience. I was pleased about the stipend I received. I had learned to live on almost any amount of regular income and thus felt like one thousand rupees was a good professional salary. Colleagues at the college where I was teaching were nuns and brothers, so I didn't have anyone to compare my earnings with, and as could be expected, no one talked about pay in my presence. I'd later learn that depending on the type of institution, instructors may well have gotten much less than I did; however, housing and other necessities would have been included in their compensation.

Pat Rogers, another PCV, from Lubbock, Texas, had majored in theater, and as I was an English major, we had much in common and became close friends. By the time I met him, he was the picture of health, but he had recovered from a drastic bout of dysentery during which he lost a large amount of weight. Like Bill, he had moved from his village to a flat in Nagpur for the remaining days of his tour. An enthusiastic cook, he made a mean, rich spaghetti sauce. Once we gathered to eat it, each of us brought something to add to the meal. I contributed a half kilo of *mosambis*—sweet, juicy, locally grown oranges, which could be pulled apart like tangerines, paired nicely with the meal. Though Pat fretted about not having red wine, as it wasn't widely available in India then, we made do with the trusty Coke substitute; and while I'd go to great lengths to drink only sterilized water, I'd stack my glass with ice cubes made from tap water anywhere! I had gotten in the habit of drinking lime juice and water like Indians did for digestion and to stay cool. Fortunately, while I contracted mild stomach bugs and viruses, I stayed pretty healthy.

Pat seemed to always be staving off boredom by proposing novel things to do. Once he talked about *Waiting for Godot*, by Samuel Beckett. I'd heard of the famous play but had not read or seen it performed. To keep up with Pat, I located a copy and read it. One day we experimented with a new way of eating lunch: sitting on low, foot-high stools, we turned our backs to one another as we ate and carried on a conversation. So absurd was it that I couldn't eat for laughing. I got a good notion of the aimless waiting that was the point of the play.

My Nagpur American friends and I had our best times going to the Ashoka Hotel Restaurant near where we lived for Friday evening dinner. This was something our group did almost every week. We'd sit at a table covered with a clean white cloth in a simple café. The tall, bronze-complexion manager with conked hair reminded me of a singer in an American doo-wop group; he would wait on us and treat us like the other customers, which we appreciated. Blending in was what we craved but usually couldn't have in many places, for as foreigners we were free objects of curiosity.

I'd begin the meal by ordering cream of tomato soup with a dollop of the fresh whiteness in the center, and then have fried fish and French fries. While I didn't eat salad, as I couldn't be sure the veggies had been washed properly, I couldn't say no to fresh fruit salad. I'd have it over a rectangle of Kwality vanilla ice cream. Those meals took me back to Friday nights growing up in Louisville, to *I Remember Mama* on television and Campbell's soup, which was "mmm, mmm good."

With Pat Rodgers in Bombay, as we called it then, autumn 1969

One day as I was standing in the midst of the hustle and bustle on the side of the street near where we lived, in my above-the-knee dress, I was attracting lots of stares, which of course made me feel self-conscious and uncomfortable. Children often trailed me when I walked down the street. That day a group of them were chatting among themselves trying to identify my nationality. Though they spoke Marathi, from my scant Hindi I could make out what they were saying. I must be Russian, one of them proffered, but no, my nose and skin didn't match that of the Soviets they must have seen. Startling them, I interrupted their private talk and told them I was from America. The one who thought I was Russian laughed, thinking that I was joking. Americans didn't look like me, he insisted, pointing to the skin on his arm, meaning that my shade was closer to his. With the deep tan of my copper-toned skin, big face, and tussled hair, I must have looked like someone from another planet. I couldn't help smiling when one of them tilted his head up, asking, I figured out, "North Korea?"

On the street, what bothered me most were the goats, which would not leave me alone. They liked to walk close to me. Equally alarming were the cows who roamed with flies alighting on their backs, wagging their scrawny tails. Their sacred status in India meant that they couldn't be harmed, slaughtered, or eaten. Missi and others had told me that I'd feel more comfortable if I wore Indian dress, but I was still resisting this strange land where I had to spend the next months, and I guess I was being passive-aggressive by resisting her advice. After all, I'd been told the same thing in New Delhi. But I told myself I'd do fine in my lightweight summer wear from the USA. I didn't want to pretend to be something that I wasn't, and wearing Indian dress seemed to be doing that.

Still, my American clothes were of man-made fibers; they were made of some cotton but mostly lots of easy-care polyester. While perfect for air-cooled insides and outdoors on Washington nights, they clung to my body in high temperature. I did feel more comfortable in the two cotton outfits that I'd bought in Delhi, but they had to be laundered after each wearing, and while we employed *a dhobi*, a washerman, he couldn't run them through a machine, for we didn't have one. The custom of doing laundry was different in India. The *dhobi* washed our clothes and house linens by hand at his washing business. This laundry was on a lake. Items were pressed and scrubbed against large rocks. He'd hang them out to dry and iron those pieces that needed it, returning them after a few days. As I didn't have enough Indian-made garments to rotate, I had to wash and wear my American clothes, continuing to be uncomfortable.

The final blow that made me convert to wearing complete Indian dress all the time was the funniest and scariest thing that had happened to me so far in this place that I was getting to know: When I was waiting for a rickshaw on a Nagpur street, a cow began taking an interest in me! The bull started running after me when I suddenly moved away from him as he began sniffing my bare legs one morning. That did it. Had it not been for the red-and-yellow seat of the rickshaw, which I could see from the corner of my eye as the driver sidled next to me, which I jumped into, I don't know what I would have done. That afternoon, I went with Missi to the bazaar and bought *saris* and cloth for blouses and more sets of *kurta pajamas*, then to the tailor to have them made.

14

College Confident

Greeting me from its perch atop Seminary Hill as I rode in the backseat of a man-pedaled rickshaw was Saint Francis de Sales College (SFD). As with past challenges, the Catholic church and my father's spirit gave me the sense of purpose I needed to make the most of living in Nagpur. While Nagpur was not well-known in the world and settling in was hard, SFD was where I belonged. A respected institution, known for its thorough preparation of men and women in liberal arts, the Sisters of the Holy Cross made up the teaching staff. I was grateful to be placed there and suspected that my Catholic background had a lot to do with it. I was not disappointed, nor was I to let down the college or the Fulbright Foundation; and the glow of pride in my Morgan State alma mater kept me confident as I embraced my first teaching assignment.

Sister Eleanor was my department head. She had a compassionate manner and discussed ideas with me about my work before making final decisions. Since going to Mass for the first time in Nagpur, I had been struck by how different the religious service was from one in the United States. It was outdoors; and with everyone in their native clothes, as of course they would have been in their country, I felt very much the outsider. And, believe it or not, monkeys were actually swinging from the trees! Cocoa skinned and relaxed in her sun-bright habit, Sister Eleanor was from Goa, the former Portuguese colony on the west coast of India. She was the first Catholic sister of color I had met.

At the college I taught third-year students who were in their final phase of study; second-year students who were slated to take a final exam in English; and a pre-university class (PUC). The PUC was made up of senior high school students who were preparing to enter college and could benefit from being with a native English speaker. That I was American and not British was special to them. Back then, Indian students were used to British English speakers; but with the War in Vietnam raging nearby and United States post–World War II prominence in Asia, they could benefit from the exposure to American culture that I would bring. My faculty colleagues were welcoming and supportive, and SFD's standard of excellence was consistent with what I had strived for, never wanting to race with those at the bottom.

From day one when I walked into the classroom of the second-year students, I was spun around by the faces that met me: rows of Catholic sisters dressed in gleaming robes the color of snow and full head coverings and as many young men swathed in the same shade of cassocks that it was like a group of doves looking back at me. A few students in street clothes were in the class too. As narrow-minded as it sounds, I could not help but be grateful for having students who, because of their vow to obey, would be willing to learn. That they would not openly present problems was incredible luck for me, a first-time teacher.

SFD Student, Seminarian Charles Pinto

SFD Student, Brother John Quandros

Even with this promising situation, I was a bit afraid of spoiling it. Would I say the wrong word? Have to speak in religious terms? I had struggled to get a B in religion at Ursuline by memorizing stock answers to problems and questions, which was nothing to be proud of. Now, I was going to have to instruct college students in my second-year class on a leading work of modern American literature: Ernest Hemingway's *A Farewell to Arms*. I hadn't even read it! I knew it only from the film of the same name starring Rock Hudson with Jennifer Jones, a steamy love story set against a background of war and delicate issues of relationships and the seldom-discussed topic of sex. What was worse, the version of the edition I taught was censored, making it difficult for me as the reader to discover the author's tone and ultimate meaning. I didn't have enough class time to explore the World War I setting of the novel, in Italy, much, but I had no choice but to cover as much as I could, taking another deep breath . . . and continuing my journey.

As soon as I was assigned to teach it, I read the book over the following weekend. After doing so, I deconstructed the plot to focus on the structure of the narrative. Since I've always appreciated teachers who could go beyond the textbook and add to a lesson, I delved deeper into the writings and life of Hemingway using some other books I'd gotten my hands on in Nagpur. Naturally, having majored in English, I was familiar with this famous American author's work and reputation. Since I had read a few of his works, *The Old Man and the Sea* and *A Moveable Feast*, I recalled what I'd read and pored over critical reviews as well. Over the moon to have the rare opportunity to teach a great work of literature, I was full of myself.

A Farewell to Arms is a story of love and war, told against the backdrop of the start of World War I. Henry, a soldier who has become disillusioned with war, and Catherine, the nurse who tends to him in a military hospital, fall in love. The reader is caught up in their intense passion. Catherine becomes pregnant, but the heartbreaking climax comes with the baby's still birth and the mother's death afterwards. When clumsy responses arose on one of the surprise quizzes I gave—to answer the question of what happened to the umbilical cord after Catherine gave birth—I got some one-of-a-kind answers.

That was what I got for putting the emphasis on such an intimate area, but as discussion was necessary to understanding the story, I dealt with the issues that the students' comments raised. For instance, I got all sorts of answers about Catherine's still birth: "The umbilical cord was wrapped around the baby's neck "because Catherine didn't take enough rest," and "What is all this talk about a cord?"— that sort of thing. The students weren't at ease talking about such intimate matters. Using what must have been my developing diplomatic skills, I tactfully advised them on how they could give simple, straightforward replies to the normal but perhaps embarrassing incidents of the novel. They were only a year or two younger than me, and I was only one step ahead of them. We were learning together.

The third-year class was more like I imagined a class at an English college would have been. The syllabus required that I teach a collection of English essays, which, again, put my newly earned bachelor's degree in English to good use. My incredible luck continued when I was presented to my students, again, mostly sisters and brothers and a few laypersons. The laypersons, young men, came from the city and barely showed up for classes. There was no exam in English for them during this final year, and they felt they could read the material on their own.

Asoke (I'd get to know many by this name spelled in various ways), a Westernized guy who struck me as having spent time in England, was my best student. He read all the works; could say a lot about H. G. Wells, Conan Doyle, G. K. Chesterton; but showed up so seldom that when he did, he acted like a guest. Hard to take was that he was rather condescending: "You're doing a splendid job, Judith," he'd say, adding "Mam" only hesitantly. I couldn't get mad at him, for I secretly found him amusing with his thick glasses and sincere manner, but I had to be firm with him, as I didn't want to fail him for exceeding the limit of allowable absences. How he tried my patience! Thankfully, he finally got my message that I would not pass him if he didn't bother to come to class. As things turned out, I got to know Asoke well after he started showing up each week. I acted more as a tutor, which really was what I was, a Fulbright English teaching assistant/tutor,[14] although, to my great satisfaction, SFD gave me the role of a professor!

The PUCs were fun to teach, but as with Asoke, they could be cocky. At seventeen and eighteen years old, they were in a year of preparation for three formal years of college study to earn a diploma. Boisterous and awkward, most with poor English, in their body language they reminded me of boys back home. The class was huge—almost a hundred; several would be weeded out and not accepted for first year. Every Monday afternoon I'd meet them for debate class. Of course I was happy and honored to lead this class that had been specially arranged to take advantage of my experience. We'd discuss a topic, and then two students would argue the pros and cons. I was given free rein to cover what I wanted, which didn't' tie me to a theme, and best of all, I did not have to prepare the students to pass an exam. Sister Eleanor or one of the teaching brothers would sometimes look in on us, but I was free to work with the class on my own.

One day, in late 1968, I was feeling my professorial oats and waxed on and on about the incredible accomplishments of America's space program carried out by NASA (National Aeronautics and Space Administration). Hearing about how astronauts were soon going to orbit the moon in Apollo 8 and how revolutionary this was took me back to when I'd get up very early to watch the launches on TV with Daddy before leaving for Ursuline. Almost right away, much to my surprise, for I was expecting the three hours to unfold in an orderly discussion of the space race, I was bombarded with critical comments and questions. I was ready for questions on the Russians, who had gone to outer space first with Sputnik, and later with a dog, but the remarks that came to me were out of left field. A young man stood up and said something like, "Miss, America may be sending

---

14 I was in the last group of English Teaching Assistants, called "Tutors." We were Fulbright recipients with Bachelor of Arts degrees.

men to the moon, but India had the first men to climb Everest." When I pointed out that Everest was in Nepal, he dismissed that as irrelevant, for in those days India dominated the foreign policies of neighboring states: Nepal, Bhutan, and Sikkim. He then went on to extol the greatness of the 1953 Hillary–Norgay ascent.[15] I wanted to stop him and pull him back to the subject at hand, because I hadn't given Everest any thought in preparing my lecture, but on the instinct that the goal was to get students to speak English, I let him talk. He was comfortable in speaking English, and I got to learn more Indian points of view and a lot about the historic ascent. To conclude his diatribe, he said, and I marked it well, for it was not to be the first time I would hear it, "The United States may be the world's greatest democracy, but India is the biggest."

Even though this was said in a patronizing way, it motivated the class to continue the conversation. "Miss is a visitor in our country, and we are happy to have her," another student rushed to the podium to add when the comments got too boisterous. That was one thing I was getting used to: the way Indians would come to my aid because I was a guest in their country.

---

15 The ascent to Everest was made from the south side, in Nepal, not India. Edmund Hillary was from New Zealand, and Tensing Norgay, the Sherpa, was from Nepal. But as India dominated control of Nepal's foreign and defense policies, my students, like many others, credited India with the historic feat.

15

Sitars and Solos

Music was like breathing. I never thought I had a talent for it. I just did it naturally. When I had to deal with the requirement of the Fulbright program that I work on a research project, in addition to teaching English, I drew on all the singing I'd grown up with and decided to use it for my project. I had only scant knowledge of the region and culture, but after settling down in Nagpur, I promised to present a written paper on Indian music at the end-of-year conference in spring 1969. As Missi had become a devoted student of sitar and had demonstrated serious skill on the instrument, everyone assumed that I would do the same. Afraid of putting a foot wrong, I accepted the assumption, *a big mistake*. I had no skill in playing an instrument and though I loved to sing for personal pleasure, music was not something I saw myself excelling in. I should have articulated these gut-level feelings before I undertook studying sitar, but I was still in my "going along with what people told me" phase, and like riding a wave, I let that carry me on.

Mr. A. K. Mukerji, who came to our home to instruct Missi and Kathleen on sitar, and, eventually newcomer Ellen, on sarod, readily agreed to teach me the sitar. A dashing figure who looked like Ravi Shankar, we called him Guruji. He had glossy black hair, long and combed back from his full forehead. Although his teeth, smudged in red from the *paan* he constantly chewed, did startle me at first, he had Hindi movie star good looks. Sitting on the floor in a white kurta and matching loose pajamas, he tried in vain to get me to sit with my legs crossed to the side while I stroked the taunt wire frets of the graceful stringed instrument. He had ordered the golden tan sitar from Calcutta (as it was known then), his hometown. Four feet long, made of a dark hard toon wood, its hollow gourd carved from a pumpkin, the instrument was a work of art. Inlaid imitation mother-of-pearl curled into figures decorating the outside. So delicate and expensive was it—fourteen hundred dollars—that I feared breaking it as I strummed. While the Fulbright Foundation paid for it, I had to handle the transaction. I had never shelled out so much money on a material thing and was in awe of the fact that it had been crafted especially for me. The precious work of art did eventually break, or get knocked down and broken, but that's another story, not for this book!

Notwithstanding that I was African American from the same college as Missi, I reminded people of my predecessor, Marcia (not her real name) who preceded me as the Fulbright teacher at SFD. Unlike me, she was white, but she was, like me, as my New York friends would say, *saftig* (plump). Rumor had it that she returned to California and was acting in "art" films, a hard act to follow. Yet as Marcia hadn't studied Indian music when she was in Nagpur, in sitar-playing ability I could only be compared to Missi. She had been studying for more than a year when I arrived, and there was no way I could measure up to her accomplishment. I was not going to be Guruji's prize student.

Not only could I not sit sidesaddle on the floor, I also could not tolerate the long nature of the *ragas* in sitar music, which can go on for hours like free jazz. And I literally had a dirty tongue! Guruji told me so and gave me a tongue cleaner to correct the matter. While I would later appreciate the virtue of the small, pliable stick, I didn't appreciate the candid remark and started to distance myself from him.

After a few months of acting out the charade of playing sitar, it became obvious that my heart wasn't in it. At Guruji's suggestion, I shifted to the holy songs, *bhajans*, of Mira Bai, the legendary Hindu mystic poet of the sixteenth century. These, too, proved not to suit me: I couldn't appreciate the music, since I was just getting to know Hinduism. I didn't want to sing a *bhajan* when I didn't understand, let alone believe in what was said. In her songs, Mira Bai addresses a very personal Lord Krishna, sometimes it seems erotically. As a Catholic, I well understood the idea of giving one's life to Christ, prostrating oneself on the floor in a wedding gown; but I knew that singing *bhajans* would have made me look foolish and seem disrespectful if I wasn't sincere about it. I couldn't imitate the sustained high-pitched rendition of Mira Bai's songs as popularized in Hindi films. This had become the standard for female voices. Trying out the titles, I'd hear myself squeak and squeal like some kind of bird outside at night; I wanted to laugh and cry at the same time. My goal of a successful end-of-the-year project was slipping away as the days flew by.

Finally, Guruji, whose main job was as a broadcaster on All India Radio, came up with the right idea: how would I like to learn and sing the folk songs of Rabindranath Tagore, the 1913 Nobel Laureate in Literature—and the first non-European, who was from India? A brief listen to the melodic simplicity of his tunes was all I needed to agree. Guruji wrote the songs down in Bengali and taught me how to sing them. Tagore songs, *Rabindra Sangeet*, are a range of over two thousand vocal pieces from dirgelike to melodic, from the rhythm of classical ragas to Western folk.

I was able to perform eleven, enough to get me to think from a different point of view—that of the person living close to the soil, connecting intimately with the earth and sky. Based on my findings, I wrote a report for the end-of-year conference. In it I gave the meaning of each song I had learned and its significance. For example, one of the songs I gave my thoughts on, *Klanti Amar* (*Forgive Me*) translates as follows:

> Tiredness is my excuse, Lord.
> If I am not on the correct path,
> it is simply because I have become confused and
> lost my way.
> My heart is trembling in nervous anticipation.
> Today I am greatly moved with fear, and I am
> still confused.
> Please excuse me, Lord . . .[16]

I wrote, "This is the first Tagore song I learned, and it remains my favorite because of the deep devotional intensity it requires when singing it. These are the signs of a confused soul struggling to find the Divine while stumbling along the path." Studying those songs gave me a lot of time to

---

16 Translated by Guruji, A. K. Mukerji. Another version, translated by the poet himself, Rabindranath Tagore, can be found on the Internet.

think about where I was taking my life. As I did so, I whispered, "Please excuse me, Lord."

Little did I know that this last-minute, but successful effort would become a lifelong interest, leading me to learn more about Tagore and Bengali culture. Best of all, in the future I'd experience the ultimate for a fan: visiting the home and touching personal items belonging to the artist himself.

Guruji with Missi

16

Coming to the Culture

Swathed in traditional dress and getting used to the people, I wanted to explore more of India. I began to shed my anxiety and to dive into the culture. I accepted the way events were unfolding and put away my regret that I hadn't been better prepared for what to expect. The purpose of the Fulbright, after all, was to learn by experiencing and to build bridges of understanding. With me, it started from the bottom up. When our Nagpur household was complete, we were three young women; Kathleen had left early in my stay, and Ellen Weaver had joined us. Kathleen's parting was painful for someone who had been in country so long and who, it turned out, was in love with Guruji.

I had come to respect Kathleen's generosity. Had she not given of her time to help the child in the hospital, the girl probably would have died, for the hospital wasn't set up for children. Kathleen cared. But she could wear her emotions on her sleeve. Before she abruptly left, there was a "but I thought you loved me scene" between her and Guruji that was like in a movie. I would learn that this was not as uncommon as I thought, for in classical Hindu learning the teacher can be like a god demanding full commitment. Before that tearful outburst, she, who had seen it as her duty to inform me of things I should know, had gone too far.

I had related a story to her about an incident at college, a miscommunication between me and the students that I had succeeded in clearing up. Such moments happen all the time between native English speakers and those of other languages, for even though it's the same tongue, the meaning comes from each person's cultural context. Until I became familiar with the context, when a student would say, "Just now I'm doing it," I'd think he meant he was getting the missing assignment out of his book bag right away; however, I would find, he meant he would be bringing it to me within some days. After I shared my anecdote with Kathleen, she said, "I can't imagine how they understand you anyway. Your accent is so thick." Hearing this, I was breathless, but I didn't give her the satisfaction of seeing me upset. She may not have liked my Kentucky twang, but the Fulbright office in Washington had found it refreshing. I thought her New England accent was lovely. Closed-mindedness, it seemed, was not limited to the American South.

Once I got to know it, Nagpur was a kaleidoscope of Indian culture. Turn it one way, festivals, holy days, and the streets dense with crowds appeared as loudspeakers blared music. Rotate a little more, and there would be flower-festooned statues of deities parading on makeshift vehicles, women with jasmine in their hair following behind. Turn left and I'd be bending my head as a garland of marigolds was put around my neck.

As I'd find living throughout the world, there is always a person who volunteers to introduce outsiders to local specialties. In Nagpur he was a formal, swarthy middle-aged gentleman I'll call Mansur. In October as the weather cooled down, our group of Americans went with him to see all the sights of the October celebrations. This was the annual procession of Ganesh, the Elephant God, who was taken to the river to be immersed. We followed the red, orange, and gold colored figurines of the god with his long trunk and people carrying clay elephants and bags of sweets and fruit as offerings. After that, I liked getting out and observing native customs and was constantly in the midst of such events.

Once, when I was with Missi at a small temple in a village, I was surprised to see a picture of President Kennedy grouped with miniature statues of Hindu gods and goddesses. After the worship service, *puja*, we were the guests of honor at a home-cooked lunch. We sat on the ground in the middle of individual circles decorated with yellow and pink flowers and green leaves, all done in colored chalk sprinkled by hand. What followed made my eyes get even bigger: large banana leaves were placed in front of each of us, and the food—rice and subtly spiced vegetables and a small bowl of a yogurt-like accompaniment, *dahi*—was dished onto the large dark leaf "plates." As I was remarking on this unusual new way of having lunch, I was taught yet another way to partake of a meal: taking my cue from

Missi, I used only my right hand[17] to scoop a small ball of rice, roll it into the vegetables, and dip the wad into the bowl of *dahi*. Such personal and thoughtful experiences showed me the rich life of "simple living" Indians.

Eating that home-cooked meal got me to try more of the local dishes, and before long, with trips to other parts of the country, I acquired a taste for a number of South Asian recipes. One afternoon in Nagpur, some friends and I ate at an outside restaurant, something I was leery of doing in view of all the warnings I had received about being aware of what and where I should eat to avoid getting sick. But as I became more familiar with my surroundings, I could adjust the rules to suit myself. Hot, freshly cooked food was the safest to eat, bought on the street or inside, so I readily sat down with my friends at the corner table in the open-air café. We ordered the plate of the day: stuffed *parathas*, which were slices of unleavened bread, stuffed with a filling of vegetables and a sauce zinging with black pepper, coriander, cardamom, and cloves. Washing them down with cool glasses of *nimbu panni*, I didn't want to stop eating the flavorful feast.

Good for me that Missi taught at LAD (Lady Amritbai Daga) Women's College. Through her contacts there, I got to know several people, even got to meet a representative of Alliance Française, the organization that promotes French language and culture around the world. With the reel-to-reel recorder and spools of tape the Alliance representative gave me, I was able to volunteer to teach a class in beginning French at LAD one afternoon a week. Teaching French to the young women who came because it seemed they liked to be with me was fun. I'm not sure I got them to learn any French, but I did become like their big sister, which made me feel very much at home.

I also got to know the fascinating lives that Hindu women can live. Passive and submissive as they struck me in the beginning, some of the women and girls I got to know were grappling with challenging stories that drew me to them. One such was an outgoing, very articulate English-speaking LAD student who openly worried about her chances of marriage. As her mother stated one day while we sat over tea in the spacious living room of her family's grand home, and the student agreed, "She is too dark." I was speechless. Her chocolate skin and long wavy hair had a tropical

17 As I've pointed out, the right hand is used for eating; the left for cleaning oneself with water after using the toilet.

luster; her big ebony eyes set off her operatic face. But color was a factor when it came to finding the right match for a life partner. Ads in the paper would read, "Wheatish complexion," which meant light brown. How could it be that in this diverse and proud nation, skin color could be as significant as it was in racist America? Little did I realize that I was forming theories that would later motivate me to delve deeper into the topic.

Another matter concerned a crush that one of the LAD instructors had on a Catholic priest who had broken away from following the rule of the local bishop and was acting independently. He held his own version of Sunday Mass in his home. This priest, who was German, welcomed us into his Scandinavian-style bungalow to listen and, if we chose, to dance around with him, flailing our arms and leaping to classical music playing on his hi-fi. While I looked forward to going there, I was contemptuous of him for being what I thought was a fallen priest. He sensed this in me and gave me, the only Roman Catholic in our group, some stinging looks when I wouldn't revel in his sense of fun.

What was just as disgusting was that he encouraged the instructor, a mature woman, well past the traditional marrying age but who considered herself good-looking due to her alabaster skin color. "Father" would tease her, and afterward she'd share her feelings with us of her hope that she was attractive to him and that one day they would marry. This was my first encounter with a breakaway religious person, though I'd run into more over the years: former close friends, teachers and former students. That first time was somewhat traumatic. And the time we spent on "he loves me, he loves me not" was like being back in sixth grade. This is what could happen among the well-off class when a lady saw herself only as "in waiting" for marriage, something that happens all over the world.

Before September 11, 2001, and talk of global terrorism, the world was quite different. When I was in India in 1968, I never noticed tensions among people based on religion. They were there, for sure, for the great spilling of blood during the partition of British India had happened just over twenty years before, over Hindu and Muslim rivalries. But an outsider didn't see the fissures on the surface. The beauty of the monuments that the Moghuls had left after hundreds of years controlling large areas of the subcontinent was widely acknowledged. That the Moghuls were Muslim was understood, and I heard no one deny the magnificent stamp that they had made on Indian culture. The differences I noted were peaceful and in religions resembling Hinduism.

One such was Jainism, an ancient religion that emphasizes absolute nonviolence and asceticism. Maharashtra, I have read, has the highest percentage of Jains, over 31 percent. They practice strict vegetarianism even to the point of not eating potatoes or any plant that when it is uprooted would disturb the organic matter in the soil. As with many extremes, this way of living requires much assistance to follow in ordinary life. We visited a Jain village where it was faithfully practiced.

As our hostess's car brought us in from the train station, I gasped when I saw a tall naked man walking on the side of the street. Were it not for the ashes that covered his lanky frame, I would have thought he looked lewd; but as he was like a plastered statue, I realized he was an ascetic. We were driven to the compound of our hostess and, throughout the late afternoon and early evening, feted with delicate morsels, fresh fruit, and unending cups of tea.

After so much tea and bananas, I was bursting to go to the bathroom, which turned out to be an adventure. In India taking care of one's personal hygiene was a matter of ritual significance, as well as, like anywhere, physical well-being. Meaning is attached to bodily secretions, and how one cares for them is complicated, particularly for women. Thus the female newcomer had to tread gingerly. I was doing okay in my time so far in this mysterious land until the Jain household visit stumped me, making me question some basics that I thought I knew.

Shown to the room where I could relieve myself, I went in and was immediately flummoxed when I faced a long winding stairway. Next to it, to my left was a shining stainless steel water tank, whose steam vapors clouded my vision, letting me know not to touch lest I got scalded. Gingerly lifting my open-toed sandaled feet up the narrow polished, open wooden steps, I took care not to fall. Finally reaching the top, I opened the door in front and found myself in a two-foot square space outside enclosed by a tin wall. I looked up at the sky and, with no other choice, squatted down and did what came naturally! Afterward, I compared notes with Missi, who had the same experience; we never did find the actual water closet.

Brushing our teeth the next morning was also a new way of doing an everyday thing: we sat around a pool of water in the courtyard of the vintage house and were served with trays born by house attendants who had towels on their arms ready for us to use. It was like being served a glass of champagne, only on the trays were cups and pitchers of water. Using our toothbrushes, we then swished and swashed and rinsed, spitting into the gutter that ran along the side of the pool under where we sat, the most formal brushing of teeth I've ever done.

The evening before, only after sundown did we meet the men: we went into a room and joined our hostess's husband and other male family members for snacks followed by dinner. Sleeping, too, was done separately, all women in one room. Sexes were often separated in public spaces in those days; I'd gotten used to riding in the women's car of trains and to sitting on their side of an auditorium. But the Jain house was where I first saw women and men living in separate parts of their own home.

What's more, the hostess asked in her soft little girl's voice, "Can I sleep with you?" startling me. We felt awkward telling her that, sure, she could sleep where she wished in her own home. Later, Missi and I agreed that she had said it as a courtesy to us, "the honored guests." Although these rare times that I was privileged to glimpse the privacy of a generous family's home struck me as odd, I appreciated what they taught me. Inviting foreigners into your home is one of the most generous, risky, and personal acts one can do. In India the kindness of strangers happened to me often.

Over time I'd meet more members of the Jain community, but I'd come to see that few of them can practice their beliefs in the purest forms, as they did in the village we visited, because they had to make compromises in the real, multireligious, modernizing world. Later when I was back in India as a Foreign Service Officer, the daughter of a close friend, who had been raised and educated as a Christian, married a Jain. This naturally caused her mother, my friend, concern, because of the orthodox lifestyle that her precious only daughter would have to lead. It would put a lot of restrictions on her.

My friend had escaped the traditional role of a widow after her husband was killed in the 1965 Indo–Pakistan War. Left with no husband and two small children when she was still young, her husband's family, not deferring to her Western education and background of having grown up in a maharaja's court, expected my friend to give up her love for living, abandon her pride in looking attractive, and no longer wear bright *saris* and spangled jewelry. She refused. Instead, she set out on her own using her background as a court tutor and her skill in appreciating the value of antiques, which she had acquired growing up in a palace. She fretted that her daughter would not have the wider opportunities that were opening up for Indian women in the late seventies, opportunities that she had not dared to dream of, tied, as she had been, to the cushy, reclusive life of the court. In the end, everything worked out. Her daughter married her Jain fiancé, who turned out to be open-minded and progressive, and we all became good friends. As the wealthy son of a jeweler, he was able to care for her daughter as if she were a queen. They could afford to hire others to ensure that they lived in a completely nonviolent Jain way.

In Nagpur even the most mundane task was a cultural lesson. Shopping in the bazaar was at the top of that list. We'd spend hours trolling through the fabric stalls gazing at cottons, synthetics, and silks that the cloth *wallahs* would roll out for our inspection. Decorative borders of red and gold batik-printed bolts of cloth; yards of tie-dyed hot pinks, blues, and yellows—all were abundant and on view.

While there are many ways to wrap *a sari*, the most common style in cities then was to use six yards of material, pleated using the index finger to measure, folded and tied at the waist. A petticoat, which is a slip, had to be made to match the *sari* and was worn underneath. It guaranteed that when the hem moved, an underskirt, not bare legs, was seen. Made of cotton, it is tied with a drawstring at the waist. Finally, a blouse (*choti*) has to be fashioned, in matching material or in a shade to complement the *sari*. The blouse is closed with snaps in the front and ends below the bra line; how low or high is a personal choice that can make a big difference in the overall effect.

Until I began wearing one, I could not see myself in the dramatic costume, and I didn't think I could do so as gracefully as Missi, who looked more like a native. Being from Texas, she no doubt had come in contact with Central Americans and other different ethnic groups in their traditional dress. I, on the other hand, coming from a then more isolated state, had never seen such diversity. Women at Morgan from other countries, except for my Liberian friend who freely wore West African fabric and head wraps, favored Western dress. Yet when I saw how well Missi carried off the *sari* and how easily she blended in with Indians, I was motivated to try it.

Tying a *sari* seemed impossibly complicated. How could I get in the habit of folding pleats with my hand and stuffing the folds into my waistband every morning in time to go to work? How could I be caught dead baring my midriff? That was for belly dancers and bikini sporters. I had never been at ease in a bathing suit, which was what made not giving up and wearing one in college swimming class a remarkable achievement.

I could just wear the *kurta pajama* with its *dupatta* (scarf), which also required making and matching; it could be stunning and easy to wear.

As it turned out, I wore both. I liked the *kurta* and *pajama*, but the *sari* became my everyday dress, for, except for the time when I draped it in the wrong direction of my left shoulder, it made me look more like an Indian woman, helped me blend into the crowd, and made me feel appropriately dressed. Most important, my legs were covered, and the *sari*, as Indian women were fond of saying, "hides a lot of sins." I even got accustomed to wearing what I thought was the scandalous blouse. The trick was to make it long enough to almost touch the petticoat and to make sure the fabric was wrapped tightly enough so as not to show my midriff. When some of it did peek through, as was inevitable, I learned not to worry about it, for I had good skin, even if too much, and Indians did not object to, perhaps some even liked, seeing it. A Sikh man followed me around Connaught Circle one day in New Delhi, saying, "Health is wealth. Why don't you share some of yours with me?" This Ursuline girl stepped out crisp and confident in a *sari*.

Wearing a *sari* in Amritsar

Buying items was a continuing lesson in speaking Hindi and confronting new cultural situations. Something about exchanging money for goods forces one to communicate as clearly as possible, and I learned early how to haggle. The secret was not to go too far in holding out for something I really wanted. I paid too much for many things, but considering their value, they were a steal. The hundreds of merchants I dealt with were usually polite, but I understood that in their dealings with me they could be seeing me as the "ugly American," a brash, impatient foreigner with deep pockets who didn't want to spend much money. I had to accept my status as an outsider who would live among them and then leave, as the British and other invaders had done, so it wasn't a good idea to make a scene just to save a few rupees.

Still, I did my best to get the most for my money, and besides haggling over prices, some other shopping episodes were high comedy. One was when I was trying to find a deodorant, for as hot as it was I quickly ran out of the few jars I'd brought from the United States. The entire evening Missi and I trudged through Sadaar Bazaar looking for it. "D-e-o-d-o-r-a-n-t?" we'd plead. A storekeeper would smile, saying, *"Hun-ji,"* tilting his head from right to left, in the expression that means yes. But after minutes of searching, I'd be presented with the most bizarre tins and bottles: a room deodorizer covered in dust, a bottle of cologne, and a can that could only be reached with a borrowed twelve-foot ladder. When the storekeeper took it down and opened it, out fell dusty flakes of whatever had been in it long ago. He laughed with us as the ashes of whatever had been the contents floated out.

I fretted that I had not brought from America enough deodorant but I had transported many rolls of toilet tissue, which were not used much in India. I'd still bring the jars of French's yellow mustard, which I couldn't live without, though. To solve the no-deodorant problem, I did what the local women did: kept my underarm hairs cut, washed myself as much as I needed throughout the day, and doused my body in fragrant lilac talcum powder. My favorite brand came in a tall, ten-inch slim light purple tin. Use of talcum powder is discouraged today, but I've never had problems from using it (in the right places).

In Nagpur the year passed, and I thrived on the lessons that each new day taught. We moved to a newly built light gray house away from the town in Gandhinagar. Shiny tile floors, modern water pipes, and floor-to-ceiling windows in ten-foot-high rooms were a step-up for me, Missi, and Ellen.

As we each wanted to strike out more on our own and be independent, the bungalow fit our needs because each of us had our own room with separate outside entrances. As in the flat in town, we'd sleep under the fans with the windows open, for there was no modern air-conditioning. I had gotten used to the lizards crawling down the walls or clinging to the ceiling. At first, they had terrified me, as they looked like tiny dinosaurs. I'd tuck the sheets over my loosely clad body, put the fan on the highest setting, and sleep hoping for the best. But with time I learned not to even flinch when a lizard scampered over my foot in the bathroom.

The blasting-fan method was also the best way to keep the mosquitoes away; I used it then and continue to do so whenever I'm in a hot climate. I did, however, get a shock when we discovered that I had been regularly entertaining a Peeping Tom. I had only heard of them and was sorry I had provided such a spectacle; however, I didn't let it bother me. I put a window shade under the dark purple curtains, which I had made and installed and hoped that the embarrassing incident didn't happen again, and it didn't.

One night all three of us screamed and huddled together on a high ledge in the dining room when a wild little furry creature galloped into our house. The *chowkidar* (watchman) came running with a stick and other men and shooed the bushy beastie away. *Silly American girls scared of such a small harmless creature*, they must have thought.

We had hired a cook who looked like he came straight from the pages of the British Raj. Mahadev was up in age, with a white bushy mustache neatly combed and curled up at the ends and a turban tied in a style not unlike those worn on the Northwest Frontier. He had worked for English-speaking people connected with the military and had been glad to find a position with three new *memsahibs* (Western women), for a rumor had spread that he had tuberculosis, and that had made finding a job difficult. Pat Rodgers had found him for us, and compared to our previous *paan*-juice-spewing, *sigri*-couching cook, Mahadev was many steps ahead. We were elated to hire him and devoured his sumptuous hot meals like heiresses who had gotten what was due them.

One afternoon, however, the table was empty when I came home from college for the afternoon meal. "No money, no food," Mahadev moaned as I expressed my astonishment. He went on to explain how in the first days Missi had given him money and told him what to do, but that week, she had expected me or Ellen to take the lead. I walked outside with him to talk as we stood under a tree. I shared with him my frustrations about everything: how hard it was to get a rickshaw, which was why I left too early to discuss housekeeping issues with my roommates; that while I liked some foods that he fixed, I couldn't bear the taste of mutton and water buffalo, which were the meats in the market that he bought; and by the way, while I liked his fried vegetables and lentils cooked in butter, I needed to cut down on the grease as I was gaining too much weight. He stepped back and looked down from his six-foot-plus-high view straight into my eyes and said, "Life is difficult, Baba."

Mahadev with his family

I realized how trivial I must have sounded and felt rather silly. Immediately, I decided to change my strident tone to coordinate better with my roommates. Ellen had not been as adamant as I had about matters. I had to admit that although I thought of myself as housekeeper, mother, big sister, I had been taking a holiday since I arrived in this new land. Now I had to take on more responsibility. Still, while it lasted, I did like being spoiled.

17

Passenger in India

After the Ganesh Festival, the places where my housemates and I were teaching went into exam-preparation mode; with that came free time and cooler winter weather perfect to explore more of India. With Missi I set out by train to Delhi; from there we would go on separate routes, linking up before returning to Nagpur independently. The 628-mile journey from Nagpur by train and other trips during the three weeks were a cultural crash course. We stayed in tourist hostels and low-cost hotels.

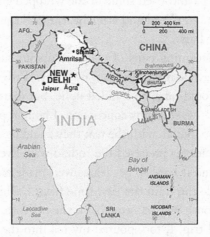

Public domain, CIA World Factbook

A variety of ticket types and classes from first to third made the railroad the connector to all of India. This was infrastructure that the British had left behind with the sweat and toil of huge numbers of Asians, in railroads that linked Undivided India including what are now the countries of Pakistan and Bangladesh. While Missi and I had enough money to go first class, we went in third to save money and for the experience. I confess that as someone who had grown up making do on little, I didn't enjoy sitting on a hard wooden shelf seat, much less sleeping on one, but I was a good sport about it and did get to know more of how the lower economic classes made do. Often we rode in the women's compartment: children of all ages and babies in arms, mothers nursing, and old women staring into space, some swathed in pale widow's cotton.

On another train trip to Bombay, we didn't get a seat. We squatted on the floor with villagers who were going to a city to take their child, huddling under a shawl, to a doctor. We chugged along feeling the clang of the rails just under us, talking to the villagers. Suddenly, all the windows opened. The travelers who filled our car escaped through them before the last stop, leaving us, the foreigners, the only ones with tickets to collect.

Everything was for sale on that journey to Delhi: *Wallahs* gawking fried stuffed snacks like *samosas* (stuffed pastries) and bright saffron-colored *jiblebis* (a donut-like sweet). Chunks of fresh coconut and sugarcane stalks passed through the car and near the tracks in arms held high by vendors. While we didn't sample the offerings, we got down to stretch our legs during stops and tried some of the wrapped goodies—little bags of popcorn-like grain, spiced and crunchy, caramel squares, peanuts, and Cadbury chocolate bars.

Stalls selling steaming cups of tea were ubiquitous along the route. Served with rich buffalo milk, the tea was robust. With sugar, the mixture was more than I could take, so I added none, but many people relied on the tonic lift of the sweet, soupy concoction. I bought plain English-style biscuits (cookies) to munch with the tea; they could be found everywhere. Then as now, I prefer tea prepared the Indian way. Even in London then and since, I've found it hard to get tea as well made and hot as it was in India. When I rode the train the first time from Delhi to Nagpur, I had scoffed at the uncouth way passengers on the platform slurped their tea. But on my second trip, I, too, poured my tea into the saucer of the cup to consume the brew before the all-aboard whistle sounded to jump back on when the locomotive left the station. Drinking the tea from the saucer cooled it down, I discovered, which was why everyone did it that way. On these journeys I got used to eating fried onion omelets with thick slices of bread, the perfect meal to consume in waiting area dining rooms.

Most fascinating was how Indians could go into the cramped space of a train restroom, with a hole of a toilet in the floor, and come out refreshed, shaved and neat as if they had just left home. Asians, I was discerning, had mastered the art of living in small spaces. Once, however, the carriage suddenly came to a halt. A woman had lost an expensive ring while using the facilities, and workers were on the track searching for it!

In Delhi, that November of 1968, I saw more sights than I'd seen when I was first there four months before: places like Rajgat, the placid memorial to Mahatma Gandhi. I quivered when standing there; I thought of how he had influenced Martin Luther King Jr. and how the American civil rights leader had used nonviolence, only, like the mahatma, to be struck down by gun violence, barely six months earlier in April 1968.

From Delhi, Missi and I went on a five-hour train ride to the Taj Mahal, one of the Seven Wonders of the World. I had been impatient to see it before I left India. In those days, arriving in the city of the most beautiful monument to love was an unpleasant experience: flies swarmed and cloyed me as I made my way along the monument grounds after a rollicking taxi ride from the train station, when we had to bargain vigorously with the taxi driver for a fair price. The throng at the entrance had made me anxious. Sweat rolled down my back, and my feet hurt in my open-toed, no-support *chappals* so that by the time I got to the Taj, I was in a bad mood. *Impress me, I thought*. No place could be as outstanding as this one was supposed to be. But of course, I was mistaken. Just one look and my heart was swept away: the glistening marble, marks where encrusted stone had been, the perfect balanced design, and the fact that I could go through it and view it up close made it personal to me. The magnificence of this palace that Shah Jehan built for his favorite wife Mumtaz in the sixteenth century made me feel their deep love story.

Some Peace Corps friends had joined us, and, as evening fell, we lounged on a cooling floor in the corner of a balcony of the marble masterpiece. Strange but true and lucky for me, the guards had let us remain inside the grounds after closing. We basked in the ethereal splendor under the light of the full October moon of 1968.

The Pink City, Jaipur, enthralled us next. Fellow Fulbrighter Cathy was there teaching English at a university. She showed us all the marvelous palaces of the city that had been in the princely state of Rajasthan. Before

India had won back its freedom in 1947, a number of other such states all over the subcontinent had also been independent.

Back in Delhi, Missi and I split up setting out on separate agendas. I went the 248 miles by long-distance bus from Delhi to Amritsar. This old city where the Sikh religion took root is in in the state of Punjab just thirty miles from the Pakistan border and that country's city of Lahore. Now that I had a greater appreciation of the subcontinent's history after being in country for nearly five months, I was excited to be going close to the border, near to a part of the country that had only been created when the British were preparing to leave India.

Not only is Amritsar in Punjab, India, but Lahore is in Punjab too— Punjab, Pakistan, a geographical anomaly I found hard to get my head around. I was also fascinated by the Sikhs, as I'd never heard of them, coming as I did from the middle of America (although, unbeknown to me, they had been living in the Pacific Northwest United States for a long time). With their neatly cared for beards, little boys with top notches of hair high on their heads, and women light-complexioned, tall, baring their full abdomens unashamedly, they were something to see, and they were friendly and easy to be with. The women on the bus made me feel welcome, asking me where I was from and offering me food. When we arrived in Amritsar, they helped me get my baggage from on top of the bus, and they chose a coolie to carry my bags, settling with him what I should pay him. He had popped up beside me as soon as my foot touched the platform. He carried my bag to the left luggage counter waiting room, where I stored it for the day while I saw the sights.

Getting off a bus or train or deplaning at an airport is hectic in many places but was especially so in India fifty years ago. The masses came to life; bodies came toward and beside me, the hum of assorted dialects of the many languages of India pierced my ears, the get-out-of-the-way suddenness of a big bundle barreled through, and always there were the bright eyes of the children and the calm shuffling along of ordinary men and women. Move with the crowd, I had learned early in my stay. And so I did, directly to the tourist desk, where a man wearing a government tourist guide badge was already coming toward me to tell me what he could show me. Amritsar is known for its significance to the Indian Rebellion of 1857 and for being the home of the greatest shrine to Sikhism, the Golden Temple.

Following the guide, I traipsed down a narrow, yard-wide alley of a market with stalls and vendors hawking aluminum pots and pans, tools like pliers and hammers, and small cans of what looked like car motor oil. I dared not stop to linger, because the air was hot and heavy with flies. I kept my mouth tightly shut while discreetly drawing my *duppata* over my face to shield myself from the bugs and not call attention to myself.

I was shown to an abandoned well and invited to look down its chasm of stale darkness. The guide said that women, children, and other civilians had hurled themselves into the void in fear of oncoming British-led soldiers. Later, when studying the rebellion, I learned that it was more widespread and complex than I had understood that day: Discontent had been brewing across northern and eastern India, eastern parts of Pakistan (now Bangladesh), and in the center in Madhya Pradesh. The dispute was over control of parts of India by the British East India Company. The final straw that led to the overall outbreak had to do with Indian soldiers finding their guns had been greased with animal fat. Soon Hindu and Muslim soldiers were protesting in a wave that spread physically and sentimentally all over India. Even where there was no action, reactions were strong.

The many rebellious acts, like at the well in Amritsar, were the beginning of the end of a hundred years of control of India by the East India Company and the start of almost another hundred years of colonization, before independence in August 1947. India "the jewel in the crown" was so precious that Britain had held onto it at great costs to its empire. While the control of other countries Britain had conquered was managed by the Colonial Office, because it was a continuing source of abundance, India was handled separately under the India Office.

Scholars have been probing the rumblings of the discontent at the Amritsar well for a long time. In March 2014, an excavation revealed the remains of 282 Indian soldiers who had been hurled into the same shaft that I looked down that day in 1968. As our guide told us his version of the story, I shivered, imagining the horror of the tortuous deaths; the lightless, dank hole showed me how, as docile as they may have seemed, Indians despised being under British rule. I compared it to the heavy life of my forebears in American slavery.

From the evil to the sublime, I walked to the Golden Temple close by; it pulled my emotions 180 degrees in the opposite direction: I saw piles of gleaming gold stacked in the middle of a ringed area; worshippers at this shrine to Sikhism were tossing rupees, paisa coins, shiny bangles, sparkling jeweled necklaces, and reams of colorful cloth bordered in precious stones and threaded in the thin flaky yellow metal that gave the temple its name. Suspended in a lake of holy water, making the brilliant gold-plated structure appear to float, I felt like I was walking into a scene from *One Thousand and One Nights*. It was unreal, and I felt no one would believe me when I'd tell them what I'd seen. The dazzling scene was almost more fabulous to behold than the Taj, which I thought was the zenith of what my eyes would see in this life. I had to keep on looking at the magnificent temple, because unlike the Taj, which I knew I'd see more times, I didn't think I'd visit this site again. I wanted to fix the details in my mind's eye forever.

I had and would hear about the self-sufficiency of Sikhs—Punjab was feeding itself already—and their care for one another bespoke their faith: I never saw a Sikh begging. Their sometimes discriminatory treatment in the United States, especially since September 11, 2001, is a disgrace.

After the tour, I went back to the bus depot, picked up my bag, and set out to rendezvous with Missi in Chandigarh, backtracking 145 miles on the bus. After meeting up with Missi, we got on another bus, reversing direction and traveling east, crossing from UP into Himachal Pradesh (HP), 187.5 miles to Shimla. Called the "Queen of the Hill Stations," "Jewel of the Orient," and other poetic superlatives, it was these and more. We took the hairpin-turning long-distance bus to slowly make our way up the steep hills. My stomach and head ached, but I had the breathtaking landscape to look at and keep me calm.

Over seven thousand feet high in the Himalayas, Shimla had been the summer capital of the British, when all the government shifted there to get away from the oppressive heat of the plains. All the trappings of imperial power—vice royal house and government buildings—were there, as were the quaint English houses and gardens where officials had lazed over long dinners around full tables and children had frolicked in the summer. I hadn't been to England yet, so I didn't know how much a duplicate Shimla was of an English village. I found it reinvigorating and lovely, the fronts of cottages and gardens so perfect, that I felt like I was in a storybook.

While we were planning the trip, I hadn't been very keen on seeing Shimla, but once I got there, I was eager to experience what a hill station was like. The concept was alien to me; however, after my student's little lecture about the mighty feat of the ascent of Everest, I wanted to know more about how the mountain chain affected Indian life and lore. I too could associate with people who had lived in the hills. What was so different about the Indian experience?

I had grown up in a valley, the Ohio Valley, and was used to living in four distinct climate seasons. While it had been hard to adjust to the stifling heat, after living in India for four months, my mind and body were now set on surviving in the unrelenting climate that I'd finally settled into. My goal was to persevere until spring when it would be time for me to return home, and I wasn't in the mood for physically taxing adventures. I really didn't want to climb the long, rough, rocky stairs up to the hotel in Shimla where we would stay just so we could look out on the mountains and appreciate the view. Cold and afraid of moving around in the unknown environment of hillside slopes, I could see the merits but wasn't thrilled about them.

At my grandmother Mama Harris's and Uncle William's home in Tazewell, Virginia, I was about 3,500 high. I didn't know that twice as many more feet could make all the difference. As I struggled to keep pace behind the coolies who carried our luggage on their backs, I saw the great difference between hills and mountains—or more precisely, hills and the foothills of the greatest mountain range in the world.

I did have to deal with the moral discomfort of relying on coolies. I felt as terrible as they looked trudging up to our hotel, faces frozen with deep lines, numb and tired. Though pink peeked through their cheeks, their leathery hands were deeply tanned; they were like beasts of burden. At the time, this was the only way it seemed to get to where we were going. Years later I'd make one more trip with my daughter to this grand hill station; we'd take the elegant two-and-a-half-foot-wide gauge red "toy" train, on the railway constructed by the British in 1906. But in 1968, Missi and I didn't want to pay the price of the expensive ticket.

A church in Shimla

At that later time with my daughter, the transfer to the hotel would be much easier on the man carrying our luggage, but my first experience in Shimla showed me how dramatically different life could be high above sea level in developing India. Little did I know that I'd get accustomed to going to hill stations, even soon living in one. That first time was a breath of blessed fresh air. Pitch-dark, after dinner on the eve before Divali, the all–India Festival of Lights, I looked out on the candles that lit the rise and fall of centuries old peaks and vales. "Silent Night" wasn't playing, but I could hear it, the stillest time I'd had on earth.

Horseback riding in Shimla

I traveled straight back to Delhi to meet up with Ellen, while Missi went on her own way. As I unpacked my bags at the Y, I felt like I was coming home, recalling the events of the orientation, which though only four months ago seemed like a year. I arrived on a Saturday morning, and in the evening I was going to go out and "do the town" with dates that had been arranged for Ellen and me. Ellen was being seriously wooed by a young man who worked in New Delhi. He was from Nagpur, where they'd met. It was obvious that they would be getting married, "getting hitched" as the man who would be my date liked to say. A third girl, also a Fulbrighter, was to have joined us for the evening, but she didn't show up. In the meantime, we went shopping for *saris*, jewelry, and sandals, happy in the cool early-November weather of the north and giggling about our blind dates for the evening.

Spying Sunder Kaula out of the side of my eyes, I said yes! He's for me. Sunder literally means good-looking, and he was that. Tall, with an urbane manner, and speaking fluent modern English, the fact that he was a writer, a copywriter at J. Walter Thompson, an American advertising agency, made him irresistible. My whole body was tingling when he took my hand to step out on the dance floor. The band struck up the classic tune that I'd only heard in movies: "Isn't It Romantic?" Indeed, I thought, as I looked up into Sunder's liquid brown eyes, it is.

Sunder, 1968

18

Too Soon

Dr. "Feel" Good was our fairy godfather that Thanksgiving of 1968. His real name was Philip Good; he was an official for USAID (Agency for International Development), who lived in a modern bungalow with a refrigerator, electric stove, sofa, and chairs—all the conveniences one would find in a typical American home. In Nagpur on his own, like most of us, he became a part of our group, easy to do because of the chocolate chip cookies he'd bring to our soirees and his fatherly attitude and the confident smile he'd pose while listening to us. He rode a motorcycle, dressed in khaki with a topi hat, like someone in a Tarzan film. But he certainly did not act as if he was carrying the white man's burden; with great respect for Indians, he was doing critical work teaching villagers how to improve their living conditions. He was the first of many AID officials that I'd be honored to know, and while I didn't realize it at the time, he was the first American I met who was in the career that I was aiming to join: the U.S. Foreign Service.

We were a motley crew: three American PCVs; three Fulbrighters; a Canadian nurse, Jocelyn; and her Japanese fiancé, Joey. Both worked in Canada's foreign aid program. Jocelyn had been Joey's nurse when he was in hospital after an accident in which he turned his motorcycle too much in one direction and bounced off into a pit. He would have died, he swore, had it not been for Jocelyn's tender loving care. Those two were crazy about each other: their lifesaving bond and mixed ethnicities — she French Canadian, outgoing with frizzy auburn hair and caramel complexion; he Japanese with beguiling eyes, monochromatic dress, and a quiet inscrutability—made them an appealing couple.

Dr. Good supplied the turkey for our feast at that one time in the year when all Americans hate to be separated from their families, and he hosted the Thanksgiving dinner at his home. I was to contribute sweet potatoes, but since I couldn't find the orange ones, I made creamy mashed potatoes with butter and full-fat buffalo milk.

We couldn't find a substitute for pumpkin pie and for that taste of cinnamon and cloves of the traditional meal, so we went with Jocelyn's orange pudding for dessert. She got *santras* zinging with taste; as they were always piled high in the fruit stalls, they were cheap. Jocelyn bought a barrel and made a soufflé that rose to such a height I thought it was going to ooze onto the floor! After filling our stomachs with the comforting food and reminiscing about our homes, we all seemed to think that Jocelyn's orange concoction was the perfect light dessert to top off the rich meal. That night made me more aware of America's neighbors to the north and that Thanksgiving is celebrated in Canada in October, of which, I'm ashamed to say, I wasn't aware at the time.

Since getting back from our long trip to North India, I had been in a reflective mood: I had met this most attractive man and was smitten with him; I wanted to get to know him, but how could I, so far away? My determination to embark on this new route may have been reinforced by the notion that I was toying with the idea of settling down in India. Missi had introduced me to an American woman married to an Indian living in Nagpur; they seemed happy. Neither was rich nor glamorous; they were middle aged, and the wife spoke with an American Southeastern accent like mine. Now Ellen and her friend were an item. I decided that I wanted to make a home and have a career, to have it all. I knew Mother would have approved; I thought Daddy would have also. How the Foreign Service would fit into all of this, I didn't give much thought.

Another force may have pushed me in the direction of making a home outside the United States: my promise to myself. I had said I'd never return after Bobby Kennedy was assassinated on the night of my graduation; now, Richard Nixon was president. I could not imagine living in a country where the gains of the civil rights movement and the Great Society were turned back. *Had my absentee vote, sent from New Delhi in November, even counted?*

Child of the sixties that I was, I missed being in America during the revolutionary summer of 1968, the seismic shifting democratic convention in Chicago; Hubert Humphrey's and Eugene McCarthy's campaigns for president; the riots and police shootings. Nonetheless, not being in America at that time was all for the best, for although I would have liked to have claimed that I witnessed that definitive time, I'm glad I didn't. The ugly reaction of the right-wing "push back" and comments like "the silent majority" were couched in racist speak, and being there to hear it would have depressed me. Like now, when the talk is about the working class. African Americans have always been in the working class. While I have always been progressive, I—like other African Americans—*have* and *had* much to "conserve" and not destroy, since the United States is my native land too. Had I witnessed the political events of the summer of 1968, I may well have lost all faith in my country.

In my letters home that Christmas, I had written to some of my former teachers at Morgan. In a letter to Dr. Ulysses Lee, professor of English, I thanked him for his inspiration and told him how it was paying off in the class I was teaching on selected British writings; I regretted that Burney had not stayed longer and that I should have persuaded him not to leave. What he wrote in his reply boosted my spirits at a crucial turning point in my life when I was deciding whether or not to stay or leave India when the Fulbright ended in the coming spring. It has stayed with me throughout my life with its many challenges. Dated early January 1969, it must have been one of the last letters he wrote, for he died only a few weeks later. In flourishing blue ink he assured me that Morgan had always known I was in the winner's circle.

Tom splashed with paint, Holi, spring 1969

Spring of 1969 came in mid-March, and the weather got warmer. One day people were squirting each other with colored water in the streets, and our friend Kelly, who was in the Indian army, was tying a *raki*, a thin decorative band, around my right wrist, making me his *didi* (sister) and promising to protect me. Confident as a teacher, I hated to be ending my time at Saint Francis de Sales. I had seen the students grow in their knowledge of what I had helped them discover, and that was satisfying, making me have more faith in myself. I also was pleased with my ability to sing *Rabindra Sangeet* and was writing the final report on my project to present at the Fulbright end-of-year conference in April. As things turned out, I went to the conference but didn't turn in the report until a year later.

Sister Eleanor had observed that I was well nestled in my teaching, so when I told her that it was too soon for me to leave India and asked her advice on finding another position, she told me she'd see what she could do. Staying at SFD was out of the question, of course. She didn't tell me, but I'm sure the college was bidding on another Fulbrighter to replace me. Moving on and being replaceable was a cold reality I would get used to.

In truth, behind all this wanting to stay was my infatuation with Sunder. I called it love.

We were like magnets. After our first date that night in Delhi in November, I canceled my plans to do more sightseeing to nearby towns and stayed to spend time with him. We had a ball: going around Delhi pouring our feelings out over long, iced, milky drinks in a popular outdoor coffeehouse; going to restaurants and dancing on their postage-stamp-sized floors, like in a movie, something long out of fashion in the States. And we'd go to see films, Western ones, from America, England, and Russia, in one of Delhi's huge prewar-style cinema houses. As we shared an attachment to English literature, we spent a lot of our time talking about writers and books and browsing through stalls. Sunder was up-to-date on modern best-selling authors, while I could talk about novelists and poets in history.

After I left and was back in Nagpur, we kept up our relationship in an exchange of letters, which I put in a heart-shaped blue velvet box covered with mirrorwork. The Beatles sang, "All you need is love," but I needed more than that, for three months after we met, he told me he was married, though separated. While my emotions thudded and I was upset when he confessed this to me, I knew that it was too soon to leave India. I'd stay on another year and see what would happen.

As early as late January, I had been thinking about how to properly say goodbye to my students. Where I got the confidence to throw a big party I don't know, but I decided to do so on the roof of our house and I had to do it before the heat would make it impossible, so I aimed for the next month. The roof had been an ideal place to sit under the night sky and to welcome the sun on cool mornings. Since the roof was flat-topped and surrounded by a wall, it was like having an extra room. Simple mats could be put on the concrete surface to sit on, and Mahadev could make finger foods and lemonade for the student guests. Sister Eleanor and the brothers' eyes twinkled when I proposed the idea, and they readily agreed. They would send the students and anyone who needed to go down Seminary Hill on a college bus. I got Missi's and Ellen's okay and personally invited all my students. Just planning the party fired me up. I discovered that I had a knack for doing it.

Mahadev was the only person who saw a shadow in my bright idea. We were discussing snacks that he could prepare. Appreciating that homemade food anywhere was always the best, I proposed that he make *samosas*. These little packets of crispy dough stuffed with savories from onions and potatoes, and often minced meat, were scrumptious. Their rich spices and kick of hotness were hard to resist.

"Yes, Baba, I can make *samosas*," Mahadev said, sadly shaking his head, and went on to tell me about someone he'd worked for who had required him to make *samosas* all day. "Him say, 'Make *samosas*, make *samosas* . . .'" I was too tin eared to pick up on the hint. I should have thought of a way to buy them freshly made by someone else. But Mahadev agreed to make them, as well as *pakoras*, another stuffed pastry. The fete, as the students liked to say, was a success. On a clear February 13, 1969, the students came, resplendent in their sun-bright robes and fresh shirts. While not one sister or any female students came, I was glad that many of the male, pre-university students and a number of the priests and brothers showed up. With the good food, and the music that Guruji provided, the day took care of itself. Still, the students had the upper hand. Indians tended to be formal in events; occasions ended with a "vote of thanks" usually after one or two prepared remarks. Since in black American culture we tended to be this way, the formality helped me feel more at home. A student from the PUC class rose to thank me. Taking from a silver-foil-wrapped tube a legal-size document, the cover page displaying a green, pink, and blue pencil-drawn angel, he read from a speech typed in blue ink on thin tissue paper:

> We express our appreciation to your unflinching devotion to duty and your willingness to help us at any time . . . you planned a programme of conducting debates.
> This undoubtedly has been a real success. Education in the literal sense of the word signifies educing something. Now by conducting a number of debates you have tried to educe the various talents that lie buried in our minds.

Lofty but heartfelt. I have kept the scroll all these years.

SFD staff came to bid me farewell

My students at the rooftop party

I had given Ramdas a note to be excused from school for the day to help at the party, but without my knowing it, he used the chit for the time that I remained in Nagpur. One day I got a note from his teacher demanding that I pay him money not to fail Ramdas for missing so much school. I was so distraught with my preteen helper. I told him that he knew better, that he was dishonestly using my signature as an excuse for not getting an education. He pleaded that he was sorry: "Judy Bai." What could I do? I asked a friend to meet with the teacher and clear up the matter. I never knew if that did the trick or not and if Ramdas finished the eighth grade.

Shortly after, Sister Eleanor called me to her office and read from a letter she had received: the Convent of Jesus and Mary ("Waverley") in Mussoorie, in the foothills of the Himalayas in Northeast India, was inviting me to join their staff. What an answer to my prayers!

19

Himalayan Hush

Looking out on the panorama of peaks and valleys on the first evening of my arrival in Mussoorie, I thought I was dreaming. Those first days moving around getting to know the place I'd see houses named "Tipperary" and remember Daddy, hat tilted back, jacket open, tie loosened, singing, "It's a long way to Tipperary . . ." Since I hadn't heard the tune, I was sure that he, ever the joker, had made it up, but eventually I learned it was sung during World War I. Now, I was learning that this quaint-sounding place was in Ireland. And here I was in my new home seeing "Tipperary" on a house as I passed through an enchanting hamlet in the hill station of Mussoorie in Northeastern India. Did leprechauns lurk in the mist when the Irish lived there?

Public domain, CIA World Factbook

A fairy-tale froth of woods, flowers, and sweeping vistas greeted me while I lived there from April to June 1969. At that time it was in the state of Himachal Pradesh; now it's in the newly created twenty-seventh state of Uttarakhand. While not as grand as Shimla, Mussoorie's proximity to Delhi, 181 miles, made it a quick place to get away to, for relaxation and, as one source I Googled claims, according to legend, "intriguing assignations." Six thousand one hundred and seventy feet above sea level in the Himalayas, with one of the premier Indian schools of administration nearby, and with a number of boarding schools, it was the ideal place for study. Seeing the special features of the town made me feel like a character in a book, and I was there to study more about India by teaching and, coincidentally, because of love.

Four men pulled me up to the walled gate in a hand-driven rickshaw like a real *memsahib*, which I was, when I first arrived. After meeting the businesslike, rosy-cheeked European mother superior, another sister showed me to my room on the second floor of the white-washed cottage. It opened out onto a veranda from where I stood soaking up the forest green and terra cotta wide view amidst the dance of dark mountaintops covered in snow, like ice cream sundaes.

Angela (I'll call her that), my roommate, was also a new teacher. With family from Goa, I could see her Portuguese roots—long hair worn behind her ears as if she could stick a flower in it like an islander. She came from Dehradun, the next town down the hill. She was kind and gentle. I would have a hard time saying that about all the staff at this all-girls school. She was a Christian, although not Catholic, the denomination under which the school was founded. What loosely linked us and the other teachers were our English-speaking abilities and Christian backgrounds.

Wearing Western dress, Angela spoke the language of Great Britain as well as her native tongue, and we got along well. Another teacher, Anita, was a heavyset Punjabi woman who wore a *sari*, spoke English, and taught math; and there was Agnes (not her real name), a tall older woman who wore Western dress and had never worn a *sari* and was careful not to be thought of as someone who did. Tension between me and Anita and Agnes developed almost from the start.

I was relieved that they only came up from town during the day, unlike Angela and me who lived at the school. Waverley was quietly situated far from tourist attractions on the second-highest peak in Mussoorie; the trek up put the elevation close to seven thousand meters. Testing the limits of my nearly twenty-three-year-old body, I walked up the hill often.

The tensions between me and the two local teachers had to do with the stress all over India of allegiance to the dying colonial ways and the new openness. Since independence Anglo-Indians, those of Christian and Western education with some British blood, had to make their way in the new Indian-dominated society. They were the government clerks, the musicians in Western-style bands, the copywriters, and the teachers in English-medium schools. A sensitive issue then, I never got to discuss it with any of my new colleagues at Waverly because I wasn't aware of it, and because in their eyes, I probably complicated the matter.

I suppose the first shock was that I was African American, not of European descent as they probably assumed before I arrived. That I always wore Indian dress and didn't look like a skirt-and-blouse schoolmarm no doubt also disturbed them a bit. I continued *Rabindra Sangeet* lessons with a teacher who came up from the town on Sunday mornings. Singing in Bengali to the loud sound of the sitar was not a wise thing to do; certainly not what one would expect at a Catholic convent.

Moreover, there were long-standing cliques, common when a new person joins a staff that has worked together for a long time. As the new girl on the block, I wasn't brought into them, and Angela was also shunned to some extent. Like many young Western-influenced women, she alternated between wearing Western pants and Eastern *kurta pajamas* but never a *sari*, and that seemed to be the dividing line.

Dress said a lot. Legs, I was learning, were the operative feature all over India, for only *memsahibs,* Western women, showed theirs, so when Agnes wore a frock with nylon stockings, she was making a statement about leaning toward Western ways. I was doing just the opposite: I was supposed to wear Western dress but didn't. That must have confused my new associates and made me too complicated to get to know. Not being accepted by the day teachers worried me, and as my time with them was limited, I didn't have the chance to discuss my feelings about being a minority group member. Looking back, I wonder if had I worn Western clothes and acted more like a "Miss Jean Brodie," if I would have fared better.

Mealtimes were where these culture wars played out; in class the students were fascinated with me, and like children everywhere, my uniqueness captured their attention. But in the cozy staff dining room, downstairs from where we slept, the tug of wills began. I was always thankful that breakfast was spared. I'd have my porridge and several cups of brimming hot Indian black tea to which I'd add a little bit of milk, not as much as my Indian colleagues did, but like them, I insisted that the milk was hot. Bearers (waiters) had laid the food in a closed oven built into the dining room wall; we'd help ourselves, and as we didn't have to ask for anything, I could enjoy the morning silence. I'd help myself to thick slices of bread toasted over fire; I'd add butter and delicious English-style jam and gaze at the mountains. By midmorning, however, the day teachers and I would rush into the room to gulp down tea and biscuits during our twenty-minute break.

That's when the innuendos, overpolite conversation, and jabs would begin. At first, I didn't know what was being discussed, but as time went on, I caught on to the intrigues. The Western-educated young couple that I visited in town in the evenings, friends of Sister Eleanor in Nagpur, seemed not to want to have children, some of the teachers were saying, according to the gossip. Among the nuns, who of course lived and ate separately, there were also two groups—Indians and Europeans—so the chances for cultural misunderstandings were many. I didn't know if they were a part of the rumor mill, but I was uneasy being between the two groups.

One teacher reached to bridge the gap. Tall, with loose raven wavy hair and wearing a soft fabric *salwar kameez* that cascaded down her willowy figure, Roshan blurted out one day so everyone could hear, "They say that every year!" She was talking to another teacher who doubted if a new person like me could be included on a committee. "Judith," she said, confronting me after she had helped herself to a plate of rice and steaming, chunky curry, "why don't you let me propose your name?" Roshan was like most of the women I had met over the wide swath of India I'd glimpsed in my travels: modern, pragmatic, eclectic. I'd meet many like her in the years ahead. They made my stay not only bearable but, more importantly, worthwhile. Despite the difficulties fitting in, I'd never trade anything for the chance I had to live and work in an Indian boarding school. Through it, I got to see the old India changing into the new and how a minority group, the Christians, was adapting. My time at Ursuline Academy had surely prepared me. My strong suit was that I was not intimidated by the stern nuns.

Another good teacher friend was Rekha; I'd meet her during the lunch break. She had the most mesmerizing ebony eyes. Once, as she looked straight into mine, hers glistened with empathy as we were discussing my problem of whether to stay in India to be near the man I loved. We were on one of the long walks we took together, talking about what many women of our age around the world were probably discussing: marriage, children and increasing opportunities. In India, we had the mind-blowing example of Prime Minister Indira Gandhi. If ever there was a woman who lived and breathed her mission in life, whether you agreed with her politics or not, it was Mrs. Gandhi, Nehru's daughter (no relation to the Mahatma, by the way). Most of our girl students were in a sort of marriage waiting room, and the sisters had made the biggest commitment, many would have said, and were wedded to and spending their lives in service to Christ.

"Come to the rink one evening," Rekha said. She and her brother were North India's roller-skating champions. I was wowed by the idea that she even knew about roller-skating, a pastime that I'd enjoyed during the first eight years of my life, until the Ku Klux Klan put a stop to it. My sister Anita skated regularly at the rink by Sheppard Square, at Grace Presbyterian Church, a center that Mohammed Ali had contributed to.

In that hill station, school evenings could be rough. Dinner was so early that often I skipped the meal so I could walk down to the town. By that time, I'd trudge up the hill on those cool summer nights, after managing to keep on walking even as bats swooped down almost on my head as they hovered around the tall lamp poles. Since childhood and the bats flying out from the shutters on the side porch of Preston Street, I'd been deathly afraid of them. Having to confront the flapping creatures each night to get back to Waverly got me over that fear.

As the night fell, the bearer would leave a bucket of hot water in the bathing room off of an inner veranda that backed to our room. I looked to that relaxing time as a way of ending my day. I'd remove my clothes and lather soap all over my body. Then I'd dip a cup into a second bucket of lukewarm water that I'd mixed—half cold and half hot—and using a clean cloth, I'd wash my face, scrub my body, and then, the high point of the whole process, I'd take the bucket of now-cooled just-right hot water and pour it over my head. The force and feel of this bucket bath settled me down to climb into bed.

Before that, as I'd be ravenous after walking forty-five minutes up the hill, I'd take out my lifesaving stash of Nestlé's condensed sweet milk and a jar of Nescafé instant coffee. I'd mix a heaping teaspoon of the caffeinated powder with boiling water from a hot pot and add the milk to sweeten the mixture. I'd take the warm brew and a few plain biscuits to bed with me to eat before I read myself to sleep. All this—from bath to bed—was done in the cold, for by then the temperature would be in the low fifties Fahrenheit, which felt like freezing.

I'd do all this stealthily, so as not to disturb Angela, and she never complained (though she must have been awakened by my rustling about). One night we both jumped up wide awake, screaming and hugging each other: "Rats, rats!" someone was shouting. Roshan had warned us about them. Falling asleep was hard enough without having to worry about pests. A few years earlier, I'd lain awake all night in the bedroom of a house in Harlem, in New York City, in fear of one of the dreaded vermin. At Waverly, I'd lie awake under a painting of the bleeding sacred heart of Jesus, which disturbed me. There were pictures of holy scenes on walls throughout our living quarters and the schoolrooms. I had had enough of these in Catholic schools when we got them on holy cards as prizes for good work.

When we heard that the rodent had attacked—someone had felt one tug on her hair over the pillow—Angela and I moved our metal-framed beds out from the wall, got in, and pulled the covers tightly around us and over our heads and waited for sleep to come. The next morning, the bearer made some noisy gesture to show that he had taken care of the problem, but I didn't believe him. Counting my blessings that I didn't have to worry about my curly tresses spilling over my pillow, from that night on, as I did for the lizards—and harkening back to my childhood when practicing what to do in case of a nuclear attack—I "tucked" and covered!

One day I got a letter from Francis. "Why have you joined the convent, Judith?" he asked; I could almost see him throwing up his hands in exasperation. Replying to him after putting it off for days, I tried to explain the transformation that living in India was having on me and that teaching and living in a convent was not the same as joining one, but the right words failed me. I could see how my old friends would assume, to borrow from Shakespeare, I'd gotten thee (myself) to a nunnery. I told him I was seeing someone else; the proverbial Dear John letter was excruciating to write.

Teaching at Waverly made me appreciate the skills required of trained teachers. While I did my best, I didn't have the preparation to do my job. I figured this out during the first week in the two very different but equally challenging classes I taught: seventh form English literature class in which I covered *David Copperfield* by Charles Dickens and KG (kindergarten) in which I assisted the head teacher, Mother Agnes.

Unlike my experience of being taught by nuns for twelve years where the title of "Mother" was reserved for the mother superior who was the director of a convent, at Waverley all the nuns went by this title. For me, "Mother" meant my mother; and having to call all the sisters by this title didn't sit well with me.

Fortunately, the nuns didn't interfere with my seventh form teaching; however, it might have been better if they had. While I looked forward to guiding the students through Dickens's tale, their knowledge of English was too low for them to comprehend the meaning. Of thirty girls, only one was up to the task, and she wasn't very interested. Most of the others were daughters of families, mostly Sikhs, living in Thailand. They were at Waverley to get a convent education to make them more eligible for marriage. They should have been in a course of English as a foreign language, not in one demanding higher-than-average proficiency and based on a Cambridge syllabus.

To make matters worse, their lack of readiness made them shy and unresponsive, to the point that I spent most of the hour reading to them from the book. As the class was in the afternoon after lunch, some of them would fall asleep as I intoned Dickens's intricate Victorian prose. This made me more frustrated and feeling that I was reading them a bedtime story. One day as I was narrating the section in which Davy is told how his mother and her newborn baby died, I couldn't help but shed a few tears myself, and when I looked up, all the girls were crying too!

The only girl who showed understanding of the English demanded by the course was the one who feigned interest during class, a Punjabi who also seemed to be biding her time. Good-natured and quick to smile, I liked her despite trying not to show favoritism. She had a big heart and would speak up during lessons more to encourage me, it seemed, than because she cared about *David Copperfield*. When I was monitoring the class on the playground as the students got to go for their "tuck" breaks to buy sweets at the school snack shack, this girl would stand next to me and get me to talk to her. Try as I did to resist her attempts, as I knew that I was going to have to give her low marks for her schoolwork, I finally softened up and made small talk with her one day. Not a beauty and rather chubby with fly away curly hair, reminding me of myself at her age, she reached down into her sack of nibbles and forged ahead to keep up the conversation. She offered me a chewy chocolate and caramel Five Star Bar after I'd told her of my love of the luscious flavors. Weak-willed as I was, I accepted the bribe!

The KG class was challenging and fun. The children liked me and at that young age were willing to try whatever I came up with. A large class of twenty-four, it included boys from the town as well as girls from boarding. On my first day at Waverley, I had been taken on a tour of the dormitories and was touched by the sight of the five- and six-year-olds away from their parents in the dormitory. Children everywhere are wondrous to look at, and Indian children, with their diverse heritage, can be gorgeous. The older children were also joys to behold. Some of the seventh formers included several of Chinese descent. They intrigued me as I was just being exposed to East Asia in those days.

A rather tall girl with translucent skin and cherry cheeks had long jet hair, which she wore in braids looped up at her ears. In keeping with her Sikh genes, strands of black hair covered her arms, and I found her beguiling to look at. When I'd ask her name, she'd say in perfectly practiced English, "My name is Naa-rip—jeet," quite a performance for her tongue and for my ears.

And there was Sanjay, another dark grape-eyed, rosy-faced cherub. He was only four and too young for the school but somehow had been accepted. His grandfather would walk with him up the hill in the mornings to the classroom, which was in its own cottage. He'd come early and immediately hunt for me wherever I was in the large room, which was fully lit by the morning sunlight let in by the wide windows that wrapped around it. "Good morning, Miss," he'd say, tugging on my floral-printed *sari*. Of course I wanted to scoop him up into my arms, but that was against the rules.

Sanjay would cry when he couldn't keep up with the others in drawing or simple pencil work, probably because the muscles in his fingers were not yet fully coordinating with his thoughts. One day he got so frustrated that he scribbled all over the picture he was trying to sketch, and it turned into a maze of lines. All the children started laughing at him and calling him a baby, making him cry. I wanted to put my arms around him and tell him that everything was all right, but all I could do was encourage him. I had to be careful; young as he was, I had to get him to show results. A few years later, I fought hard not to be devastated when I heard that he had slipped into the gutter that ran along the hilly road as his grandfather brought him to school during the monsoon rain, and drowned.

I had been going to Delhi on most weekends. I'd take a bus to Dehradun and from there go to Meerut, from where I'd hire a seat in a car. I would be the only woman riding with four male passengers but never had any problems in those days when Eve teasing (harassing women in public) was publicly shamed. I'd stay at the Y hostel in New Delhi, which was very inexpensive.

Meeting up with Sunder, I got to hear about the ad campaigns he was working on. One, selling soap, showed that Arabic numerals had actually originated in ancient India, a revelation to me. He was fascinated by my Western culture, and I, by his Indian; however, I soon found that I had been exposed to more of his country than he. He was a lost soul even in those days when his youth and energy hid it. He pretty much thought of himself as Scottish and stood out because he didn't look or act Indian enough. I came to understand these conflicts within him as we got to know each other. Yet, the question of his marriage never left us. All I could do was hope for the future. I denied that it couldn't work out for us and looked upon my situation as normal, which obviously, it wasn't: coming down from the Himalayas, staying in New Delhi, and returning to my mountain retreat — all over two days.

Back at Waverley, I continued to explore Mussoorie. One weekend I hiked the fourteen or so miles down to Dehradun with a fellow Fulbrighter, a redheaded young woman from Oklahoma, who was visiting. Not having hiked or camped before, I jumped at her idea of going to the next town this way. *How hard could it be to walk fourteen miles?* I thought in an excess of confidence. Not halfway into the trek and my feet were the sorest they'd been in my life. While I completed the journey, I never again attempted even a fourth of that distance in the kind of thin-soled shoes I was wearing.

Another time, I joined the other teachers on an excursion with senior students to Kempty Water Falls, fifteen miles from Mussoorie. We had a relaxing picnic and fun climbing around the hills at the foot of the foaming cascade, which formed a spectacular panorama 1,364 meters above sea level, with the mountains in the background. But the occasion was marred by a freak accident that prompted me to make changes in my life.

Agnes, the Anglo-Indian teacher who wore Western dress and was aloof, fell out of the bus! She had been standing apart from the rest of us, leaning against the door. As the vehicle was struggling to bend sharply up the hill, the pressure of her body catapulted the passageway open, and she barreled down the slopes. Although quite shaken up, she was miraculously unharmed. No one said what they were thinking—that she had brought it on herself by remaining apart. I was startled by it all. We all acted like what had happened to her was a common occurrence. I may have asked her if she was all right, but no one expressed emotion about the close call she'd had. That got me to thinking. *If I had fallen from a bus, I'd like people to think of me kindly, like they did my father. I'd like to be missed.* The next week, I got a letter from Sunder telling me that he had found me a position at a well-known private school in Delhi. I said goodbye to my Shangri-La home and prepared to say hello to New Delhi.

Before leaving, I had a special last class with my KG students. Among them were two boys named Tsering, both were Tibetan, from the settlement close by, established after their families were forced out of what is now China in the late fifties. One of the boys wore a red woolen pullover with holes in it and had candles of snot running down his nose. He was a refugee. The other boy, who sat at the same desk, was dressed in a dark blue blazer with matching pants, pale blue shirt, and tie. The picture of health, he looked like the son of one of the leaders of the Tibetan settlement, which he was.

One day something sacred happened. As the children were coloring, one of them whispered in the dulcet tones of a child's awe, "Miss, look at Tsering's!" We all stopped and stared at the impressionistic vision of dancing yellow wildflowers that Tsering the orphan had created.

With teacher colleagues at Waverley

20

Delhi Delights and Delusions

With Permission of Rajni Kumar, Founder, Springdales School

Delhi was like an oven when I arrived in early July 1969 to begin my new job of teaching at Springdales School on Pusa Road. A well-known, progressive English-medium school that charged a fee, it was founded by Rajni Kumar in 1955. An Englishwoman married to an Indian lawyer, she had established this new type of school that stressed internationalism and diversity. The prospect of being part of such a forward-looking venture excited me, and I couldn't wait to begin teaching there.

During the first two weeks of moving to Delhi, I rented a room in the home of an Anglo-Burmese lady, whom I'll call Mrs. Buckley. Needless to say, I had been anxious about finding a place to live, and although I was glad to find a room, I was a little intimidated by my new landlady. Yet I had no choice but to stay in her home if I was going to begin teaching at Springdales and living in New Delhi. Mrs. Buckley had pseudo-British airs. Her conversation was full of snide remarks about Indians: "these people" and "they're dirty" rolled off her tongue. Despite the threadbare condition of her flat and her worries about money, which she shared with me all the time — "Sugar costs," she'd say as she put the bone china bowl on the table, and "Tea is so expensive"—nonetheless, she seemed grateful to have me as a boarder and took my rent in advance. After the first day, I went to the Y for breakfast to avoid provoking her. Another lodger, an Indian man who worked as a bank clerk, got a more spacious and better furnished room than I did. Mine had only a soot-colored rod-iron bed. I had to put my bags in the corner on the floor as there was no rack or chest of drawers. Mrs. Buckley wore broad-brimmed hats entwined with ribbons and floral cotton dresses as if the British were still around. Calling me "Maude," she talked to me in a demeaning tone, like I, not she, was from another era.

I stayed out of her way, went out in the evenings, until, thank God, Mrs. Kumar invited me to live in the apartment on the roof of her house. It was similar to the top of our house in Nagpur, but in Delhi, was referred to as the *boshoti*, a Bengali word meaning settlement. This proposed living arrangement was almost too good to be true, and I'd get a decent salary to boot! (I had a hard time making it on the smaller one at Waverley.) Lydia Clark, the same age as me, was also coming to teach at Springdales, from England, sponsored by the Society of Friends. We could share the flat, each having our own ample-sized room and a kitchen; I'd have a roommate and a friend, lifelong, as it turned out. Before that good news, however, I almost didn't live to see that happy day.

Having put me off from taking a bath for a few days after I arrived, Mrs. Buckley relented, but she insisted I wait until afternoon when the water would be hot. I did, and when I walked into her dim and dank Western-style shower, the metal pipes were exposed, and the floor was a solid surface with no tile or rubber mat to stand on. I had missed the warning that she said she had given me, and when I turned on the taps, "ZAAM!" an electric current jolted my body. I don't think my hair stood straight up, but I was shocked. Howling for help, I tried in vain to dislodge myself from the stinging suction that glued me to the ground. After a few minutes, Mrs. Buckley came to turn off the deadly running water but left me to rinse off the soap by myself. That's when I decided to get out of there.

The Kumars welcomed me to Springdales in the best tradition of Indian and British graciousness; Lydia, though reserved, as the English can be, seemed like someone I could get along with. Her direct, can-do attitude was like an ice-cold drink on a dripping-with-sweat day. Laser focused and organized, she would listen, sum up a situation, and then get on with doing something about it or telling me what she thought. And she was a good cook who made us tasty meals in the evenings. I must have come across as a bit of a know-it-all to her, I concluded, as we reminisced about those days in recent years. Still, we hit it off and lost no time making our situation work.

Someone had told me that the Kumars were communists, but if that was true, I thought, as I got to know them, it was of the armchair variety. In my year with them I was put in the position of having to do two things only slightly having to do with the Soviet Union: One was taking charge of the Russian Folk Singing Club. The second was seeing the well-known Communist Party member and former freedom fighter Krishna Menon, who visited the school one day. Towering above everyone with his enormous height and dressed in a Nehru jacket and cap, the former freedom fighter was someone to see; he made me want to know more about India's history and struggle for independence.

Except for those two obvious nods to the United States' Cold War foe, I would describe Mr. and Mrs. Kumar as democrats who had come out of the Nehru social justice tradition. Mr. Kumar was a well-known barrister and judge of the Supreme Court. The couple had met, so I came to know recently, in the thirties while both were at the London School of Economics. At that time, LSE was assumed to be a nesting space for left-leaning political thought. Rajni embraced Indian culture unreservedly when she left her native England and came to marry Yudister. She seemed determined to educate young minds to prepare them for the newly independent India and the changing modern world that it was opening up to. I wasn't surprised to learn that her dedication came from her Gandhian spirit. As a principal, she was forthright and strict, but sympathetic, and she always smiled.[18]

Their daughter Jo was a pleasant teenager who showed me more than one random act of kindness. She had the most haunting, sympathetic eyes. Mrs. Kumar, Lydia, and I all wore *saris* to school and must have presented a posse of determined Western women set on pouring knowledge into curious children's minds. The Kumars made their household staff available to us from time to time as needed, and we rode to school with Mrs. Kumar in her chauffeured car.

Most valuable was the chance I got to know Mr. Kumar's American brother-in-law, a humanitarian who worked for CARE, the foreign relief organization, and his wife, Mr. Kumar's kindhearted, fascinating sister. Diagnosed with cancer, she came to stay in the last days of her heroic life as a humanitarian. Being in the presence of such a woman who was facing death squarely left a lasting, positive impression on me.

---

18   See online, *Gulf News, People,* "The Woman behind the Legend," April 17, 2013

Roll call at Springdales

Vultures stood guard on the walls behind us mornings at the school assembly outside. I was afraid they'd swoop down on my head as they did when they snatched potato crisps from the hands of an unsuspecting child during recess. Springdales put me in the middle of the action of a wide-ranging, bustling scene, more like a well-off public school in the United States. Refreshingly forward-looking, it was a change from the solemn, traditional Catholic convent and college where I'd taught and studied. The students and my colleagues were urbanites in a fast-paced, powerful, growing world capital. This made me smarten myself up. I tried to look and act sharper.

Mrs. Kumar blended well in her adopted culture, but I never felt that she wasn't British, and with Lydia coming from England too, I was thrilled and threatened. Thrilled because after studying English literature for so long, I could now learn directly about it, for I was surrounded by people who came from the culture that spawned it; threatened because of that old colonial complex that I, like many Americans, had.

Given U.S. involvement in Vietnam, anti-American sentiment and skepticism about U.S. expansion in Asia must have been rampant in India. Yet I never felt it or had it talked about to my face. Once, I did get a call from the U.S. consulate: "Call your family," the Middle American–sounding voice scolded. Increasing attacks on U.S. forces and broadcasts of America losing South Vietnam had been shown on TV since the Tet Offensive had begun in January 1968 while I was still in Baltimore. Nearly two years later, as Christmas of 1969 neared when I was in New Delhi, and war raged in Southeast Asia, I had reconnected with my family through letters and cards.

Not too long after, Mother was probably talking over the phone with her brother, Uncle William, about my being in India. That must have provoked a hysterical reaction: *Sissy's over there!* they were probably thinking seeing the Vietnam battles shown on TV every night. Uncle William must have called the State Department to inquire about my safety. At first I was a bit embarrassed that my uncle, whom I thought the world of, had assumed I was in danger. India was far away from the fighting in Southeast Asia. With time I came to feel their overreaction as the strong embrace of love.

Years later, I'd understand how important it is for Americans overseas to register with the U.S. consulate; but back then, I didn't. I told myself that I would never be caught going into an American embassy. The sting of antiwar protests, the draft, boys in my childhood neighborhood who joined the military and some, like Andrea's boyfriend Butch, getting killed in Vietnam; and those who avoided going, like a fellow Fulbrighter who had asked me to write his draft board attesting to his conscientious objector status—all these left a bad taste for the U.S. government in my mouth.

While U.S. foreign policy wasn't in my purview, being among those who had been English-educated did keep me on my toes about representing America and, when my back was to the wall, put me on the defensive. This may have been why I was glad to be starting at Springdales during the opportune time of the moon landing. During the week following July 21,

1969, the day Neil Armstrong took that giant leap for mankind, I took my geography class to see an exhibition on the historic first at the American embassy's cultural center. (I was already violating my rule of not going close to the mission, but I told myself that the American Cultural Center didn't count.) The monumental landing on the moon made me beam with pride renewing my faith in America. Within ten years, I'd eat my words of never going to the embassy: I'd be working there. Within twenty, I'd meet Neil Armstrong!

Teaching geography to sixth formers, also one of my tasks, took only an hour of my time per week, the rest of the time I taught English to seventh, eighth, and ninth forms, roughly equivalent to the same grades in the United States. The students were as full of life and talkative as Americans, or growing children anywhere. I was homeroom teacher to an eighth-form class. They could be a handful. I was called to the administrator's office more than once to account for their boisterous behavior. The worst was when one of them stood on top of my desk while I was out of the room, and I was called to task for not controlling my class.

Nevertheless, the students liked me, and most of them were sincere learners. I had to take stacks of copybooks (notebooks) home with me to correct their homework nearly every afternoon. At thirty students a class and four classes, that got to be a heavy load in more than just sheer weight. Yet when I'd come upon work that students had put effort into, I was happy and satisfied that I was getting through to them. I met one of my students, Dilip Kuchibhatla, a few years ago at the World Bank in Washington DC, where he was an officer. As we reminisced about his eighth-form class, I was brimming with pride in having played a miniature part in getting him to believe in himself to achieve his high level of education and attain the position he did. In an e-mail he said, "I still remember how you liked my short essay and gave me a 10/10 . . ." He'd done it as homework in his copybook.

With former Springdales student Dilip Kuchibhatla at World Bank, 2012

Heading up the Russian Folk Singing Club was something I had to take a deep breath, jump in, and do. Refusing to do it would have caused misunderstanding, but agreeing to do it made me worry that it would come back to haunt me in the future. I'd filled out forms for the Peace Corps Internship and for the visa to India and knew about that disqualifying "Have you ever been a member of the Communist Party?" question. Plus I had no familiarity with Russian folk music!

When I shared my doubts with the senior instructor in charge, she told me not to worry and gave me a folder, a tape, and copies of song lyrics; some were in Russian with the words written phonetically in English in the Roman alphabet. Two titles that stick in my mind are, one, "Soviet Land," which I guided the children to sing in English and went like this:

Sovietland so dear to every toiler,
peace and progress build their hopes on thee.
There's no land the whole world over,
where man walks the earth so proud and free.[19]

The other, in Russian, was a tongue twister and full of catchy slogans with exclamation marks. Over the years I remembered the tune but forgot the lyrics. One day not long ago, in America when a Russian-born technician came to service my home heating and air-conditioning, I asked him if he'd ever heard of the song. I tried to sing it for him in my best, but very bad-sounding, imitation of Russian. To my surprise, he recognized it immediately. In good Russian, it sounds like, *"Klich pionera segda boj gatof . . . !"* Roughly translated, "Pioneers, always be ready!" "Oh," he said, "sounds like something we used to sing in the Young Pioneers!"[20]

Halloween rolled around, and the school staged a haunted house and all-day fun fair for the students, with booths, games, and theme park snacks, like cotton candy and popcorn. I'd not had a day of pure play like this since being sprayed with colored water during Holi months ago, and I thought it was wonderful that the school was celebrating a popular American tradition. Used to seeing the students wearing their gray-and-red uniforms, I was glad to see them dressed in costumes. One sixth former came as an astronaut, the "getup" all homemade with cardboard, plastic, and aluminum foil. Her parents escorted her around before they took her home that afternoon, her dad grinning with pride, for she won first prize. Best of all, I got to be a witch!

In impersonating an evil enchantress, I made scary-sounding announcements over the loudspeaker. I jumped at the chance and had a blast in the shady-as-night dress and tall conical hat with a stiff brim that I'd stitched, glued, and pinned together. "Come to the *haa-aun-ted house, the haa-aun-ted . . . house,*" I shrieked in my best Wicked Witch of the West voice.

19 See "Memoirs of a Dutiful Red Daughter," by Amirah Inglis, *Australian Left Review*, Nov. 1987, p. 38, for reflections on this and other 1930s Soviet rallying songs.
20 Translation, courtesy of Alex Orlov, Russian born and raised, now my neighbor.

That October, I was a featured contributor to the *Springdalian* magazine: "An American Teacher 'Sounds Off' about Indian Students."[21] Extremely direct in its tone, my commentary talks about the preference of Indian students to go abroad after their studies and offers the view that they should stay in their own country to build it up. "In this Moon Age patriotism is 'out' among young people in the world . . . Indian students overlook the fact that theirs is a democracy in its infancy . . . [India] has a terrific potential for utilising [sic] student involvement . . . Students can say . . . we the students of today have an obligation to clean up the politics of the future." You'd never think I was on my way to becoming a tactful-talking diplomat from reading that article, and you'd see how open-minded Springdales was in wanting to show uncensored points of view.

A raw chill came over me as the lights of Divali settled into the twilight of a North Indian winter. Sunder and I had been going out for a year—restaurants, dancing, talking—but still no resolution to our dilemma. To be fair, he never "led me on"; he was clear about not seeing when he would be free to spend his life with me. I was sure that he would and that somehow things would work out for us. As he was rapidly advancing in advertising and had moved to two different companies since we met, he was secure in his career in India. He expressed no desire to go to the States, didn't ask me to help him get a visa, and seemed to see his future in his own country. That appealed to me, for as I had suggested to the students, Indians should stake their future in their own country, and I could imagine living the rest of my life there.

At the same time, we found we were fellow travelers in that we were different among the very different: He with a Scottish mother (who had been totally segregated from the rest of his family) and Kashmiri Brahmin father; me with my African American background. We were both Catholics, although he only nominally. And we had both been educated in the same style: me with the Ursulines, and he with the Jesuits at Saint Xavier's in Bombay. We both reveled in that big open city by the sea and spent more than one time together there when I was still in Nagpur. Those differences between us kept us interested in each other. And as Sunder had spent his childhood in Shimla, which I had visited, and since I had lived in Mussoorie, we had a fondness for hill stations in common. We mixed with Sunder's associates in public and a few times in their homes. All were

---

21   *The Springdalian*, October 1969, p. 4

reputable people who seemed to accept me. Ours was not an "American Girl Comes to India and Goes Native" tale. Rather, it was an "as old as time" love story.

By Christmas, Lydia's fiancé, James White, was visiting, and I hated that I couldn't keep up with Lydia and him, for we had such good times and spontaneous laughter, but inevitably I was heading for—what Lydia called, and I soon borrowed the word—the loo, the toilet! Looking down from the rooftop flat where we lived, I gazed at the stars wondering if and when the mornings of sickness would end. A couple of weeks later, I went to a doctor and found out I was indeed going to have a baby.

For someone who believed in happy endings, I was beside myself with worry. Weeks passed, and all I could keep down were quarts of Kwality vanilla ice cream, which I'd eat as one big snowy block. The smell of butter sickened me. I couldn't even bear the sight of chocolate. Since as a child I had lived close to a chocolate factory on Preston Street, I'd harbored a vision of eating endless bowls of the divine concoction, but now I couldn't stomach it. By the second visit to the doctor, I'd lost so much weight that until she examined me, finding everything was fine, she thought I may have lost the baby.

I walked around in a fog for days. Not proceeding with the birth was presented as an option, but I instantly rejected the thought. I knew deep down that I could never get rid of Sunder's child. I loved him and wanted his baby. As time dragged on, I pulled my *sari* securely around me and went to see another doctor. She proposed that I have the baby and leave it at an orphanage. Thoughts of ragged street urchins bombarded my head; I found the scenario so horrific that I went into a gloomy spiral of lying on my bed weeping, to the extent that Lydia cautioned me about taking care of my mental health. She was my link to reality; without her, I do not know what I would have done.

She got in touch with Missi, in Calcutta by then, and got her to come to stay with me for a while as I went through my long nights of despair. Lydia had proposed that I go to stay with her mother, a doctor in Bath, England, have the child, and stay there while I got my footing. As I regained my strength, I knew I had to return to America to face reality, but it was comforting to know I had the alternative of going to Lydia's home.

Throughout it all, I went to class, never missing a day at Springdales, working well with the other teachers, even making new friends, like Chandra Bose from Bengal and Mrs. Sen from Kerala. I didn't like having to keep my pregnancy a secret, but I'd seen Mother give up the job she loved, teaching in the Louisville Catholic schools, when she was expecting Helene. She went on to have Rodney and Evelyn and, because of the unfair rule, hadn't been able to return to her profession. Like my family, most Indians had economic needs, but Indian women had babies all the time; they'd deliver, and when the child was walking, they'd take him or her to the field with them.

On the other hand, there was the shame, the fitting the stereotype that I hated to be compared to. Growing up as I did, I knew a lot about shotgun marriages, the hush-hush, and the girls who were teenagers one day and turned into grown women the next. Sunder had said he was glad about the baby, but then he seemed to distance himself from talking about a solution for the future. We hoped to be together someday, but *when* was my constant query. My dream would come true in the future, but as time went on, I truly couldn't see it happening.

In the meantime, I had a plan B. After I got over the shock of what I'd let happen, I could see clearer. Interested in someone with my academic and South Asian experience, Dr. Charles Heimsath had invited me to do graduate work in South Asian studies at a new Center for South Asian Studies that he was heading up at American University in Washington DC. I wrote to him accepting the offer but asking if I could begin after a year. He agreed, and thus I decided to return home, have the baby, and earn some money to move to Washington to begin graduate school in September 1971.

Springdales staff; second row,
from left, Lydia and Mrs. Kumar

With Lydia and
Springdales colleagues

With James and Jo Kumar

With students

Throughout my bluest time in Delhi, when I was well along in my pregnancy, I went through a period of desperation, but I never thought of killing myself. Years before, a priest had knocked that idea out of my head forever: "That's the coward's way out," he said, and I certainly never wanted to see myself or be seen as a coward.

By mid-May, the time was nearing for my already-extended round-trip return ticket to expire; if I didn't use it, I'd have to pay a hefty sum to change my departure date again. Lydia lent me the $230 I needed to use the ticket before it expired. After a lot of hassle in getting an exit visa—here Lydia again played a pivotal role, putting up with the attentions of an obnoxious member of parliament to help me get my papers—it was time to say goodbye to Springdales and to India. My colleagues honored me with a large farewell party, which meant so much and inspired me to carry on.

Sunder and I had talked, but I couldn't see a resolution of my status in his plans, although I did note that the last time we met, he brought along a woman who worked with him. *Was this backup a new girlfriend?*

An American from California I had met who was living in a commune invited me to move in with her. While her blonde curls and warm smile lifted my spirits, I couldn't see myself becoming a hippie and declined her invitation. The Beatles were breaking up too. *Abbey Road*, their last long-playing record, lulled me to sleep those worrisome warm nights:

> Once there was a way to get back homeward . . .
> Sleep, pretty darling, do not cry.
> And I will sing a lullaby. Golden slumbers fill your eyes . . .
> You gonna carry that weight,
> carry that weight a long time . . .[22]

Sunder and I were to meet in a few days, but by then, I was on a flight for London, on my way home.

---

22 From "Golden Slumber/Carry That Weight" by John Lennon-Paul McCartney, 1969

III
Belonging

*"You are only free when you realize
you belong no place...
you belong every place -
no place at all..."*

MAYA ANGELOU

21

London at Last!

Life has a way of backing me into learning things. I should have gone to London before, but the chance came only after two years in India. Finally I would see the city of my childhood imagination. As I neared the roundabout in the neighborhood where James lived, the first thing I noticed were the gray stones of the buildings and the shiny black iron fences. The oval driveway also wasn't lost on me, nor were the welcoming hellos of his female flatmates, one of whom worked for the BBC. The coziness of their kitchen with the electric kettle full of water ready to be heated for a cup of tea anytime warmed me inside—literally and emotionally. Full of life as I veritably was, I was ready to fulfill a lifetime ambition to see as much as I could of England in only one week on my way home to America.

Lydia was staying a few months longer in India, but James had returned after his visit back at the start of the New Year 1970. Now meeting him again in late May in his country, he was the perfect guide for all of the sights that I had to see during my first time in the great city: the Tower of London where many, like Anne Boleyn, had had their heads chopped off. I felt I was at court when looking at the imperial state crown, scepter, and sword through the revolving glass display of the crown jewels. I had seen these first on television, in black and white, when they were placed on Elizabeth's head at her coronation in 1953. More than pomp and circumstance, taking in the scene on that warm day in 1970, I felt a rush of the ages: Beefeaters guarding the tower in bright orange-red and yellow, looked sharp; the Queen's Guards in royal red tunics, black trousers, and tall bearskin caps on watch in front of Buckingham Palace smartly marching in the Changing of the Guard.

I reverently walked through Westminster Abbey, stopping to take in the scene: I was standing over places where kings, queens, writers, and poets that I'd studied were buried and memorialized. Among the literati: Shakespeare, Robert Browning and Elizabeth Barrett Browning, William Wordsworth, and Henry James. Among the scientists: Isaac Newton and Charles Darwin. These shapers of the world I knew were resting beneath my feet and in the air I was breathing.

In addition to seeing the famous sights, I got to taste English delicacies I'd only read about. One day James drove north from London and stopped in York, three hours away, where we had tea with crumpets. The delicious light dough—tasting like sweet Southern biscuits—with a dollop of fresh cream and a teaspoon of golden honey rolled over my tongue.

Many visits to London since have crowded out memories of that first view of the splendid sights, but three remain fixed, so unique that they cannot go away:

One was a practical joke. All I had talked about was the poet Robert Browning. I had done my senior thesis on him and, with the confidence of a nearly twenty-four year old, considered myself somewhat of an authority. And by extension, Elizabeth Barrett, whose sonnets I had read and admired and whose story of getting to know Robert through his letters before meeting and marrying him was an ideal love story suited for a romantic like me. James took me to the famous address of her house on Wimpole Street[23] and bent over in stitches of laughter after I mounted the steps and stood in front of what was now a bank! An engraved placard indicated that the well-known house had once stood there. Disappointed. All my plans of London had centered on going to that house. James, though, ever full of fun, thought my bafflement hilarious.

The second unforgettable first experience had to do with—brace yourself—rhubarb! James dropped me at a movie theater, pressed some coins in my hand, and escorted me to the ticket window. I would watch a ninety-minute Sunday afternoon flick while he went to the baptism of a client's child. Settling into my seat, I was looking forward to a good movie, but as the film unfolded, the only word uttered throughout was "rhubarb."

---

23 See *The Barretts of Wimpole Street*, MGM film, 1934, and remake, also MGM, 1957.

Of course, I could see that it was a comedy—the others in the audience guffawed nonstop—but I couldn't understand the humor. After jumping into James's car when he picked me up, I told him what had happened, trying not to make him feel bad about it. He seemed as surprised as me and explained that rhubarb was a word for the mumbling of crowds in films. That was many years before I acquired a taste for Basil Fawlty and Hyacinth Bucket,[24] with that zany, nuanced British sense of humor.

The third revelation I had on my premier visit was a mind-opener: Westminster Abbey, where William and Kate wed in 2011, to name but one recent and historical moment there, is the sine qua non of what to see in this world capital. James, an Anglican, took me to the evensong service there that same Sunday after the rhubarb movie. James liked to carry on jokes and double entendres and was a little nonplussed by me. I was fascinated by him; Lydia I knew better after our intense time as roommates. I liked their Englishness, their authenticity, their reliability. After living in a former British colony, getting to know Brits and visiting London, my colonial complex was fading.

James, who studied (read, as they said), history at Oxford, referred to the Order of the Bath when he was explaining something historical at a museum, and while I took most of what he told me about England seriously, after the Wimpole Street prank, I had to watch what he said. That evening my eyes got bigger and my ears reddened as I heard the incredible: during the service, the vicar speaking from the lectern in the lofty hallowedness of the cathedral, the boy choristers in their cassocks sitting to the side, said, "And let us pray for the Order of the Bath."[25]

---

24 BBC television characters

25 According to the Online Encyclopedia Britannica, the Most Honorable Order of the Bath was an order of British knighthood established by King George I in 1725. In the eleventh century bathing was probably introduced in a religious context with knighthood, although the tradition goes back even farther, to the court of Charlemagne in the eighth century.

22

Home Again

Neighborhood girls in front of Sheppard Square home

Chappals on my feet, I slid into the Kennedy terminal after getting off the flight from London. A black cloth bag with mirrorwork rimmed in orange dangled from my right shoulder, and I was pulling a red Samsonite Royal Traveler carry-on case with my left hand. My lighthearted mood was so obvious that it caused a man in a business suit with a briefcase walking beside me on the tarmac to say, "I wish I was as relaxed as you look." That made me feel good; I *was* relaxed, did feel confident and happy that I was back in the USA. The week in London had done me good. As the plane landed, I'd been taken aback a bit when looking out of the passenger jet window and seeing an African American baggage handler in, of all things, a cowboy hat, removing luggage from under the hold. Was this New York? Was I ready for the America of the new decade?

Things got scary when the customs inspector spying the plastic bag of talcum powder in my carry-on reached in, took some, sifted it through his fingers, and taking a whiff declared, "You can't bring this into the United States!" Realizing that he thought it was drugs, I heard my voice faintly telling him what it was, but he wasn't listening and confiscated it. I did, however, muster up a plea when he was running his fingers over the large smooth fruit pits in a plastic bag: "Oh, please these are the mango seeds I've saved for my little brother." The good-looking blue-uniformed, bronze-toned man gave me a half smile as if to say, "You must be kidding," and took away Rodney's gift.

Francis was waiting for me in the reception hall; we hugged and didn't say much. There was so much to say, yet we couldn't say anything. We talked over Cokes for a while and then parted as we had begun: friends. "There is nothing half so sweet in life as love's young dream," wrote Irish poet Thomas Moore. The verse is from a book Francis had given me.

I got a flight to Louisville later that day and arrived to the open arms of my accepting, big family. Almost six years had passed since I'd left Louisville for college that day in August 1964. Although I'd been back many times, on that first departure I was full of hope and was certain I was leaving home for good. Now, in May 1970, I felt like I was on the bottom, overwhelmed and somewhat defeated. But I was thankful that unlike the popular sentiment, I could go home again. And the love of my family who seemed genuinely happy to have me in their midst gave me courage to face the future. To their undiminishing credit, they didn't probe me for answers about my situation. Still, I couldn't bring myself to tell the whole truth outright, for fear that they'd be too disappointed in me, for living up, or down, as some might say, to the stereotype of an unwed mother. Of course, this was my problem. What I had, I later learned, was probably a messiah complex — the belief that I was responsible for things beyond my control — and also a lot of survivor's guilt for having benefited from great experiences that my family hadn't shared.

While I was still getting back on my feet, I lived in my own reality to get through the bad patch until I could face facts. I grew out of that blur by dealing with each day as it came, and I'm thankful to my family for going along with my make-believe. Their unflinching emotional support kept me sane then and since.

My family, Christmas–New Year's Eve 1972; back, from left: Mother, Helene (with tall hair), Billy, Andrea holding her firstborn Colby, Anita with baby Raymond, Rekha, and Evelyn "Poochie" holding Dancing Bear

Mother, at age forty-nine, was still adjusting to widowhood while raising my youngest brother and sisters. Billy had graduated from Louisville Male High School in 1962, the same school that had sparked the KKK to burn the cross in our Kentucky Street front yard. He was with the Department of Commerce, in the Census Bureau, in Jeffersonville, Indiana. Andrea, three years my junior, had finished high school—Male

High, in fact, which was by then integrated. She was working and had married Rick Allen. With her golden hair and good figure, she looked like a magazine snapshot of a typical young American woman. Anita, five years my junior, was also out of high school and was working and living away from home. Her partner, Raymond Cobb, and I hit it off right away, as I did with Andrea's husband Rick. They were almost like brothers to me. When I looked at Anita, I saw myself, especially in her expressive broad face; however, being taller, she looked more like I wished I'd looked. Helene, in pigtails with a radiant smile and big marble-brown eyes, was twelve and the perfect younger sister. Mother told me how Helene so reminded her of me when she looked at herself in the mirror in her school uniform. Rodney was ten and had a lot to say about everything, among which was that on the night of my high school prom, seeing me decked out in white, he'd thought I had gotten married! Evelyn, Poochie, was six. She was the babe in Daddy's arms when I took the train to Baltimore six years ago, and though she was about to enter first grade and was talkative and had her own personality, we all still considered her the baby. All my siblings and my mother welcomed me back home and helped me prepare for and take care of my own baby. I wouldn't have made it as a mother and gotten back on my feet as fast as I did without their steadfast caring.

Poochie, Helene, and Rodney, growing up while I was away

Summer evenings, while waiting for the baby to come, I'd take long walks from our home in the Sheppard Square housing projects to downtown Louisville's Fourth Street, on sidewalks I had trodden as a teen when I was going to Ursuline Academy. Poochie would come with me. We'd get as far as WAVE television station, where we could rest, but when we'd head back on the two-mile journey, she'd beg me to carry her. "I'm already carrying one child," I'd tell her. "How can I carry two?" She'd look at me with her big, liquid brown eyes surrounded by two ponytails of ash blonde hair that set off her face, and my heart would melt. Of five girls, she most resembled Mother. As I said, she was still a baby herself in our family of seven sisters and brothers; but she had been the first to show me the sweeping changes in race that had happened since 1968: "I'm black, and I'm proud!" she proclaimed, lifting her light-skinned right fist in a black power salute. *Was I ready for this new America?*

Poochie in 1970 when I returned from India

As a new kind of "lady in waiting," I spent most of my time sitting in my mother's living room in a comfortable chair, watching TV or listening to Dionne Warwick songs on the record player. Her voice became an anthem of determination for me. "Don't Make Me Over" and "Promises, Promises" kept me going that summer.

One evening my family left me alone after preparing and leaving a delicious steak dinner in the oven. When one of them called to ask if I had enjoyed it, I heard a voice come out of my head saying "It was terrible! The beef tasted bad and the vegetables were inedible." When they returned it was obvious I was in much pain. Before I knew it, I was off to Louisville General Hospital, three days early, due to complications. During that time I was in a bed in a room with three other women who also had special pregnancy issues. We were equally of black and white races. No more going to the hospital for coloreds; Louisville hospitals had at last integrated. One woman, a mother of three, had an Rh-negative blood type; she had to go through painful pricks and procedures before giving birth. Another woman, in her early forties, had only one leg and, naturally, needed special attention. She was having her eighth child. Like me, she was Catholic, and like my mother, she had many children. The other African American woman, besides me, was preparing to have the birth of her child induced, as she was way overdue. She joked that she was going to beat the baby every day because of the grief he was giving her—she was sure it was a boy, in those days when one couldn't know the child's sex in advance—by taking his time being born. She did not mean what she said. When rushed to the hospital because I had begun hemorrhaging, I felt so bad that I insulted my family about the meal they had taken time to prepare for me. Now, feeling better, I was being monitored to make sure that my child was okay. Getting to know the other expectant mothers further prepared me for the huge change my life was about to undergo.

A bad taste to the sweet memory of my daughter's birth was the physician who attended me. The caring doctor, whom I had been consulting at the prenatal clinic, was not available that Friday night when I went into labor; the one on duty was a hellish healer, rude and insulting. He was young and good-looking with dark hair, but he had such a flat Southern, country accent. I, not ever having had close contact with someone like him—certainly not as close as we were on that night, and having been away from the South for so long—was terrified. When he stuck what felt like a hat pin into me, a needle to break the sac cradling my baby, the water burst forth. The rush of wetness startled me, for I didn't know what was going on. My regular doctor had been comforting and reassuring; he would have kept me informed throughout. This man was beside himself in the mess he had of forcing my body to give forth life. "Having a baby is not easy!" he scolded when I moaned.

His outlandish bedside manner must have set a new low. As uncool as it sounds in this day of natural childbirth, thank God, finally during that long, hard night, someone stuck another needle into my spine, and when I came to, on August 8, 1970, a little after 7:00 a.m., I saw a tall round-faced nurse in a gray uniform, grinning from ear to ear, holding a living doll in her right arm. For a split second, I thought: *what a beautiful mother and child.* But then I snapped into consciousness and heard her say, "It's a beautiful girl," and I realized this was my daughter.

Maybe it was the freezing cold of the delivery room or the sight of the doctor hovering over me with his hands on my abdomen, but when I heard him tell me to massage my own stomach, it didn't boost my morale. I knew the practice: women in India had their stomachs massaged immediately after birth to encourage the skin to snap back and tighten into place, but I was too confused to move, and the doctor was quite disgusted with me. It wasn't like in a movie when everyone is all aglow and the nurse puts the baby in your arms. In August 1970, hospitals all over America were bursting with babies. Although much lower in scale, the explosion of newborns was like when I'd entered the world just after the war. Hospital beds in some maternity wards spilled into the aisles.

As soon as I woke up from my first nap, the nurse's aide suggested I go to the bathroom on my own; this rather startled me, but I waddled off, still dazed and drowsy. Of course, I later understood that getting the blood circulating was important, but confronting the filth in the restroom turned my stomach. No one had cleaned it in a while. There were feces all over the place, and I had a hard time figuring out how to wash my hands. I felt so clammy and wanted to take a shower, but I discarded the idea, feeling I was in a sea of germs, and limped back to bed. The hospital in Nagpur was immaculate by comparison. I spent one night in that Louisville hospital of horrors. Thank God when Anita came. Since delivering her, I first saw my daughter through the window—after Anita had viewed her.

The next morning, while waiting for the "good doctor" to come by to let me know I could leave, I had the disheartening experience of hearing him bad-mouth the woman in the bed next to me, the white, Catholic woman with one leg: "You got to cut this nonsense out . . .," he was saying. I felt so embarrassed for her. Finally, Rekha—whom I named after my friend in Mussoorie, the skating champion—was brought to me, and I got to hold this wondrous, warm, pulsating ball of life for the first time. She was so still and so perfect; her lazy left eye was only half open, making her look as if she was slyly checking me out. I told her that I'd be good to her if she just cooperated with me. I think she heard me. She was the best baby; and like people did with all infants, everyone wanted to look or hold her. She was so quiet in the first days after I brought her home that everyone kept teasing me, saying, "Doesn't she cry?" until one night she let out a soft cackle.

When we left the hospital, Anita held Rekha as we descended the elevator, beaming as she cuddled her. But when we entered the lift, we were stunned by more unpleasantness: The woman who had been in the room with me and the other women before giving birth, the other black woman, was weeping uncontrollably. She told us that she had spotted what she thought was a problem with her newborn son and had asked a nurse about it. The nurse, also African American, had said," Nothing's wrong with him. He's just a plain little black baby." I was indeed back home. The same old black-on-black negative thinking that I had been on guard against while growing up hadn't gone away. *Didn't that nurse know that black is beautiful?*

Mother with Rekha,   **Radiant new mom!**
her first grandchild

While I was settling in with my new baby, I used Dr. Spock's *Baby and Child Care* as a guide, not that I needed it much, for having been around when my siblings were born, I knew how to take care of a baby. As Rekha got bigger and crawled around, she deviated more and more from what Dr. Spock said she should do. For example, Spock specified four ounces of milk, while she would drink only an ounce and a half and then slobber out the rest. One day, I came home, and Helene, who was babysitting, was in tears: "Rekha won't eat her food," she wailed. This was true. Rekha would only eat small amounts; she loved to reach up and grab the butter when the refrigerator door was open. Appropriate, I thought, given her Indian roots: Lord Krishna, who was said to have been fond of eating the same thing, was called the Butter Thief.

My friend since grade school, Garnetta Jackson, gave me a baby shower where I received all the baby items I would need for a while. She and her brother Bobby graciously agreed to be Rekha's godparents when she was baptized at Saint Peter Claver's. The ceremony, before the wide alabaster fount, was beautiful and solemn, Rekha letting out a loud burp to break the silence! When she was six weeks old, I began looking for a job. I was sure that with my college degree and Fulbright experience I'd be snatched up by a Louisville company.

My plan of joining the Foreign Service was on the back burner, for if I could stay near my family and raise my daughter, it would be easier. Soon, however, my enthusiasm was thrown back in my face. From the renowned, nationally known *Louisville Courier Journal* and *Louisville Times* newspapers to the Chamber of Commerce, I was rejected for not being qualified enough or for being too qualified. To be turned away in my hometown almost broke my heart.

Integration was happening, but taking its time. For two weeks, I sold encyclopedias, enjoying the novel world of the door-to-door salesperson. With my ability to parrot back the memorized pitch with wide-eyed sincerity, the company liked me a lot. I made a sale on my first try, which pumped my ego, until I quit and the company refused to pay me. I found going door-to-door at night in the suburbs scary and difficult—dogs barked, and my kidneys couldn't take it so soon after giving birth. But the good thing was that I got invited into homes—white people's homes—just, it was obvious, because they felt sorry for me. I'd give my spiel, once even having a hot drink, and chat with them. One woman told me about having sold cosmetics for Avon and suggested I try doing that.

Just as I was losing all hope, my brother Billy came to the rescue and got me an opening at the Census Bureau. I started as a GS-3 clerk, very low on the scale then, but I was grateful to get the job, a temporary position, which would last for eight months. I got to code the labor and industrial section of the 1970 census, a valuable endeavor from which I learned about the wide range of jobs in America and through which I made several acquaintances. Working gave me time to plan my move to Washington and to save money for it.

By August 1971, I was getting ready to move; Andrea and Rick were driving me. I had bought a few odds and ends of furniture and a television with a stereo for the apartment I had found. As if in a movie, one day the phone rang with a call from *The Courier- Journal*: would I like to work for them? Writing for a newspaper was the chance of a lifetime I would have grabbed months before, but I was set to continue on my course of getting into the Foreign Service, and I wasn't going to wobble. "Thank you for the offer," I was unabashedly proud to say, "but I'm off to Washington DC to do graduate studies at American University's School of International Service."

Billy and Connie with infant Dezi   Andrea and Rick with baby Rekha
(before they had their two sons)

Anita and Raymond (in hat), their son Raymond on far right, and
my nephew Brandon (Andrea's younger child), July 1978

23

Rekha and Me against the World

As soon as I waved goodbye to Andrea and Rick, I felt the crushing thud of the 180-degree change in my life. Rick had driven the nine hours from Louisville to move me into my new apartment in the 1800 block of New Hampshire Avenue, Northwest, in Washington DC. Now I could take on the life of going to university and being a single mom. The former I was sure of, the latter, less so. I was winging it, trying to do my best, uncertain that it was good enough. Caring for a child and living with no other adult, for the first time in my life, at age twenty-five I was alone. Like Helen Reddy would sing in her 1974 hit,[26] sometimes it felt like Rekha and me against the world.

A happening place in the sixties, in 1971, Dupont Circle was calmer and coming back as a neighborhood after the destructive riots of 1968. Located at the convergence of five streets, the sculptured fountain adorning the circle was a feast for my eyes as I'd approach it from our home five blocks away. From its two-tiered white marble basin, water spilled into a sweeping pool that was more than eleven feet wide. In the hot weather, when the fountain was full, I'd let Rekha slosh in the cascade. When it was cold and empty, I'd push her in her stroller around the foaming stream, across the street, and down Connecticut Avenue. Crossing the circle was an adventure, as the pedestrian light only gave us a few seconds to make it to the other side. I got in the habit of taking my chances and hurrying across wherever there was a space in the flow of traffic. Once when I was

---

26 "You and Me Against the World," recording by Helen Reddy, June 1974

pushing Rekha across on a frigid winter morning, a car sped toward me as I sprinted: "You don't care much about that baby!" a man shouted. Shaken by the taunting, I was even more upset at myself. Rekha was the most precious person in my life, yet none of the child-rearing books told me what to do. I had to write my own guide as I walked the tight rope of single parenthood.

Rekha at Dupont Circle Fountain

Houses and apartment buildings on our block were red brick or gray stone with grass, trees, and shrubs. My third-floor flat, however, stuck out as it was in a more modern structure, and I was delighted by its spaciousness. Though only a one-room studio, it seemed larger. The six hundred square feet of space was sectioned off to appear to have separate rooms. Opening the door, I stepped into the main area, and the daylight from the window on the other side greeted me. I liked it right away and wanted to cozy it up and get busy building my new life.

I put a sofa against the long wall that spanned the width of the room and placed the TV and stereo system in front of it, five feet across, against the wall. In the right corner I positioned a double bed under the window, and directly in front of that I made a dining area beneath the second window. Next to it was the kitchen, separated and made private by a part of the wall that was the other side of the main area.

To the far left, on entering the flat was an alcove with an open closet. I put a playpen there for thirteen-month-old Rekha, who, although she had taken her first steps, was not yet walking. This was the nursery. With little to spend on trimmings, I cut out shapes from shiny cadmium-blue contact paper and stuck them on the freshly painted eggshell-colored wall, continuing the motif into the adjoining bathroom.

The pristine fixtures of the sparkling bathroom made it a refuge. I'd soak in the tub, savoring the music and relaxing warm water while Rekha jabbered in her fenced-in area. But that didn't last long. One night as I was lost in thought in my aquatic cocoon, I looked up, and my little monkey was standing over the tub, grinning from ear to ear, pleased that she had figured out how to climb out of her cage!

Now, with an active toddler about, I continued arranging the space. For the kitchen, I cut out orange and yellow flowers from the design in some other contact paper I'd bought and stuck it on the walls. I took a gallon-sized empty brown-tinted glass bottle and glued flowers on it. The stainless steel sink gleamed, and the electric range sparkled as the coils brightened hot when I cooked in my kitchen corner. In Louisville I had found an old dinette set, a round table with four chairs, which looked like it had been the center of a lot of meals in the fifties and sixties, and brought it to Washington. Taping over the stuffing protruding from the seats, I covered the entire set in the colorful floral stick-ons. Liking to look out of the three-foot-wide windows facing the street, I kept the Venetian blinds open to let in light during the day.

On my visit to Washington before I moved from Louisville, I had tried to get lodging near the American University (AU) campus; but despite the "for rent" signs, no one offered me an application. Although I had to walk ten minutes to the stop, and take two buses to get to AU from Dupont Circle, I was grateful that I had found a place to live. Only years later, when I got to know about fair housing, did it dawn on me that the many denials to my rent requests were acts of discrimination.

Since good childcare was vital to starting courses on time, I lost no time finding a babysitter. I put an ad in *The Washington Post*, and a couple who lived nearby answered. After taking a look at their home and checking out the woman's scant references, I employed her, but since they did not have children, I didn't feel comfortable with the arrangement. Within two weeks, a new friend, Loretta, a black woman who was working on her PhD at AU, put me in touch with a West Indian woman across the street, and she offered to care for Rekha. June, I'll call her, was a full-time mother with a husband and three children; her flat was comfortable, with gay, colored rugs and spotless hardwood floors. She was happy to look after my daughter while I got myself settled, and as June would not discuss what I should pay her, swallowing my pride of not accepting free things from strangers, I lost no time in taking her up on her generosity and kindness. Loretta and June took me under their wings and helped me get settled, advising me on where to buy second-hand furniture—the Goodwill Store—and the least expensive children's items— the basement of a department store. I'd get off the bus at Sears in Bethesda, Maryland, on my way home from AU and shop for kiddiewear.

The people in the NH Avenue building were cordial. Our next-door neighbor, a retired government worker, and a neatly coifed lady of Austrian extraction, was like a fairy godmother. She invited us into her grayish white-and-gold French provincial apartment for tea one day; I imagined I was stepping into Paris. Thinking back on it, she probably gave me some subtle hints about the building, but all I remember is the plate of cookies she sent us home with, next door, and the little bags and paper plates of goodies she'd sometimes give us.

My cream-suit-and-fedora-hat-wearing neighbor across the hall reminded me of a "colored" version of Nathan Detroit, a jive-talking gambler character from the musical *Guys and Dolls*. "Mr. Cool" followed me into my apartment one day, barely knocking as he cocked his wide brim and leaned back in his polished tan shoes. He asked me how I was doing, did not have anything in particular to say, and was in no hurry to leave. My natural aversion to small talk, especially to people I barely knew, saved me. Mother would say, "You need to flirt," but that time, not knowing how to helped me avoid seeming interested. He must have felt really rejected. While I liked his suave and nifty clothes, his easy manner didn't move me at all. It took me only a few minutes to figure out what he had come for, and when I did, I opened the door and speeded him on his way. He never tried again. That was in late August, shortly after I'd arrived, and no matter how down on my luck I was, I knew I didn't want a sugar daddy. Later in life, girlfriends would tease me about my seeming success with men, but back then all I wanted was to raise a healthy, educated child and get my master's so that I could join the Foreign Service. I had no time for a love life.

During those same first weeks, a lovely man I had met in Louisville when I was getting ready to move to DC buzzed my door one afternoon. A pleasant-looking tall guy who had told me that his descendants had come from Eastern Europe had moved to the nation's capital to take up a job at the Treasury Department. Before I moved to Washington, we had met at five o'clock in the morning in front of one of the first big-box stores in

Louisville. Wearing a medium blue T-shirt, jeans, and sneakers, I was not dressed to look my best. Like today, when people camp out in front of the Apple Store to buy the latest device, we were in line to be the first to get our hands on one of two TVs on sale for $79. After standing and talking for so long in the line, we joined forces to help each other locate the sets.

When the wall of glass doors opened at 9:00 a.m. sharp, we led the horde of screaming shoppers rushing through the aisles. Despite our strategy, we were out of luck. My new friend found one of the two reduced-price televisions and, without hesitation, gallantly insisted that I buy it. He was a kind, engaging man whom I would have liked to know better, but when he surprised me with his visit, I feigned an excuse and couldn't even muster the courage to ask him in. I regretted being so abruptly unsociable, but the best I could do was let a male classmate from Utah, with hippie-length blond hair, follow me home a few days to talk about India, where he'd also spent some time. I was not yet ready to let a man into my life again.

One day I came home to find my door ajar. Gripped with dread, I froze in fear as I saw that my apartment had been robbed. The stereo and TV, which I had saved and scrimped for; most heartbreaking, the red-and-white snowsuit that I had bought to keep Rekha snug in the burning winter cold; even the meager stack of pennies, nickels, and dimes that I had left out—all were gone. After all my saving and doing without, all my planning, I was wiped out.

I became paranoid about staying on NH Avenue; I couldn't sleep and began thinking about finding another place to live. I didn't know how, where, or when, but I knew I would not stay there much longer. What made it worse was that everyone in the building seemed to know what I was just learning: drug dealers lived there. Before that, Washington's notorious crime problem had not touched me. I had lived in and moved around the city in the summer of 1967 when I was working at Peace Corps with no problems, and in 1966 when I visited with my classmate from Liberia. In my stress I forgot that although those times were recent, they were *before* Washington was broken apart by the riots of 1968.

The doorbell sounded in the middle of the night. "Who is it?" I'd shout before inaudible noise and laughter came across the intercom. It was as if people were harassing me on purpose, taunting me for being such a fool, for not having taken more precautions against someone stealing my modest belongings. I yanked the buzzer out of the wall and kept waiting for the next harm that I knew would befall me. Looking through the peephole one night, which had become a compulsion, I saw a young woman naked from the waist up, her skin the color of brandy, with long legs perched high in stiletto heels and long hair falling down her back. She was wearing tiny red panties and silver hoop earrings that dangled as she begged my neighbor across the hall to let her in. He opened the door and then slammed it in her face, leaving her to run down the hall to the elevator with nothing on. I thought of the seamy stories I'd peeped at in the green "colored newspaper" at home: private parts in freezers, the glaring white of a shirt on a bright black, dead body, and the low-down life that I'd been taught to avoid. *Dear God, please get me out of here,* I prayed.

Christmas Day of 1971 was bleak. I did nothing to celebrate, not daring to spend money. I'd relied on my family so much in the past year that I didn't want to ask them to bring me home for Christmas. As I pushed Rekha in her stroller, bundled up against the cold when we were out on a walk, I must have looked as downhearted as I felt, for a man in the elevator told me things couldn't be that bad and pressed $20 into Rekha's hand.

24

Heaven Helps

Just when I was despairing of things getting better, an angel came into my life. If ever I needed a miracle, this was the time. I was doing well in my studies but unsure if I could continue under the mounting pressure of the threat to the personal safety of me and my daughter. The childcare arrangement with the lady across the street was only temporary, and I felt that I was increasingly losing grasp of reality. I needed a clean break from Dupont Circle lest I continue to remain immobilized by fear and stop doing anything. That's when I put another ad in the *Post* and met Catherine Weatherall—Sister Cathy, as she asked me to call her—and that made all the difference in Rekha's and my life.

Every woman in need of help with taking care of her child should have a Sister Cathy. For that matter, they should also have an uncle like her husband, Tom, who happened to be an African American, but not at all a groveling stereotype of a yes-man. They were a unique couple to be sure, albeit with no children, but I was sure Cathy would take good care of my daughter.

Some weeks passed before she, who was English, let me in on her secret, which I had already guessed. The way she dressed in high-necked sweaters, wore a neatly tied scarf anchored in a triangle that fell perfectly from her head, and wore her chestnut-brown hair parted in the middle in two long braids reminded me of the women I'd spent so much time with. Watching her sit with straight, erect posture and seeing how she extended her arms were also clues. She had been a nun—hence, Sister Cathy.

After she gave up the ruse, she fascinated me with the story of how she met Tom while they were both living in Paris: Having been a missionary, including in China, and after leaving the convent, she was working as a layperson with other sisters in the City of Light caring for the poor. She met the fine man who had blended in with Africans residing in Paris in the course of her charitable work. As was a common practice for a number of black Americans, Tom, from Texas, had stayed in Europe after World War II.

From those first days when we met over the phone, Cathy said the $20 a week I'd pay her was fine. She had invited me to her home, a high-rise apartment overlooking the Potomac, and the four of us hit it off immediately, becoming the perfect square. One time when we were dining at Washington's Statler Hilton, someone thought that I was Tom's second wife! By then, he and Cathy had regularly taken Rekha with them when they met his business contacts. As he had meetings with officials from Guinea-Conakry, I got to know people from that African country. This exposure added to my perspective on the part of the world my ancestors came from, which had been developing since college. When I traveled to French-speaking West Africa, including Guinea-Conakry, twenty-eight years later, I felt those days with Tom and Cathy pay off.

Cathy's Englishness helped make her an ideal babysitter in my eyes. I thought that being around a native English speaker would be good for my daughter's verbal skills, and I was right. Yet strange to those of us who know her now as loquacious and never at a loss for words, Rekha was slow to speak beyond the usual "ma ma" sounding words. And when she did begin at seventeen months, her first words were, "See th'aahter!"—"See the water" in an English accent.

Sister Cathy, Tom, and Rekha

Cathy not only took care of my child, making it possible for me to go to evening classes, but also steered me toward finding a place to live near her, away from the threatening atmosphere where I lived. In the months before I relocated, while she cared for Rekha, picking her up on Monday and bringing her back for the weekend, I could concentrate more on my studies. Secure that not only was Rekha safe but she was benefiting from Cathy's care, I was free to do research and exploit the many sources of learning in the metro area, such as the Library of Congress and those in Washington's consortium of universities.

Cathy, Tom, Rekha, and I were like a family; I spent a lot of time in their home. The wife of one of their African friends had shown me how to wear her local dress: a long skirt with a matching tunic and two yards of the same fabric tied on my head. I wore it in a waxed grassy-green fabric, which made it shine and made me feel like a queen.

25

Back to the Safe Halls of Ivy

At twenty-five, I felt old and overwhelmed being a mother and a householder. Still, from the start I did well in graduate school. Diving into earning a master's in South Asian language and area studies in the School of International Service at American University, I immersed myself in a wide range of courses: from international relations, history, politics and government, to cultural anthropology; from advanced readings in Hindi to an introduction to Sanskrit and studies in non-Christian religions. Excited to delve into what I had experienced living in India, I was happy to be back in the safe halls of ivy.

Uncovering the origins of modern India lit up my mind. Eager to know more about the Indian freedom movement, I spent hours combing through issues of *Young India*, the newspaper through which Mahatma Gandhi had begun to spread his message of nonviolence and self-reliance when he was a young lawyer in South Africa. Martin Luther King Jr. had drawn on the South Asian struggle for independence to evolve his philosophy for leading the American civil rights movement. In India, King found validation for his strategy, which grew out of his commitment to the Christian way of life. As a witness to and beneficiary of the movement, I was naturally inclined to learn more about its history and culture.

In my studies, I was fascinated by details of those who had played decisive roles in India's quest, such as Jawaharlal Nehru, India's first prime minister, and Indira Gandhi, his daughter, India's third prime minister and the first woman to lead the world's biggest democracy.

My relationship with Sunder probably motivated my interest to study his native country, but going as far as I did, literally and academically, to learn about its background and culture came from a deep interest within me. After all, I chose to go to New Delhi before I met Sunder. In the future, Sunder would boast of my prowess in South Asian studies, especially Hindi, which he had not excelled in when he was in his Jesuit high school.

Also, he was not shy in talking about his grandfather who was the first Indian comptroller general of India while it was still under British rule, a historical achievement if ever there was one. Sunder had spilled his heart out to me when we first met, recounting the Romeo and Juliet saga of his mother and father meeting and marrying in Scotland. The marriage was against the will of his grandfather, a strict Kashmiri Brahmin, who refused to accept Ellen. He tried to bribe her into divorcing his son, but tough Scots woman that she was, she wouldn't budge and he treated her as an outcaste. In time, I would come to know and feel close to her, as would Rekha. In New Delhi, she had to maintain her kitchen in the family home, separated from the rest of the family because she was a foreigner and therefore an outcaste, but Sunder refused to abandon her. No wonder I was propelled toward probing the depths of the caste system.

The independent study course I took with visiting Bengali Professor J. Bandiophadyaya on the emergence of Bangladesh was rare and exciting. His expertise and authenticity—he was from Calcutta—and my intrigue with Tagore songs and Bengali culture were a perfect match of teacher and pupil. What was even more special was the "breaking news" element of the course. It *was* happening then. The course began in January of 1972, just as Bangladesh was winning its independence and becoming a nation. It was in the news, and I was delving into its background and could better understand the current event. So heightened was my awareness that ten years later, I sought and was given a posting to Dhaka. Some may have thought I was odd to want to go to such a fledgling nation, what Henry Kissinger had, in a rare undiplomatic moment, called "a basket case," but I knew why: to experience firsthand what I had followed at the university and gotten a feeling for in getting to know about Tagore.

Having been exposed to Indian culture for an extended period, I was deeply drawn to exploring the belief systems that underlay its society. How had the caste system come about, and how was it adapting to the new democracy? Although caste was illegal, I knew that phrases like "good family" were among the new code words for the old system, and while living in India I had marked the similarities between caste and racial segregation. A course in cultural anthropology led me to the writings of anthropologist Gerald Berreman, who had done groundbreaking work in comparing class and caste in North India. His writings on inequality in India lured me to explore the topic deeply and helped me see the black American struggle in an international, cross-cultural context, and as part of a worldwide quest for equal rights.

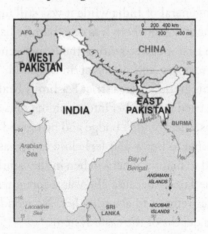

Public domain, CIA World Factbook

Among other scholarly studies, one book, *The Modernity of Tradition*, by social and political scientists Lloyd and Susan Rudolph, got me to think about how Indian traditions and ways of life met the needs of its modernizing society. Never in a million years would I have predicted the rapid progress that India has made since I was involved with it decades ago, but even in 1968, when I first lived there, the push to compete globally in education, technology, cinema, and other fields pulsated. This spirit spilled over to Indians of low status who wanted a vast increase in opportunities for social mobility. I had heard about the long visa lines at the American embassy. Those who were able to go to the United States, mostly to study, were few, due to U.S. quotas. I never could have predicted the large number of subcontinental people who have come since and the number who are citizens, nor could I have foreseen, though I admit I hoped for, the closer ties between our two countries.

Geoff Burghart, professor of anthropology, placed the bar high in his courses. My problem was that I lacked the basics of the subject, which I would have gotten had I studied it in undergraduate school. While it took long nights of keeping my eyes on pages to catch up, I was able to come up to the level demanded.

All that extra work pulled me into another world. In studying various social groups I came upon some surprising exceptions. One of those was about the toddy tappers, a group who practiced polyandry (multiple husbands) in a community on the coast of South India. The men spent the day in a palm tree tapping it for toddy (and no doubt sampling it), while the women made whoopy at home mating with their husband's kin. In another effort, a paper I did on a certain group, Kashmiri Brahmins in their native setting in that predominantly Muslim state, I gained insight into Sunder's ancestors, and thus, Rekha's. I observed how they had migrated to all parts of the subcontinent. Since they were always a tiny minority wherever they settled, they could smoothly blend in and adapt to the ways of the local people. That was the irony behind the Gandhi family's popularity in India.

Above all these topics, my main ambition had been to do a paper on the similarities between caste and race, an area that had been treated before by scholars who had observed the discriminatory treatment of some Indians in the United States South before World War II. Those explorations had not found that race and caste were the same beyond the color line, and my searches didn't turn up anything new either, a sobering truth that I came to admit, despite what had seemed so obvious when I was in India. To be sure, there was open color consciousness, but it was related to appearance, not race.

Another subject, Hindi, was a pleasure and a plight. I wasn't allowed to enroll in beginning courses, because they were offered only at the undergraduate level; yet the language was a requirement. The department arrived at a compromise allowing me to audit the courses and do extra work in reading to get the needed credits. While my fluency and practical ability in Hindi were still good, the course was trying, for both the instructor and me at times. I often thought my classmates' contributions to the discussions were elementary; however, I had to converse with them in the language to make it through. It seemed a waste of time, for none of my three classmates, who were five to three years younger than me, had visited India. Often the conversations would evolve into a dialogue between the Indian-born instructor and me. That was good for me but didn't endear me to my classmates. My pursuit of an MA was turning out to be practically all-independent study. While I was privileged and grateful to have the luxury of the individual attention and scrutiny, it was a lonely journey.

"Introduction to Sanskrit" was much more fulfilling in unlocking mysteries of Hinduism requiring me to read more and leaving no time to fret about not making friends. Since it would have been impossible to learn Sanskrit as a language in one semester, the class was a philosophical overview of the earliest recorded origins of Hinduism. That led to uncovering the seeds of devotional Hinduism. Its many gods and gilt, incense and rituals reminded me of the Catholic church. I was familiar with the mysticism of the church I was born into, but familiarity with some of the exoticisms in Sanskrit helped me better appreciate the abstract nature of Hindu thought. For example, how fire and the god Agni who represents it exert a force. The course also gave me an idea of how the caste system probably came about, a useful basis for probing it further.

These courses on non-Christian religions were windows of fresh air. I'd seen some of it practiced; now I got to understand why the believers acted as they did. Buddhism increasingly trends in the United States, and it's helpful to know that it has its basis in Hinduism. While followers of Hare Krishna in America may seem typical of Hinduism, this sect and others like it are a relatively new form of the philosophy—devotional—that only began in the West in about the nineteenth century. Our small class at AU and professor went to a Sikh temple in Washington, where we dined on bland but bountiful rice and vegetables, then meditated. It still is strange to see American Sikhs swathed in white with turbans. I am reminded of the Sikhs I saw and met in India.

Surprising, no doubt, considering my origins, but Islam was the most eye-opening religion to study among the three non-Christian faiths. The splendor of the Taj Mahal said it all: the most beautiful is the most sublime. After the pictures of saints and the stories, the relics and holy cards in the Catholic church, I could fathom the belief that followers of Islam have, that the sound of vocal prayer going upward was the only true way to reach the Highest Power. Since high school I had been struck by the belief that collective prayer, people praying aloud together, can be most impactful. Muslim thought seemed similar.

Studying Islam led me to the unique opportunity of interviewing Lonnie Shabazz, the head of Temple No. 4, of what was then called "Black Muslims" in Washington, DC. Dark as the night, with hair closely shaved, and wearing a black suit with equally somber accessories, he was intimidating. I later learned that his dignified, reserved manner made sense in light of his professional background. A renowned mathematician with a doctorate, he was indeed Dr. Shabazz, but I didn't know about his reputation when I met with him. Stressing the self-help programs that his mosque offered and the seriousness that they placed on blacks being economically independent, he answered my questions about the goals of the Nation of Islam, although he didn't share anything that I hadn't read about. And while he was difficult to talk to, and I felt awkward in his presence, the very fact that he agreed to the interview *was* something. At that time, with the memory of Malcolm X's 1965 assassination still fresh, along with the violence and Black Power movement, too quickly and simply, associated with the Nation of Islam, assumptions about the group were negative. My professor, a former Jesuit priest, had been delighted when I proposed the idea of meeting Mr. Shabazz and gave me high marks for my effort, a rare case of when being black was a big advantage.

26

Things Are Looking Up!

I was broke. It was spring of 1972, and while well settled into Washington, I needed more money. My savings were running out; my fellowship stipend of $350 a month covered the rent but was not enough for anything else. Groceries, bus fare, childcare—all had to be paid, after the rent, which was $250. When McDonald's opened at Dupont Circle that spring, it helped a lot. The burger, fries, and a Coke were cheap. I knew they'd make me put on weight but, like most people, didn't understand how bad they were for my health. I thought fast food was the best thing to come along since chocolate ice cream!

My attempts to get social assistance had been met with a reaction that was like a great big slap in the face by a social worker, who ironically happened to be black woman. Assuming that she understood that I was aspiring to do better by earning an advanced degree, I was breathless when she rejected my application: "What's more important, your degree or your child?" she asked, then told me that as a student with a fellowship I wasn't eligible for aid. The statement seared me, and I had to fight back tears. I wanted to tell her that she, above all people, should know the struggle I was going through and that I wasn't going to be a welfare queen if she just gave me a little financial help. But I held my tongue and vied to finish my master's and join the Foreign Service. I'd show her.

Sometime during that down-but-not-out episode, Cathy gave me the news that would significantly improve my situation: An apartment was for sale near her. Wouldn't I like to buy it? *How could I buy an apartment?*

I barely could make it to the end of the month, but Cathy insisted that I apply, and as if that Leprechaun lurking in the hills of Mussoorie three years ago had handed me a pot of gold, my application was accepted. I got to buy into Saint James Cooperative Homes at Second and O Streets, Southwest. Sister Cathy and my guardian angel had apparently joined forces, and my dad in heaven must have been doing his part too.

The down payment was about what I'd been paying for the rent at NH Avenue. By moving before that rent was due, I would have just enough money to make the move. Now, I would have a sunny two-bedroom garden apartment on the second floor of a fine old brick building that had been constructed for housing during the war. The monthly payment was about half of what the rent was on New Hampshire, and it was in a family-friendly, diverse community near Capitol Hill.

In those days Southwest Washington was not considered the tony place it is now. Rents were just beginning to rise, but affordable housing was still available, and the cooperative I bought into was subsidized by the Department of Housing and Urban Development. Hazel Brooker and her daughters Kim and Kaye welcomed me into the community, as did Donna Banks and her daughters Kimberley and Tiffany. They "had my back," showed me the ropes, helped me with Rekha, and rooted for my success.

Hazel Brooker, one of my Saint James good neighbors

An Iranian friend, Risa, helped me relocate. I counted out the exact $49 that the advertisement with two guys and a truck had promised, and off we went on a move that would speed me to my goals. Risa and I had bonded quickly in the last seven months. Her story was heartbreaking yet not uncommon. She'd come to my apartment to escape the beatings and violent outbursts of her boyfriend. When she came with a black eye, I let her stay for a few nights. As we sought ways for her to get away from her brutal companion, I listened to her unbelievable story. She was staying with this man for one purpose only, she told me—to get an extension of her student visa to remain in the country.

Those years, 1971 and 1972, were before the Iranian Revolution in 1979. Americans and Iranians went back and forth freely; the Shah was still on the throne. But the pathos of my friend's predicament lay not only in the abuse that she accepted from her partner but also in an error in her identity that stemmed from being born female.

Before my friend Risa was born, her father and his first wife had a baby girl whom they named Risa. Later, her father divorced his first wife and married my friend's mother. The two-year-old daughter by his first wife fell from a window ledge and died. Rather than registering my friend's birth, her father substituted the dead child's birth certificate for my friend giving her the same name. That was Risa's predicament: a haunted feeling that she had been replaced and was living the life of a dead sister she'd never met. What was worse, her passport gave her age as six years older than she was, making her appear closer to thirty than to twenty. She looked older too with the worried, despondent expression she carried on her face. Maybe that's what kept her tied to an abuser. After moving to Southwest, I lost touch with her. Did she return to Iran to straighten out her identity papers? Was she caught up in the epochal events a few years later? Neither of us knew that a tsunami of rivalries and bloodletting in the Middle East would be churned up with a revolution in her country.

When I moved into 219 O Street, Southwest, all my stars began to shine brighter: First, I had a comfortable, safe place to live in a caring community. Sunshine flooded into the high-ceilinged flat; hardwood floors led down a hall past a small kitchen and single bedroom and into an ample-sized master bedroom. My few belongings fit easily into the space, and I lost no time in making it a home, hanging yellow and orange drapes that I fashioned out of a double bedsheet, at the long, six-feet-across living room window. And after a few months, I arranged red-and-white Holly Hobbie curtains with a complementary polka-dotted bedspread in the smaller bedroom, which was Rekha's.

While bubbling from my good luck, I had the benefit of another unexpected happening: a check of $300 from my federal income tax return for the previous year. It was 1972, and I had done a lot since returning from India two years ago and needed a break. Most of all, I needed a boost to my motivation on my plan to have a career working overseas. AU wanted me to go to India to study Hindi for two months that summer. That was hard to refuse, but as I didn't want to be away from Rekha for so long, I turned it down.

Instead, I found a low-cost group charter flight to London, and we went to visit Lydia and James for six weeks. They had come to see me and meet Rekha when she was an infant while we were still in Louisville. Always my supporters, Andrea and Rick had hosted them in their home in one of the better neighborhoods of my hometown that had opened up to housing blacks in recent years.

Being back in England soothed my soul. English language and literature had brought the world to me when I was growing up. I was energized in the soil where it originated. I saw even more of London than I had when James took me to all the major attractions on my first visit, and I saw other parts of the country, including Lydia's hometown of Bath. We also went to Wales, where we vacationed with Lydia and James in a rustic cottage on a hill in the middle of a field surrounded by an earthy gray landscape.

Discovering odd and new things was, as happens in travel, the highlight of that vacation. One day I got turned around in Wales while out walking in the heather. My feet were sinking into the spongy peat, and I could not find my way back to the cottage because the path had become indistinguishable. I should have dropped bread crumbs! Diapers, of all things, guided the way. I'd washed and hung them on the clothesline outside the cottage to dry. Pampers or other good disposable diapers hadn't arrived on the market yet, so I had to make do with soap and cold water in a bucket to get the nappies as clean as I could. The ones flying in the wind that day were striped with yellow, unmasking my poor skill in hand washing Rekha's unmentionables in cold water!

Foldable strollers—or "push chairs," as the Brits called them—were also not available yet either, but I was fortunate to have a sturdy traditional type that Lydia had borrowed to take Rekha around London. On and off the tube (subway) we'd go. Someone would always help me; strangers would press sweets and coins into Rekha's hand. The same thing would happen to me forty-five years later when I was there on medical leave: people I'd never met would send me plates of chips (French fries) to show they cared. Lydia's family was warm and welcoming. We stayed in her family's elegant three-story Georgian house and I ate my first homemade Yorkshire pudding at their table. In their London flat and elsewhere, Lydia and James made me feel at home, not making a fuss when, for example, I accidentally broke their stainless steel electric tea kettle; sharing their privacy before they had their own children—three beautiful boys. We punted in the river at Cambridge University, Lydia's alma mater, and rowed up the Thames from Oxford, where James took his degree, to the place where Lewis Carroll first told the story that came to be known as *Alice in Wonderland.*

At a castle in Wales

In the heather

Getting away had done me good. I returned to the United States fired up about finishing my degree and getting into the Foreign Service. But first I had to lose weight. Foreign Service required that an applicant have a normal weight. Fearing that overindulgence could keep me out of my dream job motivated me to get back to losing the pounds. I had almost got down to a healthy size after giving birth in 1970; I was within fifteen pounds of a healthy weight. During that heady time, while I was getting used to the idea of being a mother, I was delighted to weigh so little. I kept jumping on and off the scale in the corner of the busy hospital ward.

Soon, however, I put the weight back on, thirty pounds by the time I left Louisville a year later and as many more during those first months in Washington. After making it through my first year of motherhood, graduate school, and living alone, I was carrying over two hundred pounds. Soon after we got back from visiting Lydia and James that summer of 1972, I joined Weight Watchers on August 1, and in sixteen weeks I lost forty-one pounds. I'd go to meetings on Wednesday evenings in a commercial section of the city, taking the bus from Southwest and bringing Rekha with me. On one such occasion, I rang the bell for the bus to stop so we could get off. Rekha spoke up in her clear, new voice, "Is this the stop for

Weight Watchers?" As embarrassed as I was, I laughed along with the passengers and the driver.

**First Weight Watchers booklet; permission of
Weight Watchers International, Inc.**

With my renewed health and energy, I had more confidence to get out and find what I needed to live better. For starters, I found more ways to make money. Tom asked if I'd like to write articles on business opportunities in West Africa for *The Washington Informer*, a local weekly paper, and I jumped at the chance. Seeing my name in the byline spurred me enormously to reach professional heights. But I wasn't picky about what I did to make money. Through a friend I had made at Unity Church who ran Kelly Girl temp services, I found short-term clerical jobs. Meeting working people on those jobs and getting out and about kept me up-to-date on what Washingtonians were thinking. I liked the easy rapport that I could have with others, mostly blacks, across the spectrum—the bus driver, the tight-skirted young lady who worked next to me and talked nonstop about her nights with her boyfriend, the women with the brown paper shopping bags in the social services office. These encounters made me feel I was a part of a world larger than my personal one.

Being more confident caused me to take more time to reflect on my spiritual compass. Though I held firm to my Catholic underpinnings, I felt I had strayed so far from the church's teachings that I could never be accepted back into it. That's when I discovered Unity, a school of Christianity that emphasizes using one's inner strength. Going to the services on Sundays gave me the community I desperately needed and taught me principles that I have lived by ever since, like staying positive, imagining what I want and then acting on that vision, realizing the power of my spoken words, and living from a prosperity perspective. Filled with this philosophy, I dug in earnestly to reach my goal of joining the Foreign Service. I got information on applying and made a plan to do so as soon as I completed my degree, which, now that I was working, would take almost another year.

The long shadow that had dimmed my outlook since leaving India and Sunder had finally lifted; I opened up and made more friends, and soon I had a boyfriend, Ernest. Like me, he was a grad student focusing on a foreign continent, African studies at Howard University. He worked evenings as a security guard in a government building. We fell into an easy relationship. While we knew we were not going in the same direction, we were *for* each other. Our shared interest in foreign cultures kept us together until I left Washington. While I still held fast to not cheating, I had broadened my outlook and couldn't resist his request to write a term paper for him. It was on the political systems in West Africa, and he got a B on it.

Ernest took me to see *Sizwe Banzi Is Dead* [27] at Arena Stage, already a well-known regional theater, located just down the street from where I lived in Southwest. The play, which was on the universal theme of identity, had opened on Broadway in November 1974; we were seeing it a few months later. After that night, I began going to Arena, and I started to stay abreast of the mounting quest for a race-free democracy in South Africa. Like Francis in college, Ernest led me out of myself in Washington. Why I couldn't do this for myself, as Helen Gurley Brown was telling single girls to do in *Cosmopolitan* magazine, would take me a long time to know.

As I let the sun back into my life, I tried new things. Through a course at the YWCA I learned to sew, and before long I was stepping out in a yellow floral polyester two-piece top and slacks that I made. I cut out and basted a red cotton gingham frock too but never got around to sewing it up, having to put the machine away from the ever-probing fingers of my curious little sidekick. I had gotten into the habit of preparing nutritious food since becoming a member of Weight Watchers. As I explored new things, I adopted a more adventurous way of eating, picking up bottles of wine, wedges of cheese, and two-foot-long freshly made baguettes from the newly renovated Safeway supermarket down the street.

People talked about the terrible twos, but when Rekha was that age, she was easy to satisfy. It was at age three that she entered into a terrible

---

27 *Sizwe Banzi Is Dead*, by Athol Fugard, John Kani, and Winston Ntshona, premiered in Cape Town, 1972; London and New York, 1974.

phase: She would cut the hair of her dolls, causing me to say that they all looked like they had been in Vietnam. Once, she cornered a white Persian cat we were taking care of. When I walked into the kitchen, poor Rani looked up at me over a toy teacup and plate filled with dry pet food, and Rekha's mouth smelled like a cat's. Two days later when the front of her hair was blowing in the wind, I saw that she had cut it. She had done so to remove chewing gum that she had stuck on her head! Yet another time, she wouldn't stop crying while we were waiting at a bus stop. A man passing by asked "What's wrong with her?" In the midst of the tantrum, she tossed her doll with corn-colored hair into a trash can. When she finally calmed down, she asked, "Where's my doll?" I had to tell her what she had done; after that, she didn't toss her things away so quickly.

As Rekha got older, we'd roam through the Smithsonian in those days when the museums were just beginning to be child friendly. Once we were the last out of the Air and Space Museum. A couple from Texas was following us as we snaked down the narrow walkway to the sidewalk. The man, who was tall and wore a ten-gallon hat, had struck up a conversation with my four-year-old. She had told him she was half Indian, and I nodded that it was true. Still he persisted, "Did you adopt her while you were over there?" in a voice that reminded me of Lyndon Johnson's. "No! I came from her stomach!" my outgoing child of the seventies replied.

That I had landed on my feet and was walking steadily toward my goal was a realization that I thanked God for every day. Four years ago I'd been down and feeling almost out, but my all-embracing mother, sisters, and brothers had given me undying love, supporting me in every way they could, not asking for a cent and giving their time, their resources, and encouragement. They knew I'd succeed. I knew I had to succeed because I was like Daddy. Daddy had been through hard times that, though I couldn't imagine, I didn't want to experience. One icy evening while waiting for the N4 Bus, I was so tired that I thought how warm I would be if I just lay down on the glistening snow, curled up and simply went to sleep. But just then, Daddy's face came to me, and I knew that I mustn't roll down that steep slope. He had nearly completed his master's when at around age thirty-six, he decided to leave university and take the position as principal of the black consolidated school in Jenkins, Kentucky. He soon married and had a family and never finished his degree. *Surely, with all my support and the opportunities on the horizon, I could finish mine.*

27

Small World

Being part of a larger whole was something that Daddy had always preached. He talked about not only the black struggle but also the national one. That way of thinking and what he had shown me about leading people must have propelled me to get involved in the fight for childcare for working mothers. Segregation, I was finding, in a perverted sense, had some advantages, among them was that there was usually someone to take care of the children.

That's how it was when I was coming along. As the oldest girl, I was the resident babysitter for my siblings until I was too busy, and then my sisters took over. That situation of growing up with babies still at home left me with competing feelings about working and raising a family. I had postponed deciding on it, but now I had to, for I was facing the eternal situation of women everywhere. It was a small world after all.

After shifting to Southwest while attending graduate school, I put Rekha in the care of a center at a Baptist church a few blocks away, but it didn't work out. While the workers seemed well-meaning, their concept of taking care of children was to let them watch TV soap operas in the afternoons. "Rekha wouldn't close her eyes when we prayed," was their constant complaint. *My daughter's religious proclivities were of more concern to them than her well-being,* I thought. I wasn't going to have my child's care dependent on her religious behavior. They cared for Rekha with funds from social services; as a user of that assistance, I wasn't going to let them put me on a guilt trip. Plus, it surely was illegal.

The center didn't close until 5:00 p.m., but I'd pick Rekha up earlier, sometimes taking her to the library with me, as I worried about her in that situation. I wanted more for my healthy, talented tot while I was reaching intellectual heights. While Cathy was always there, I didn't want to rely too heavily on her and Tom as my economic situation improved. I wanted to keep them as friends, the closest thing to a family nearby that I had. Cathy took care of Rekha in the evenings when I needed her.

Nevertheless, I have a happy memory of Rekha's last day at the Baptist church. Dressed in a pink sunsuit with ruffled trim, my twenty-two-month-old daughter performed her heart out: "I'm a little teapot short and stout, here is my handle, here is my spout," she sang. Then she bowed to her right side in the grand finale of the song, "Just tip me over and pour me out!" bringing down the house. Tom, who had taken time off from work to come with Cathy, rushed forward and swooped Rekha into his arms!

When we got back from London in late July 1972, Cathy had gotten a license to care for children in her home; I of course again asked her to resume looking after Rekha and she was only too happy to oblige. Now my mind was again at peace while I pursued my studies for the rest of '72 and '73. By June 1973, I had applied for Rekha to be accepted into what struck me as the best early childhood education experience for my daughter in that age of equal opportunity and affirmative action. Getting into Capitol East Children's Center was a long shot. The slim, smartly dressed, mahogany-skinned director Gloria Panton had made it clear in her West Indian accent that the chances were slim of getting into CECC. Their enrollment was a mirror of diversity and liberal ideals. It came about as close as one could get to Martin Luther King's vision of little black children and little white children playing together in this sweet land of liberty. Mrs. Panton said she would phone me if an opening came up.

When I got a call from her two months later, the cloud of child care worries that had been hanging over me was lifted. Capitol East had an opening for a three-year-old girl of mixed race, from a low-income household. I never knew if the mother of the child had to be a struggling graduate student receiving food stamps, which by now I had been able to get, but I'm sure my unique case didn't hurt the cause. People do use assistance to improve their lot. My parents had been ashamed to accept help for our family; I wasn't as shortsighted. I took advantage of social assistance programs for a short time to help me help myself.

In that first year, I paid no fees for Rekha to go to CECC but volunteered my time as needed. By the second year I was paying a small fee and serving on the board of directors. By the third year, I not only was paying the full more than $100 weekly fee, but was also president of the board, signing my name on checks.

Coming into contact with some of the leaders of Washington society was one of the advantages of being associated with the center. One evening we had a meeting in the living room of a Washington local television personality, Jim Vance; I was thrilled to meet him, the first black news anchor on Washington television, whom I watched every evening. Betty Kane, who went on to serve on the city council, was a fellow parent; and another mother became my lawyer when I was ready to go overseas and had to draw up a will. That evening nothing was lost on me as I took in the way a Capitol Hill hostess entertained: the tasty hors d'oeuvres, the low lighting, the way the drinks were laid out so guests could help themselves. I checked a box in my brain that I'd soon draw on when I had to host such affairs.

28

Watergate and Open Doors

At one of the worst times in American history till then, doors began opening for me. As 1972 turned into 1973, I concentrated on my studies and writing the paper that would qualify me for the master's degree in South Asian language and area studies. AU Professors Glenn Wood, the chairman, and Tom Timberg, my adviser, were on the academic committee that approved my topic: "Non-Alignment in the Post-Nehru Era." While it was my second choice—I had wanted to focus on United States nuclear policy toward India, but for a reason I never understood, my idea was dismissed out of hand—I was satisfied to get the green light to research a not widely known issue. Since World War II, American views had equated nonalignment with neutrality, which was seen as negative. If you weren't with us, you were against us in those days of the Cold War and hasty alliances.

The realities of the post war world notwithstanding, I found India's leadership (with Indonesia's and others at the Bandung Conference)[28] admirable and courageous. In 1973, *Washington Post* columnist Jack Andersen won a Pulitzer Prize for reporting that the Nixon administration had leaned toward Pakistan, and away from India, to keep Pakistan united and not looking toward the Soviets during the conflict that led to the birth

---

28 The Bandung Conference, held in Bandung, Indonesia, in April 1955, is generally considered to have launched the Non-Aligned Movement. It was a meeting of twenty-nine African and Asian countries, mostly newly independent.

of Bangladesh, almost causing a third world war.[29] I used the revelation in my non-thesis option paper, and finally, what I had to say provoked discussion. As a result, I was invited to speak to students at a high-school in Northern Virginia.

By the spring of 1973, while my life was taking a sharp turn—up and for the better, America was facing the Watergate crisis. Seeing myself as so much a part of America, I seemed to be growing older overnight under the load of the tumbling down of the office of the U.S. president and my own responsibilities. As a child I had not imagined that this was how it was going to be. As I got happier, I had assumed everyone around me would be happy too. But I had learned that life in our democratic republic didn't work that way. It would never be a walk in the park, and freedom always had to be monitored. "Eternal vigilance" was the price we had to keep paying.

Like millions I watched the Watergate hearings on television. To keep myself focused and make the best use of my time while not missing the testimony, I painted the entire twenty-by-thirty-foot front room of my Southwest apartment. Glued to every word and camera shot, I couldn't accept what was happening. Could the president be guilty of a crime? No fan of Nixon, I had devoured the daily reports by Bob Woodward and Carl Bernstein. They became my modern heroes, seekers of truth, justice, and the American way. Although I hadn't supported Nixon, I wasn't gleeful about what was unfolding. I was sad to see what my president had done. In bringing himself down, he was bringing me and a lot of Americans emotionally down with him. The whole country seemed to be stunned and disappointed by his behavior.

As I watched TV, spreading butter-yellow paint with a five-foot roller up and down the high walls, splashing bits on my arms and nose, I was captivated by North Carolina Senator Sam Ervin's straight country-lawyer approach, spoken in his regional drawl, and Senator Howard Baker's refrain of a question, also delivered in a Southern accent: "What did the president know, and when did he know it?"

Wonky-looking (the term wasn't used then) White House Counsel John Dean's words—sounding more like the standard TV voice—about

---

29 See Nixontapes.org: "Superpower Relations, Backchannel, and the Subcontinent: Using the Nixon Tapes to Examine the 1971 India Pakistan War."

what President Nixon had said transfixed me and kept me listening. And I couldn't get over his wife Maureen's composure and ethereal beauty, as she corroborated her husband's damning testimony. That Ervin and Baker were from the South didn't matter, for they were speaking for the Constitution, and as someone who was a part of the minority, which was finally getting rights under that document, I was on the side of those who were defending it, no matter where they were from.

That was the first time I saw Fred Thompson (also a Southerner); he was a counselor to the committee conducting the Watergate hearings. Later, he would become an actor, and I'd see him in the role of a judge in the television series *Law and Order*. Twenty-nine years later, I'd meet him in person and sit next to him in Taipei during a staff meeting at the American Institute in Taiwan.

In more recent years, at a State Department luncheon, I got to shake hands with Senator Baker, a couple of years before he passed away. Though he was much heavier and slower in his nineties, he still had the engaging smile that he'd flashed during the Watergate hearings; he warmed me with it as I thanked him for what he had done for our country during those fragile days.

On August 9, 1974, after I'd completed my academic work, Richard Nixon was resigning from the presidency while I was talking with Senator Walter Mondale in front of Capitol East Children's Center, both of us standing on the slope of a hill. At close to twelve noon, he had come with members of his committee to take testimony from parents and staff about the quality of childcare CECC provided. Since I was president of the board, it was natural for him to meet with me. His clear blue eyes pierced mine as we chatted; however, I'm sure we both were thinking about the historical event taking place at the White House at the other end of the Mall, even as we—citizen and representative—were doing the business of democracy. I rushed back home to watch Nixon's disjointed speech and tear-soaked farewell with his wife and daughters before they boarded the helicopter and flew away. An article appeared in *The Washington Post* soon after, sparked by the issue of the hearing at the childcare center, with a photo of three of the children: "What's Best for the Children, and Who Will Decide?"[30]

Rekha was one of the three unnamed children in the photograph. Disappointingly, Mondale's bill failed to pass, and it would take a long time before that meeting with Senator Mondale, a future presidential candidate, would result in federal help to childcare for working parents. Years later, during the Reagan presidency, a bill would pass in the form of help for working women needing care for their small children. That bill was a part of the welfare reform that was taking hold—too late for me and Rekha, but in time for others.

ry 16, 1974   THE CHRISTIAN SCIENCE MONITOR   Judy mudd 5222

By R. Norman Matheny, staff photographer

Federally funded day care: Push is on for uniform high standards

Quality care for mini-citizens

Congress debates, tables day-care standards

Quality of U.S.-funded day care in Congress. Second of three articles.

By Louise Sweeney
Staff correspondent of
The Christian Science Monitor

Washington

"There is no political clout for children. . ."

Double-barreled amendment

His amendment is double-barreled, providing that in-home child day care be regulated by the states in accordance with accepted national standards, and in its more controversial second part, that out-of-home day-care facilities "shall comply with the provisions of the federal interagency day-care requirements of 1968" as

problem has not been solved, merely shelved.

But questions remain.

These questions may touch the lives of millions of Americans, for Senator Mondale estimates that more than 40 percent of the mothers in the U.S. work, and the number is increasing.

Some critics question why HEW Secretary Caspar L. Weinberger,

With permission of *The Christian Science Monitor*

---

30 *The Washington Post*, Feb. 3, 1974, p. F1, "What's Best for the Children, and Who Should Decide?" by Bart Barnes. See also, pictured above, *The Christian Science Monitor*, January 16, 1974, "Quality care for mini-citizens." [sic]

That summer of '73, even as Watergate held my attention, I was flying high. My former college dormmate Sherry Nixon visited. We'd gone around Washington, taking in all the tourist sites, something I hadn't done in a while. We got dressed up and went to the Kennedy Center to a National Symphony Orchestra concert, just like old college times when we went to the Lyric in Baltimore. At Howard Johnson's near the Kennedy Center (and not far from the Watergate Hotel) we ate mouthwatering burgers and hot fudge sundaes; I gained weight, while she remained as rail thin as ever. Sherry called Rekha her niece and was very generous to her, then and for years. And she was appalled that I couldn't find work, now that I almost had my master's degree. One morning, she said, "This is terrible. I'm going to speak to my lawyer."

Sherry and Rekha

A couple of weeks later, I got a call from a doctor. At long last, having medical insurance, Medicaid, I was getting the long-neglected care I needed. I had been having persistent tonsillitis, so when the person on the phone said, "Hold on, Judith, Dr. Toote wants to speak to you," I mistakenly thought it was my medical doctor, Chinese-born Dr. Tu. But as I listened, a familiar, comforting voice radiated through my ears over the line, and I understood I was talking to an African American woman, then realized it was Dr. Toote, the Assistant Secretary for Fair Housing and Equal Opportunity at the Department of Housing and Urban Development (HUD). A doctor of jurisprudence, she was indeed also Sherry's lawyer.

"Judith, this is Gloria Toote. Can you write?"

"a pleasure to meet you, Dr. Toote," I managed to say; something told me this commanding caller didn't want small talk, so I summoned up as businesslike a tone as I could while inside I wanted to scream for joy. "Yes, I can write," I said. "I can write speeches. I was a debater and practically minored in speech!" With the last phrase, I wasn't hiding the smile in my voice, and I was talking to Dr. Toote as if she were a friend of my father.

The next morning, I gathered all my term papers on their onionskin paper, walked the six blocks from my apartment to HUD, and dumped them on Mr. Jenkins's desk. He was the mustachioed, wavy-haired deputy to Dr. Toote. Glancing at the titles, Mr. Jenkins looked at the assistant secretary, and they rolled their eyes. "The Concept of Self in Hindu Philosophy." What's that about?" Dr. Toote asked, staring at me as if to say, *can this woman be for real?* as I nonchalantly explained the metaphysical Hindu concept to her. And could I write speeches? Why, yes, I had been giving them since I was ten. I had been a debater in high school and college, going on a scholarship to Morgan State because of my skills. Fortunately, I got the job; ironically, Dr. Toote was a Nixon appointee, and a rarity, a black Republican from Harlem. Thus, I began my professional government career as a political appointee for a Republican.

Years after Dr. Toote gave me my big break, I came to know how historically important she was. Her father had continued the work of the Negro Improvement Association begun by the legendary Marcus Garvey in the late 1920s, and she had charted her own course in business and made a million dollars when most Americans, certainly not blacks, could not have imagined doing so. Her sundry ventures included founding a music recording label with James Brown.[31]

That year of working at HUD, from September 1973 to October 1974, got me to where I needed to be to get where I wanted to go. Although the job wasn't in foreign affairs, it was a full-time, well-paying GS-9

---

31 See Encyclopedia.com, "Gloria E. A. Toote, Lawyer, Entrepreneur, Political Appointee"

government position that made it possible for me to take care of personal needs—clothes, furniture, a carpet, a vacuum cleaner! The security of a regular solid paycheck helped settle my mind on taking the big step to follow my passion. More than writing speeches for the assistant secretary, the job exposed me to the ropes of surviving in a government office—all the untaught rules, like keeping track of what you've done to show you're performing and playing the game of the office culture.

The Office of Fair Housing and Equal Opportunity (EEO) was emblematic of the seventies. All the ingredients in America's melting pot proudly exhibited their cultural differences; affirmative action was allowing this rainbow to arc over offices in the federal government, showing how the policy could work. With my wide Afro hairdo, hoop earrings, and wide-legged pants, I jubilated in the times that were changing. A work ethic that had been instilled in me since grade school and stamina to keep going along the rockiest routes when I wasn't sure of the way ensured that I did the job.

Going to a historical black college and living in India had prepared me a lot, but as those standards were so high, I had to learn a lot more about working with all types of personalities: those who excelled and some who didn't share my view of a job well done. The office was dominated by people of color, mostly African American, like Deborah Seabron, who became a close friend, and Lloyd Davis, head of the Voluntary Compliance Division. He later did a lot to bring about the Martin Luther King Holiday. Latinos were on the staff, as well as a lanky American Indian man who wore his tribal feathers in his long platinum mane. Among those of European origin who swam in this diverse pond were two who had recently worked at the White House. One of them, Paul Lavrakas, shared an office with me.

The office had responsibility for monitoring access to fair housing under the Civil Rights Act of 1968 under a law, which was signed on April 11 of that year, seven days after Martin Luther King's assassination, by President Lyndon Johnson. During the Great Depression in the thirties the Roosevelt administration recognized the need for affordable housing for the middle class and passed a law to make that happen, but it didn't have much success; we know now that its policies protected segregation. Not until 1965, when Lyndon Johnson pushed for the establishment of the Department of Housing and Urban Development did the reality of homeownership for the middle class become more possible and the need for low cost housing receive recognition at the federal level.

With floors of glass-plated windows and stone walls that slink across streets, the HUD building is a behemoth of government in actual size and in the number of programs that it oversees. In 1973, just walking around it reading the names of offices was a crash course on the details of federal efforts to support housing. "Urban renewal," "model cities" and "public housing" were terms that I was familiar with. But I was learning about other HUD-based entities that helped people buy homes: the FHA (Federal Housing Administration) had made possible the cooperative housing that I had bought into and helped me purchase a family-size home nine years later.

One day I looked up and saw the name Fannie Mae on the fogged glass pane of a door. That was the government-sponsored enterprise that came out of the efforts of the Roosevelt administration. It had become a private company in 1968. In addition to being intrigued by the flippant name for such a somber undertaking and coming from a family who had never owned a home, working in the building was eye-opening, if somewhat overwhelming.

The EEO office had a number of responsibilities. As a speech writer, I became familiar with three of them: enforcement, voluntary compliance, and contracts. Enforcement of equal housing opportunities appeared obvious to me, for blacks and other minorities needed access to better housing. But I hadn't realized before that better housing improved access to good public education and thus helped integrate schools. Voluntary compliance, which persuaded realtors to respect equal rights laws, was new and absorbing. The strategy reminded me of the direct action that Gandhi employed to lead India's demand for independence. Dr. Toote promoted the policy on behalf of President Nixon to a positive headline-grabbing effect. The contracts division sought to get shares of construction work for minorities; while I never got into the nuts and bolts of it, I got to know some of the terms, like "minority set asides," for example. I appreciated "contracts" huge importance to the lucrative housing industry.

At HUD I sharpened my focus on gaining more opportunities for women. My life had been an effort to be taken seriously as a black and as a woman, and I never thought it necessary to line up formally behind one group or the other. In the parlance of the day, I was a "twofer,"[32] and I resented the notion, even when I had to play that card. But the search for

---

32 Twofer: a two for one. As a minority and a woman, I was one.

childcare was a specific women's need that I had long identified with, now in my involvement with Capitol East Children's Center, and from the days when my mother went back to work and I had to stay home from school and care for my baby sister—and when she had not been allowed to continue working as she had more children. Who would care for the children had been my mother's constant concern and had driven a wedge between us.

Providing childcare assistance was vital to giving everyone a "head start" in life. Like all federal departments, HUD had a women's coordinator. The responsibility for the Federal Women's Program was the assistant secretary's. As her speech writer, I had to keep track of what she kept her eye on, especially the number of women hired. As this was at the height of the women's movement, when all women at the housing department and in organizations all over the country were clamoring for a fairer share, I joined other women at HUD to form a women's caucus to draw attention to the issues facing employees of the department. Childcare was one that united us all, for like me, my colleagues had to deal with the need, whether directly or indirectly as it affected staff, absenteeism, childbearing, and the high costs of paying for good care. We decided to press the secretary of HUD to establish a day care center for the children of departmental employees, and I volunteered to edit the newsletter. The assistant secretary's speeches were issued as press releases, so it was easy for me to put together the regular updates on what was happening and see that they were disseminated as part of *HUD Women's Caucus Notes*.

HUD WOMEN'S CAUCUS NOTES

| Volume 2, Number 4 | Washington, D.C. | June/July, 1974 |

CAUCUS CITED IN TESTIMONY BEFORE SENATE

With permission of the Department of Housing and Urban Development

News that our caucus's efforts were paying off made the Congressional Record, and with it the reply to our request to meet with the secretary. What a heady moment it was, reporting the outcome in the newsletter:

It was June 14, 1974. Testimony before Senator Proxmire's Subcommittee on Housing and Urban Development, Space, Science, and Veterans of the Senate Committee on Appropriations was being heard. In answer to a question on the progress of minority hiring, Dr. Toote was present, and HUD Secretary Lynn responded:

> We have a Women's Caucus within the Department that the Undersecretary's Office and Administration work with closely and I think we are getting the job done.

Later, responding to Senator Proxmire's question about what the Women's Caucus did, Secretary Lynn said:

One of the best things they do is consciously prod me and the Undersecretary, and that is a very noble thing to do.

He went on to say that the caucus was doing "very meaningful work of working closely with Ms. Toote's office" on various matters.

With this open nod to the value-added contribution that the caucus was making to the HUD mission, we asked for and got a meeting with the secretary to discuss the issue of a childcare center at the department. Gathered around his wide dark wood desk on the top floor one morning, we listened to his commitment to the idea of providing a childcare center. Although I left HUD long before it became a reality, decades later, now, when I pass through the side street and see the multicolored jungle gyms and sliding boards, I feel a deep sense of having been a part of a major accomplishment.

Being in the midst of the diversity of HUD put me in the classroom of real life every day. Once, as I sat in the office I shared with Paul, who had worked at the White House with some of the names in the news during Watergate, he gave me some solid advice. Noting that I was awestruck by well-known people, he told me that when he felt that way, he said to himself, "We all shit the same way." In the not-too-distant future, I'd conjure up his advice when I'd meet VIPs.

As I got closer to getting my MA, Paul's and other colleagues' pep talks gave me the courage to telephone the CIA to inquire about the possibility of working for them. "How dare you merely call us up!" the tone of the man who answered the phone implied. They knew about everyone, he told me, as my officemates stood around my desk, egging me on. They, the CIA, would contact me if and when I should become interesting to them. What a laugh! At least I'd tried, and we all went back to work until one day I started to get Mailgrams at my address from "Bureau of the Roads" (CIA didn't use its real name) about my application to join the agency! I hadn't even applied.

Months before that pivotal phone call, I was putting the final touches on more than two hundred typed pages of my non-thesis option, the research paper that was required for the master's degree. In undergraduate school, I had been allowed to submit papers in handwriting, neat and properly spaced, of course. But in graduate school, everything had to be typed. Thank God for onionskin paper and Wite-Out mistake eraser. I used them all the time as I knocked out draft after draft on my portable typewriter. I was pretty good at it since I had learned to type at Ursuline, even though I never was known for my speed. Now at AU, the skill was invaluable, and it must have helped me get good grades (I finished with a 3.73 average). But in those days before computers as word processors, I paid a professional stenographer a hefty sum to type the 261-page final version of my non-thesis paper. On a sunny afternoon in spring 1974, I took Rekha with me to collect it from the typist on K Street. "You're little!" my three-and-a-half-year-old proclaimed as I handed the lady the check.

"Yes, I am!" she said, smiling from ear to ear as I looked embarrassed. "It's okay," she said, looking up at me, then at Rekha. "I'm your height," the stenographer said nonchalantly.

That first close-up encounter with a dwarf was just one of the myriad people my child got to experience in her early years, no doubt helping her to be tolerant and broad-minded about people and ideas. I got my master's from American University's School of International Studies a couple of months later in June 1974. I didn't attend the ceremony in cap and gown to receive it. In my "I'm off to better things" frame of mind, and busy with full-time work, I just dropped by the campus one day to pick it up.

6/28/75

Dear Judy,

We are very grateful to you for helping to make our 39th Wedding reception a happy occasion. Raylab was adorable. Everyone wanted to know if she was our grand.

Our love to both of you

Nevada & Bill Seabron

Thank-you note from Debbie Seabron's parents and photo of Rekha as flower girl at their thirty-ninth wedding anniversary; with permission of Dr. Stephen Seabron

29

Waiting for the Letter

I had done all I could: taken the Foreign Service examination, gotten my MA and submitted my application to join the United States Information Agency. In the essay "Why I Am Interested in a Career in the Foreign Service," I harkened back to my experience in India of finding that people had extreme ideas about Americans, from being of loose morals to everyone driving big cars and living like movie stars. I had been frustrated trying to convince people that although I was a minority, I was an American too. If I got the chance, I would harness my unique background and my good education to promote the goals of USIA. Quoting Texas Congresswoman Barbara Jordan, one of the first black women to serve in the House of Representatives, I said, "At last I am now one of 'We the People.'" Even fifty years later, the reasons I gave for joining the service remain the same; I lived up to what I said in that statement.

While working at HUD, after spending an afternoon talking to the Affirmative Action officer at USIA, I thought I'd quickly be called to work in their section of the Foreign Service. Debbie Seabron, a rising star in our HUD office, cheered me on to keep working on my goal of joining the information agency. As a speechwriter, I'd often been pulled from crafting remarks for the assistant secretary to writing for others in the office, which wasn't right and was a bit demoralizing. Not being in law school was also challenging: I looked around for a job on international housing issues, but none really existed. Debbie had helped me to keep my spirits up: we'd go to movies and sometimes have lunch together; we'd visit each other's homes.

She invited me and Rekha to meet her parents, and most flattering, asked Rekha to be the flower girl in her parents' renewal of their wedding vows.

My idea was that I'd make a triumphant departure from HUD to do what I had been preparing to do, a kind of "Take This Job and Shove It" gesture, but USIA left me in limbo. All "degreed," I had no job to go to. As all political appointments will do, the job at HUD ended on September 30, 1974, and I still hadn't heard from the information agency. The Monday after I left HUD, I answered an ad and began taking care of the children of a family living in one of the new townhouses in Southwest. Although I had expected it, losing my well-paying job was a hard knock that I'd never felt before. To have been so on top of the world and now to be down again was defeating. I knew I had to keep on pushing or I'd fall into a deep funk. While I was the "help" for only two weeks, I was proud to have done it and had proved to myself that I could "stay out there" and do what I had to do until something better came along.

Two weeks later, I was back freelance writing. The phone rang often, from people who needed help with producing office reports and the like. Once I was called by a man who had set up office in Alexandria, Virginia. A tall ebony statue of an African with a British-influenced accent, he was, I realized when we met, blind. He needed me to prepare a proposal of a project he was trying to get funding for. He hired me on the spot, and I diligently sat in a sparsely furnished room organizing his thoughts on pages. After typing them up and giving them to him for approval near the end of the second week, when I came in on the last day to collect my pay and expecting to continue to work for him, I found the door locked. I went to inquire from the building manager. He told me that the man and his colleagues had closed up shop and left town. Speechless that I had been bilked so royally, I understood that I had been blinded by the stereotype.

Another time, a man, I'll call him Mr. Jones, phoned to ask me if I'd ghostwrite a book about not paying taxes. *Goodness,* I thought, *wouldn't not paying taxes be illegal?* Having recently been audited by the Internal Revenue Service, the IRS, I had a healthy fear of provoking them. The rags-to-riches jump in my income caused by my salary from HUD must have triggered the IRS to questions the taxes I'd claimed. I was so nervous during the audit that the official took pity on me and helped me correct the mistakes I had made so that I wouldn't owe anything! Thus, I hemmed and hawed with Mr. Jones when he checked back with me over the weeks, until finally, he said, "If you don't want to do it, just say so." He was right, and I said no.

I didn't want to work for the CIA in those days when working for it was not viewed favorably after the revelations of its involvement in coups and killings. But never one to say never, one day I found myself hopping on and off three buses to go to an interview at CIA in Langley, Virginia. Up to then, they had carried out the most flattering wooing of me—as I said, sending me urgent messages, inviting me to meet with their Washington official, and making me feel comfortable while I chatted with him. The official I met was the same man who had rebuffed me when I'd called him from HUD, but after he'd done his homework on me, he became like prince charming. USIA had flirted with me, but CIA was asking me to dance. I found myself going closer toward joining the Agency (as we called it), even though it hadn't been on my list.

After the long journey to the Virginia suburbs for the interview, I blinked twice when the lady who answered the door looked like a Christmas tree, with a sparkly corsage that resembled a decoration on her red dress, her blonde hair coiffed and flipped up at the ends. She and the other women who received me were welcoming and all smiles. I felt like I was in their living room, until, as I took off my hunter-green wool coat, I looked down and saw that my coffee-colored dress was clinging to my body. When I caught a glimpse of myself in the mirror, I looked like Charlie Tuna's girlfriend in the advertisements, the static from my coat's lining and my panty hose having made me appear as if I was trying to look sexy! But having come this far, I had to proceed, and that's how I walked around the Central Intelligence Agency Headquarters.

All the officers—men—acted as if I looked okay and talked with me seriously, while I felt self-conscious. I did get a shock when they told me that I was going to talk to a psychiatrist "just so he can meet you," and while I felt odd about it, I didn't object. With my new masters and their South Asian area, I knew I had found the match for me, at least if I was going to work for the Central Intelligence Agency, so I was willing to go along with meeting a psychoanalyst. But when I went into his long, narrow office, instead of someone like Freud, a dreamy-looking swarthy-skin man who reminded me of the actor Billy Dee Williams smiled back at me. He laughed, motioning for me to sit down. "I'm here to make sure you can talk and handle the interview situation," he explained as if it was a joke. We both knew what was going on and shook our heads in incredulity. He told me he was from California and still getting used to Washington. I told him about growing up in Louisville and that I was used to segregation, that I hadn't been to California— yet— but I had been in Asia. That was my pleasant half hour with the shrink—affirmative action in action in the seventies!

What ended my possible career in the spy agency was when I dared again to ask them the wrong question: that I'd like to work in the South Asia area and when would I have the opportunity to go overseas? *Off with your head*, the chief seemed to retort. Only after several years of working as an analyst would it be remotely possible to consider me for such a position. I felt like poor Oliver Twist, asking for more porridge. Having been put in my place, I made a mental note that sitting at a desk poring over reports was not for me. I thanked him and started on my long bus sojourn back to DC, much wiser, for the day had been an adventure to a sort of wizzard's land.

The new year of 1975 came, and I was in the "gig economy" decades before the term came into vogue, doing a lot to make a living and keep my spirits up while waiting for that letter inviting me to join the US Information Agency. Even though I had ruled out joining the CIA, I hadn't told them so, and I took their exam, on a one-of-kind afternoon that belongs in the annals of the *Perils of a Black Pauline*, if there ever was such a book. Not only was the test excruciatingly difficult—more than the Foreign Service exam, which was terribly tough—but the circumstances under which I took it were perplexing:

The monitor, the only other woman in the room, gave out the booklets. The other test takers were thirty young men with crew cuts, who sat on the right side while I sat on the left. *The cover of their books was blue, while mine was pink!* The rest of the day was just as unreal. No one would talk to me when I went to eat in the small cafeteria downstairs during the half-hour lunch break, not even a hello or "how ya doing'" when I tried to talk to them. To this day, I've never understood why. By 4:00 p.m. when I got to the essay section of the test, where I was usually able to excel, I was too exhausted to do my best. I left sure that that had put an end to my prospects in the CIA.

Over the four years when I was living in Washington before joining the Foreign Service, I stayed in touch with my family, visiting Louisville for holidays when I could afford plane tickets after that first penny-pinching year. Billy and his wife, Connie, drove up with their new baby during the summer of 1972. Baby Dezi was a bundle of delight, soft and small; he liked cuddling close to me, and I couldn't get over the fact that Billy was a father. Mother and my younger sisters Helene, Poochie, and six feet, four inches tall "baby" brother Rodney came in summer 1974. Making enough to feed and entertain my family, I protested when Mother told me she had brought food. "You can't feed Rodney," she declared as I fussed over the meal. She was right. Rodney ate four pieces of chicken as soon as we sat down; I had only prepared twelve. Poochie stayed on that summer for a long visit. At age ten, she was six years older than Rekha but still the youngest among my sisters and brothers. That point hadn't registered with me when I put her in charge of looking after four-year-old Rekha.

I expected her to assume the responsibility of older sister and cousin to her niece, but, she wasn't used to that. Over a year later, when I was moving overseas, I was taking down a handcrafted display of purple grapes from the dining area wall. I had been fond of the piece, for it reminded me of the Concord grapes that Daddy had grown in our Preston Street yard in Louisville. When I saw that the ceramic had been smashed to pieces and glued back with clear tape, I was speechless. Rekha, having been sworn to silence, now meekly confessed all: that it got broken during a game they were playing. Poochie had put the fear of God in her!

Andrea and Rick, who had moved me to Washington in 1971, returned in 1975 with their two gorgeous sons, Colby and Brandon. By then my stars were rising, and they were with me to celebrate.

But I'm getting ahead of my story. Before that summer, by January 1975, I still hadn't received the official letter inviting me to join USIA, while I'd come home to regular Mailgrams from the CIA "regarding your position . . ." Despite my lackluster performance on their exam, they had invited me to join. I began to see myself huddled over a desk in a corner office at Langley. Visions of being in the Foreign Service began to freeze in my mind's eye, and I was beginning to think that I wouldn't be asked to join USIA. Like in the CIA testing experience, I was the "odd girl" out; I was missing something I didn't know, which made me ineligible for the dream of standing in front of an embassy like the women in the photo in the magazine I had seen long ago.

My security check for the information agency had been done. The answers I had given on the questionnaire had been investigated and found true. Lying on that form would have been a violation of the law; I would have been prevented not only from joining the Foreign Service but also from finding work in future government agencies and I could have gone to jail to boot. All my neighbors had been poised for the security interviews and were ready to speak well of me. When the investigator in his khaki trench coat came to meet with me at my home that cold day in January, I sailed smoothly through his list of questions. Although he didn't ask me, I elaborated on the details of my time with Sunder. I told him it was good to get the whole story out, like going to confession. He left me with a sobering thought: "Yes, but I can't give you absolution."

The physical exam at State Med was a breeze. Although I had feared it most, thinking that because I was overweight, having regained most of those pounds I had lost, I would be disqualified. All the promotional literature stated that applicants had to be a healthy weight. Since I was sixteen and had learned about the Foreign Service, I had been aware of this requirement. Even when I went for my interview at USIA, I had feared that I'd be "kicked out" due to my weight, but no one had said a thing. Thus, when during the medical exam, I got off the scale and the nurse said nothing as she wrote down my weight, I vowed to finally lose the extra pounds before I went overseas.

I had passed the MLAT (Modern Language Aptitude Test) with flying colors. It was given to me during my initial interview at USIA back in the fall of 1974. Without much direction, the recruitment officer had left me in his office alone with a tape recorder; I was so nervous and so unfamiliar with what I was supposed to do that I missed the first part of the test before realizing what I should be doing. It was on a made-up language in which the test taker had to respond to questions based on recognizable patterns and similarities to other languages. When I scored high enough to be eligible to study for difficult languages, I felt enormously competent and grateful for the Latin, English, and French I had studied at Ursuline and Morgan and the Hindi I had learned in India. That MLAT score followed me for the three decades of my career. I never could remember what my score was, but it was high enough. Had I not missed the first part, I'd have probably gotten over 90 percent.

As winter '75 faded and the March thaw signaled the coming of spring, I called the recruitment officer at the US Information Agency, an African American, to ask about the delay: was I going to be invited to join the agency or not? He beat around the bush until he finally blurted out, "What are you going to do with your child?"

That set me off. I was hurt and mad. "What do you think? I'm not going to leave her here." After all my work, all my waiting, all the testing, all the coming up to par—now this.

He tried to calm me down and said that I had to understand his position. Most of these places in Africa, where he assumed I'd go, didn't have schools for children. "These places are in the bush." I was starting to wonder if I wanted to join USIA after all. What did he mean "Africa" and "in the bush?" I had a shiny new MA in South Asian studies, and I was fluent in Hindi. Also, as he knew, I had lived in India for two years. I wanted to go there or to another Asian country. Again, my multiple interests and talents, my whole "well-rounded person" thing was causing problems, and a man of my own race didn't seem to appreciate the value that I'd bring to the part of the USG he represented.

But I had learned, from the support and encouragement of faith, family, friends, and teachers, that life surged between despair and triumph all the time. My friend at Unity, who directed Kelley Girls, gave me another job to carry me through. By April, I had become friends with a group of people, one of whom was a distant cousin in the Mudd family. As my bright-faced relative, a slightly older woman and successfully settled Washingtonian, told me, "We just do things together." One evening as Rekha and I strolled with them in my host's backyard in the lowering evening sun, I thought, *this is ideal. This is exactly how I want to live. I could stay in DC forever. Just the kind of social outlet I've been looking for.* (My mother had assailed sororities and racially exclusive groups, but maybe I needed to get used to this reserved club.) How I found my distant relative fades in my memory, but I recall that I wore an ankle-length spring green polyester dress, with white polka dots, and I felt very well, brimming with hope.

The very next day, a Monday, I got a letter, but not the one I'd been waiting for: "It is with pleasure that we invite you to join . . . the CIA." Telling no one, I roamed around in a fog for days, flattered but torn between what I should do. By Friday, the letter that I'd been waiting for, from USIA, finally came, a sort of anticlimax.

I was still grateful for the one from the CIA; I wrote them about my decision and smiled when they replied that the door to joining them was always open. It was nice to be wanted by two U.S. government agencies. Snatching up Rekha from the school van as soon as it arrived at our home at Saint James's square, I took her for a stroll along the Potomac close-by. *Was this the right thing to do after all? Was this the best thing for her?* As we munched on pretzels and sliced apples, *I* counted my blessings as I looked on the still ebb and flow of the early evening tide. *Yes, of course it was.*

30

You're in the Foreign Service Now!

Public domain, Wikimedia Commons

"Telling America's Story to the World," the banner on the USIA[33] building at 1776 Pennsylvania Avenue beckoned. Walking through the doors of the United States Information Agency on that first day, I was giddy. I could almost hear drums and bugles and feel the wind of a waving Stars and Stripes.

This was the government agency that Edward R. Murrow had directed. The famous broadcaster brought his reputation of facing down Senator Joseph McCarthy's efforts to label people communists on live television to President Kennedy's theories on winning the Cold War race for hearts and minds. He gave USIA a reputation that attracted young people like me. One day short of my twenty-ninth birthday, June 4, 1975, along with fifteen others, I raised my right hand to be sworn into the United States Information Agency by Director James Keogh at the building on Pennsylvania Avenue. A few days later, with other new recruits, I was sworn into the Foreign Service by Secretary of State Henry Kissinger in the building at Foggy Bottom. In time, my name would go to the Congress for approval, and my commission would be signed by President Jimmy Carter.

---

33 USIA was folded into the State Department in 1999, becoming the Bureau of Public Diplomacy.

USLA swearing in

With all the new Foreign Service Officers of
June 1975 at the State Department

Our group of public affairs trainees was a part of the larger group of Junior Officers in Training (JOTs), some one hundred new employees of the Departments of State, Agriculture, and Commerce. Our small group was part of the changes the Foreign Service was putting into place to make its workforce more reflective of American society. In our rainbow class of sixteen, three were black, two Asian, one Latino, and ten were white. A wide range of regional and national backgrounds existed within those who were white: Irish, Italian, Scandinavian, and Jewish, to name what I can recall. Those of European origin ranged from men and women who had gone to prestigious Ivy League and well-known state as well as smaller, private colleges and universities. One woman didn't have a college degree but was so fluent in Japanese, having lived in U.S. Micronesia for ten years working as a journalist, that not having a degree didn't matter. She was a single mother as well.

Most of us had traveled. One, Jerry Chirichigno, had been a Prisoner of War in Vietnam. He was a native of Peru, and his verve and joy of living was contagious. He was constantly beguiling us with his exciting activities, like meeting fellow POW John McCain at an affair the evening before. Jerry would have us over to his apartment, where he'd blend up daiquiris and spellbind us with the story of crashing his helicopter in a Southeast Asian jungle and being captured and surviving captivity.

Overall, our group got along and helped each other, which surely made a difference to my success. Seven of us who raised our hands that day were female. The Foreign Service had only recently begun increasing the number of women in its ranks. Before that, women in the service had to leave when they married, and females in general had not been recruited, nor were blacks. When he was running for president, John F. Kennedy had said there were only twenty-six Negroes in the diplomatic service in 1960.[34] Paradoxically, after the sweeping changes that had overtaken U.S. society by 1975, opening up opportunities for women and minorities, of the seven women in my JOT class, twenty-nine years later, I was the only one remaining.

When I joined I didn't know where I would be going overseas. The general thinking was that an officer wanted to be posted in Western Europe. But that was changing, as several of us were interested in developing countries. An officer had to bid on three assignments among a

---

34 *Meet the Press*, NBC TV, October 1960

list of possible places; one of these had to be in what was called a "hardship" post. Since I had lived in India, which was very much considered a hardship assignment, I thought I'd be a shoo-in for the opening there. Moreover, who else had a fresh master's degree in studies of that area? But my "no contest" thinking was soon set right as I learned that the policy was not to send officers where they wanted to go and where they liked to live and/or had experience. An officer might be too sympathetic to the local population and thus should be posted to an unfamiliar country, or so the thinking went. That way of posting officers reminded me of the British during their days of empire—which is one reason why we see people in films dressed and acting as if they are in England when they are in a sultry, hot old mansion in Calcutta.

I found out later that I had indeed been considered for French-speaking Africa since I had an academic background in the language. But by September, I got the assignment to India that I wanted. I have Carmen Suro-Brady, who was my career counselor, to thank for that. Foreign Service is extremely competitive; many join, but few remain, and I wanted to go where I had a good chance of showing that I could succeed. While waiting for my assignment, I took part in the two-week orientation course required of all new entrants. Experts exposed us to a gamut of issues related to living and working abroad—from packing, storage, travel, through the meaning of diplomatic status, housing, and official expenses, to the basics of U.S. foreign policy. Often I felt as if someone was throwing binders and papers at me: so much information, so much lingo, so many acronyms and names that I had to struggle to keep up. At the end of a session, I couldn't wait to get up from my seat in the dim, freezing cold, air-conditioned auditorium to walk out to the sun-filled sidewalk and open, if polluted, air of Twenty-Third Street.

I had been panicking about entertaining, holding representational events as it was called, until a wife of an officer spoke to us about how to go about it. She said we didn't need to have fine china and silver. All we needed was to be ourselves. On hearing that, I was greatly relieved. Suddenly feeling very rich, I went to Woodward & Lothrop department store and splurged on two sets of Pfaltzgraff stoneware and enough flatware to serve sixteen people.

What to wear was a constant concern in those days before "dress for success" had entered the popular vernacular and no one advised women on office attire. Shopping for the wardrobe I would need left me out on a limb, and I had to use my own, sometimes unwise, judgment. The times didn't help either. The extreme fashions of the seventies—winged collars, long skirts, bell-bottom pants—made it hard to decide what was acceptable for the new woman diplomat.

During and after the orientation, USIA kept my group busy with small sessions on public affairs skills. We did such things as learning how to take photographs with a 36-mm camera and how to thread a videotape player (tapes were reel-to-reel then, not yet cassettes). Most bizarre was an exercise called the "inbox test," which required that we act as if we were in an office. As the phones rang, messages were delivered to our inboxes as interruptions occurred—a person would come to the desk, a buzzer would suddenly go off—all to test our abilities to stay focused. I felt like I was in a cartoon: a woman in a swivel chair, phone at her ears, turning sideways with legs crossed.

Our group toured the first commercial satellite, COMSAT, to see how the groundbreaking technology worked. Little did we know as we walked about seeing the spectrum of maps, looking through telescopes and at all sorts of equipment, that commercial satellites would soon change communication throughout the world. Television relay and newspaper production were just two changes that would soon affect me.

In July we had to go for a week to Harpers Ferry, West Virginia, to play simulated war games. Fortunately, I could leave Rekha in Louisville with my family after flying down for the Fourth of July. So undone was my four-year-old at my leaving her that she tore up the twenty-dollar bill I had left under her pillow. Savvy as ever, my little sister Poochie taped it back together and took Rekha to spend it right away.

In Louisville at Billy's barbecue, May 25, 1975

Of all the officers at a post, those in public diplomacy (PD) had some of the most direct contact with the citizens of the country where they were stationed. My guess is that this was why much of the training had to do with working and getting along with each other in our group. Life overseas, I was learning, had everything to do with getting along with people—compatriots with whom you worked as well as the country's inhabitants. In fact, to be good in PD, it helped to like people. And as someone in our group said, one of the reasons he had joined the service was to find an esprit de corps. I agreed. I, too, needed to work in a professional community with strong ties and high standards towards a common goal.

Robert Kohls was our director of training.[35] He was always warm and compassionate. He gave an enchanting dinner for us outside on the lawn at his home in Washington, getting us ready for affairs of this kind when

---

35 *The Washington Post*, September 2, 2006, "Robert Kohls; Official, Author Led Training in Overseas Life," p. B6

we would be at our posts, but also to get to know us and let us have fun. Other USIA officers were encouraging as well. One couple, the husband and wife both in the service, made a lasting impression on me and, I'm sure, the others in our group. In time, tandems, as such twosomes came to be called, would become familiar, but in 1975, they were trend-setters.

I got on well with several of my colleagues: Pat Corcoran, Lloyd Neighbors, Dave Hamil, and Ellen Berelson, to name a few; all went far in their careers. Pat would be my boss in one of my last Washington assignments. In those early days, he and I laughed and talked a lot, often about music—once dueting on "Falling in Love Again," me in the style of Dionne Warwick, he Marlene Dietrich, on our way to grab snacks at the coffee shop next door to the agency. His wife, Renata, took care of Rekha more than once when our group had an evening activity, and I will always be grateful for that. Jerry Chirichigno and I would work together soon and in the future. Ellen Berelson would leave the service and eventually work in the Fulbright Program. Years later, she'd have a very favorable impact on my career.

One evening our group went on a picnic to Wolf Trap National Park for the Performing Arts. We each brought food—quiche, brownies, salads—and bottles of chilled white wine. We grazed on the dishes as we lazed on blankets in the cheap-ticket section on the lawn, chatting and savoring the live performance of a symphony orchestra. This was my first visit to the park, though I had lived in Washington for four years.

One day our group toured the Kennedy Center. I brimmed with pride as we walked down its red-carpeted Hall of States. For the first time, I was conscious and proud of being a Washingtonian. Like so many in the city, I had followed the progress of the center, which was largely due to the vision of Mrs. Kennedy. Now as we toured the magnificent facility, I imagined how that First Couple must have looked—Jackie in a chic evening gown, John in an elegant tuxedo—walking on the red carpet that led to the performance halls. Like me, others had been propelled to public service in answer to the late president's call: "Ask not what your country can do for you—ask what you can do for your country."

Privileged to meet the center's renowned impresario, Patrick Hayes, who spoke to our group, we were then escorted to the balcony to hear the National Symphony Orchestra rehearse for that day's matinee. Without announcing it, as soon as we sat down, the musicians struck up "Stars and Stripes Forever." Tingling with pride, I fought to hold back the tears.

We were three black women in our group of sixteen, but by fall two had dropped out, leaving me as sort of the cheese standing alone—again. A little hollow inside was how I felt when I heard they were leaving. Both, at first glance, were more impressive than me, although I knew I would shine as I got comfortable with my quick ascent from bare-bones living while raising a child to projecting the image of a diplomat. One of the women had interned at USIA and amazed me at her knowledge of all the sections of the building. The other woman was stunning with a master's from John Hopkin's University. She cut a stylish figure in our small circle, all the time, like Ginger Rogers, in high heels.

I was looking forward to taking a course in Hindi at the Foreign Service Institute in Rosslyn, Virginia. I felt my Hindi, though fluent, was fragmented. I asked for a full year of study; however, after testing me, the linguist said, "It's obvious you know the language. You've just forgotten it," and enrolled me in a six-week course. Blasting through it in time and making the proficiency level was tedious; the materials were very poor—dialogues on sweetshops and undershirts! And lugging a reel-to-reel tape recorder home and back to FSI was no fun. But I got through it.

By early December I was packed up, and Cathy and Tom were driving me and Rekha to futuristic-looking steel-and-glass-plated Dulles Airport with its upwardly swerving roof that was becoming an icon in films. In her red trench coat, hair parted in the middle and gathered into two puffs on each side, Rekha resembled a little government official herself, but as we were departing, she expressed her deep sorrow at having to leave her happy home. As the mobile lounge van taxied us out to the plane, she screamed, "Maybe you want to go to India, but I don't. I don't want to leave Sister Cathy . . ." I was upset by her reaction, not having thought she'd take leaving so hard, and I was too embarrassed to do or say anything but hope for her to be quiet. This was not how I had pictured my farewell scene. Ten minutes after we were airborne, when the stewardess brought her some playing cards and a TWA pin, she smiled at me and said, "I think I'm going to like India."

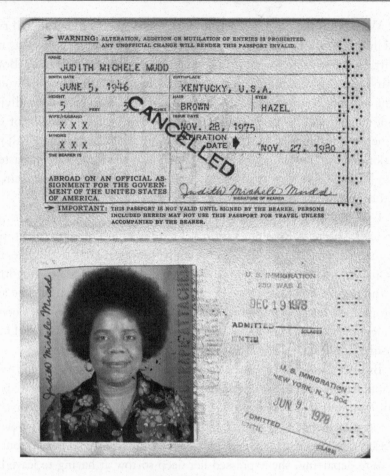

Passport, 1975

Six months before, when I was sworn in, I could hardly wait to tell America's story, which was *my story*, to the world. A friend had sent me a bouquet of red roses with a note saying, "You did it!" As I placed the long stems in a vase of cold water, I remembered the beauties Daddy had raised when we lived on Preston Street. I didn't like the thorny branches when I helped him cut some of the crimson blooms one day: "It only stings for a little while," he had softly told me. His words rang in my head as we flew off into the wild blue yonder, to India and other places I was yet to know.

Upper right, first official visa

Printed in the United States
By Bookmasters